SECOND EXODUS

OF

YISRAYAH

&

COVENANT

By
Dr. Goodwins Arikibe

Dr. Goodwins Arikibe

Unless otherwise specified, Scripture quotations are taken from the Book of the Covenant (BOC), World English Bible (WEB), or New King James Version. Some Hebrew words are sourced from Strong's Exhaustive Concordance, The New Strong's Exhaustive Concordance of the Bible – Nelson's Super Value Series, or BOC. These include words such as: YHWH [Yahweh], YAH, YAHSHUA HaMashiach, Yisrayah [Israel], etc. Most of these were derived from BOC, which restores the Names of the heavenly Father, YHWH, and YAHSHUA the Saviour and HaMashiach.

Copyright © 2025

All rights reserved. No part of this publication may be reproduced, distributed, or transmitted in any form or by any means, including photocopying, recording, or other electronic or mechanical methods, without the prior written permission of the publisher, except in the case of brief quotations embodied in critical reviews and specific non-commercial uses permitted by copyright law. Please direct your inquiries to info@livingyahweh.com

SECOND EXODUS OF YISRAYAH

First Edition 2025

Dr. Goodwins Arikibe
Assembly Of The Living Yahweh (ALY)
Stoke-on-Trent, Staffordshire, United Kingdom
Email: info@livingyahweh.com
www.livingyahweh.com

Printed in the United Kingdom
Good Reach Publishing
26 Haslucks Green Road, Solihull, England, B90 2EL
www.goodreachpublishing.com

Paperback

ISBN: 978-1-918039-31-3

Good Reach *Publishing*

Dedication

This book is dedicated to YHWH Almighty, our Heavenly FATHER, and YAHSHUA HaMashiach, our Saviour, whose wisdom, knowledge and understanding made writing this book possible. I am eternally grateful to Abba YAH for His Spirit's guidance and enlightenment in penning down the Word of truth for others to know what Second Exodus is about. YAH's unfailing Word provided the needed direction in all ramifications of this book.

YHWH, the Source of the Set-apart Spirit behind every righteous thought, inspired this work to be accomplished. It was prophesied that Yisrayah, scattered among nations, shall awaken in the last days to know YHWH after He reveals Himself to them. Through reading, learning, and applying understanding to His prophetic counsels, and diligently following the instructions of YAHSHUA HaMashiach [the Messiah] preached by His Apostles, efforts were made to begin writing down the revelations as inspired. First, Yisrayah shall return to YHWH, their Father, who reveals Himself to them. Second, they were commanded to watch, pray, and prepare for the Second Exodus to the Land of Yisrayah, as promised to the fathers that their children would return. Thirdly, the enabling Spirit of His favour instructs on what to write, making it possible for this book to be readily available to all those that YHWH shall save that call upon His Name.

Acknowledgment

My immediate family – my wife, children (sons and daughter), and close friends – provided much inspiration, helping me complete this book with the depth of knowledge that comes from the Spirit's inspiration and personal experience. Furthermore, this book is also indebted to many others who are part of the Covenant Way I am called to follow. Their names are too numerous to mention here.

First and foremost, I am grateful to my dear wife and best friend, Chinyere Arikibe, for her patience and kindness during the periods I worked late into the night, gathering ideas and organising them for this book. You inspired me every day with your incredible thoughtfulness, your encouragement to persist, and your heartfelt prayers to YHWH, which kept me going. Your sincere prayers continued to strengthen my resolve to persevere and overcome. I remain eternally grateful to you.

I am also grateful to my children for their support and assistance in ensuring that every aspect of the work was completed smoothly. Their insight and belief that the Ministry will flourish in connection to this book are like receiving numerous prayers, which signify the success of the work. I therefore sincerely and warmly thank my sons – Uchenna, Bright, Junior, Chinonso, and Udo for their good thoughts, prayers and contribution to the work of the Ministry.

Thank you, Michael Howlin, my elder and friend at heart in the mission. Your wisdom always radiates tenacity in championing a good cause. You have consistently been present, praying and sometimes prophetically speaking life into the noble work of ALY Mission that we all share. Most of your inspiring words significantly contributed to the writing of this book. I must also acknowledge your partnership in achieving one of our great works—the Book of the Covenant (BOC), on which the knowledge for this book was particularly based. Thank you very much, my dear friend, and beloved son of YHWH.

I thank all of you, my devoted fans and children of YAH worldwide, who appreciate hearing the teachings and messages from the BOC, some of which are included in this book. I remain eternally grateful to you all. Forever, stay blessed.

Preface

For I will take you from among the nations and gather you out of all the countries, and will bring you into your own land Ezekiel 36:24

The quotation above is a landmark promise of YAHWEH, the Creator of Heaven and Earth, to gather you, the reader, called Yisrayah, from the nation where you may have been scattered back to your own land, Yisrayah. This is not a promise of man but of the Creator Himself. With ancient prophecies, historical truths, and divine revelation, this book guides readers to rediscover their identity as YHWH's covenant people. He reveals why they were dispersed among the nations, how they lost their spiritual heritage, and what must now be done to prepare for the great return. This book is both a revelation and a roadmap—a call to repentance, obedience, and renewal through the Torah Covenant, leading the faithful back to the Father's promise.

The history of Yisrayah was written by YAHWEH Almighty Himself, the Creator of Heaven and Earth. He brought Yisrayah out of the Land of Mitzrayim [Egypt] with power and an outstretched arm after punishing their oppressors who enslaved and afflicted them for many years. At Mount Sinai, YHWH established an everlasting Covenant with Yisrayah. He declared:

Now if you [Yisrayah] obey Me fully and keep My Covenant, then out of all nations you will be My treasured possession. Although the whole earth is Mine, you will be for Me a kingdom of priests and a set-apart nation. These are the words you are to speak to the Yisrayah. Exodus 19:5-6

YHWH documented His Covenant with Yisrayah in the Book of the Covenant [BOC], known today as the Bible. The essence of the agreement with His people is revealed in these five key commandments:

- **Fear YHWH**
- **Hear His Word**
- **Obey YHWH's Word**
- **Love YHWH with all your heart**
- **Teach YHWH's Word to others**

If Yisrayah keeps the Covenant, they shall live in peace in the Land of Yisrayah He was restoring them, but if they disobey and worship the God of the Gentiles, many of them will perish in the Land, and their remnants will be scattered all over the world. Alas! Yisrayah did not heed His commands. They violated His instructions with impunity and worshipped the gods of the nations, which YHWH forbids. YHWH did everything to preserve and save them by appointing judges, prophets, and priests to guide them back to Himself, but all the efforts were in vain.

Having broken the everlasting Covenant and become irredeemable, YHWH therefore rose against them, destroyed them, and scattered their remnants into the Gentile nations to this day. He warned that in the Gentile nations, He would withdraw Himself from them, leaving them to serve and worship the Gods of the Gentiles made of wood and stone. However, in the latter days, after they repent and seek YHWH with all their hearts and souls, YHWH will hear them, forgive them, and return to them. He will reveal and restore His Name among them (Isaiah 52:6 NLT) and guide them through His Set-apart Spirit to worship Him. Furthermore, He promised to gather them from the nations where He scattered them and bring them back to their Land. This gathering and restoration is called the Second Exodus of Yisrayah [not rapture into heaven].

For I will take you from among the nations and gather you out of all the countries, and will bring you into your own land Ezekiel 36:24

The following Scriptures serve as proof of YHWH's promise to gather and restore Yisrayah to their Land in the latter days: Ezekiel 11:17; 34; 34:13; 36:19-28; 37:21,25; Jer. 23:3; 31:8; Isaiah 43:5-6; Deuteronomy 30:3-5; Isaiah 11:11-12; Jeremiah 32:37; Amos 9:14-15; Zechariah 10:8-10; Isaiah 49:12; Isaiah 60:4; Matthew

24:31; Romans 11:26-27; John 11:52; Acts 15:16-17; Revelation 7:9, etc.

Today, Yisrayah are still enduring their punishment among the nations because of their rebellion against their FATHER, YHWH. Unfortunately, many have not repented and still serve and worship the Gods of the Gentiles – wood and stone – as YHWH foretold (Deuteronomy 4:28, 28:36,64; Jeremiah 16:13; see Deuteronomy 32:16-17; Psalm 115:4-11 etc). Sadly, the majority of Yisrayah are still involved in various religions, such as Judaism, Christianity, Islam, Buddhism, Hinduism, etc., where they serve and worship their Gods. This is what YHWH hates. The BOC reveals that when the fathers were in Egypt, they worshipped the Egyptian Gods, which led to their enslavement, captivity, and affliction. Today, the same is happening to them despite being warned never to worship the idols of the nations. Until they repent and forsake idol worship and return to YHWH, they will remain in their troubles.

This book reveals who Yisrayah is. It describes their history and what they must begin to do to return to YHWH and be restored to their Land. The book highlights a snippet of the first Exodus and its relation to the second captivity of Yisrayah in foreign lands. It addresses the Second Exodus by reminding them of what caused their dispersion from their land. It explains the Covenant and how it affects them when they disobey it. Using much evidence from the BOC, the false teaching about rapture is demystified – because YHWH never promised Yisrayah rapture into heaven but promised restoration to their own Land, where they would live and reign with YAHSHUA the HaMashiach at His return to commence the Government of the Father, which would restore the earth into righteousness.

Read this book to discover who you are as a Covenant-keeper. Repent and prepare for the Second Exodus of Yisrayah in these last days.

Table of Contents

PART 1 1

CHAPTER 1: The Second Exodus of Israel 1

CHAPTER 2: Covenant 18

CHAPTER 3: Law Of Love And Liberty Stumbling Block To Many 31

LOVE OF YAHWEH, WILL OF YAHWEH, AND THE WORD OF YAHWEH 105

CHAPTER 4: The Covenants 134

YHWH'S COVENANTS 134

HISTORICAL PERSPECTIVE OF THE COVENANT 137

First Covenant 137

CHAPTER 5: Second Covenant 148

NOAH 148

CHAPTER 6: Third Covenant 156

ABRAHAM 156

CHAPTER 7: Fourth Covenant 158

Descendants of Abraham 158

PART 2 162

CHAPTER 8: FIFTH COVENANT YAHSHUA 162

YAHSHUA 162

CHAPTER 9: COVENANT OF PEACE 173

PART 3 177

CHAPTER 10: YISRAYAH.. 177

CHAPTER 11: WHAT DID BOC PROMISE YISRAYAH?
RAPTURE OR SECOND EXODUS?... 199

RAPTURE OR EARTHLY INHERITANCE? 199

YISRAYAH'S RESTORATION DRAWS NEAR........................... 205

CHAPTER 12: PRELUDE TO SECOND EXODUS....................... 223

CHAPTER 13: EVIDENCE ON THE SECOND EXODUS 229

CHAPTER 14: CONCLUSION 347

A Call to Action: What Can You Be Doing NOW 353

REFERENCES 357

GENTLE APPEAL 375

PART 1
CHAPTER 1:
The Second Exodus of Israel

INTRODUCTION

Many believe that soon, in this world, there will be a supernatural way of escape, tagged 'rapture' that will take them to heaven while the earth and the sinners face the beast during the great tribulation. The Christians are erroneously taught to believe that before the time of the great tribulation, they would be snatched away and taken to heaven, where they would remain until after the trouble on earth. It's incredible that, despite the Bible's teaching concerning the Second Exodus, many never found it expedient to believe the Word of the Father that promised a Second Exodus ['not rapture'] back to the Land of Israel in these latter days. The rapture theory and its deception are horrendous. Today, many are not thinking about the re-gathering of the people of Yisrayah, let alone preparing to escape into the wilderness for protection as taught in the Scriptures. They ignore the instruction that says, 'Flesh and blood cannot inherit the Kingdom of YHWH' (1 Corinthians 15:50). They pay attention to those who brainwash them with false teachings, without recourse to what the Scriptures instructively provide. The failure to get prepared for escape will result in facing the beast with his mark of worship. The false pastors and false prophets are duping many because they are promising them heaven that they cannot enter.

Contrary to the rapture heresy, the people of YHWH will be taken to the wilderness, just like the first wilderness experience from Egypt to the land of Canaan (Isaiah 11:11-16; Ezekiel 20:33-40; Hosea 2:16-17). In the wilderness, YHWH's people will be fed for a period of 1,260 days while the great tribulation lasts. They will remain in the wilderness until the trouble of the beast is over. In the wilderness, they will be taught the Torah, or the Law, and subsequently be led into the Set-apart Land of Yisrayah as soon as the seventh trumpet sounds. 'Torah' is a Hebrew word for 'instruction' or 'law' that refers to the first five books in the Book of the Covenant [BOC], i.e., Genesis, Exodus, Leviticus, Numbers, and Deuteronomy. They are also called the Book of the Law. The Torah is the Word of YHWH made flesh in the Person of Yahshua Mashiach [Messiah]. In these last days, He promised to return to save those who have faith in Him and keep the Torah commandments (Revelation 14:12; 22:14; 3:8, 10).

Read this Book of Second Exodus to get yourself prepared so that you can escape the coming trouble to a place of safety during the time of trouble on earth.

Preparation towards Second Exodus: to understand the promise of the Second Exodus and the restoration of Israel (Yisrayah) to their Land, YHWH [Yahweh] requires His people to repent and forsake their sins and those of their fathers and return to Him (Leviticus 26:20). To repent here means to atone and forsake sin and return to YHWH and obey His Word. He promised to forgive them, receive them, and save them when they truly repent of their sins; and would save and restore them to Himself during the time of Jacob's trouble or great tribulation that would engulf the earth. "Seek YAHWEH your FATHER, and you will find Him if you search for Him with all your heart and with all your soul…" (Deuteronomy 4:29-30). True repentance will lead to YHWH'S forgiveness. Having received YAHSHUA MASHIACH and the SAVIOUR, the repentant individual is expected to be immersed (baptised) in the Name of YAHSHUA for forgiveness of sin, and the gift of the Set-apart Spirit, which the believer needs for the fruits of the Spirit that empower Covenant-keepers to love and obey YAHWEH's Law and to do His good works. This is YAHWEH's favour. The BOC recognises obedience to the Law as the principles of Torah Obedience Instruction (TOI). TOI is the framework upon which the Covenant was made with the people of Israel. The TOC requirement, as captured in the BOC, strongly demands the following from anyone who must be saved and restored to the Land of Yisrayah during the Second Exodus.

- First, study the Covenant Torah, or Law, and do what it says (2 Tim. 2:15).
- Second, hear what His Torah Commandments say, Deut. 10:12, 20.
- Third, obey His voice and keep His covenant, Ex. 19:5.
- Fourth, love Him with all your heart and with all your soul. Deut. 6:5.
- Fifth, fear Him, and walk in all His ways, Deut. 6:2; 10:12, 20; Eccl. 12:13.
- Sixth, teach and lead others to His Law as Yahshua taught, Deut. 6:7.
- Seventh, acknowledge that YAHWEH is One, Deut. 6:4. (Read: Lev. 26:40; Deut. 6:7; Is. 54:13; Jer. 31:34; Jn. 6:45; Deut. Chapters 6, 10, 11, and 12; Rev. 3:8, 10).

What is the purpose of TOC? The purpose of TOC is to equip those who would inherit eternal life to get rid of sin so that they can possess righteousness for the salvation required for the Kingdom inheritance. YAHWEH, through Moses, declared, "It will be righteousness for us if we are careful to do all these commandments before YAHWEH, as He has commanded us" (Deut. 6:25; see

Deut. 5:29; 6:3). Indeed, carefulness is what everybody needs to obey YAHWEH's Commandments. The path of obedience and disobedience is too narrow to ignore watchfulness in the pursuit of the Kingdom inheritance. One may easily slip and fall into sin, yet praise oneself that he still stands. Therefore, caution is required daily, as Joshua was instructed to meditate on the Torah frequently to remain on the path of righteousness always. He was told that faithfulness and commitment are the keys to prosperity, blessing, success, long life, and the pathway to inherit the Land. Anyone who follows YAHWEH's instructions will reap His kindness, favour, and love and shall be delivered and saved from the coming trials, great tribulations, and the wrath of YAHWEH.

Answers to the questions below reveal who a true Israelite is. They probe into their preparation towards returning to the promised Land. The book reveals first-hand information about the incredible event that is soon to happen in the history of humanity. This book responds to the following questions:

- Who is an Israelite and in the Covenant?
- Why do Israelites need to embark on the Second Exodus?
- What is the Torah and Covenant to an Israelite?
- When would the Second Exodus occur?

- Is there biblical evidence of the Second Exodus?
- Did Christianity replace the Israelites?
- What is the promise to Yisrayah: Second Exodus or rapture?

In no particular order, the above questions are answered within the chapters of this book. This book teaches a curious reader the pathway of YAHWEH'S righteousness, which a kingdom-aspiring person must pursue.

Following the prophecies that require YAHWEH's people to repent and obey Him from wherever they are scattered in the nations, there has been increasing awareness about the people of the Covenant – Israel. The Israelites are beginning to be aware of who they are as people of the Covenant (Bible); they are returning to the knowledge of the true Creator, their Father, who called them. They are beginning to understand that YAHWEH is their Father, not God[1]. They were lied to! YAHWEH is the Creator and the Father of mankind, while God(s) are His creatures. The creatures are commanded to worship the Creator (Deuteronomy 6:13; 10:20; Matthew 4:10; Luke 4:8, etc.). The Covenant that the Creator made with Yisrayah, which they didn't keep and that resulted in their dispersion, has been revived.

---

[1] In the Book of Covenant Yahweh Is Not God by Goodwins (2025) – is a must-read book. It tells you everything you want to know about the Creator, YHWH, and the creature, God

The people are beginning to understand the Torah (instructions), Covenant, Commandments, Law, etc., as was given to the fathers (see Romans 3:2; 9:4-5). Without the knowledge of these, one may not know how to repent and forsake sins and walk with Him, let alone think of the Second Exodus. Indeed, to those Israelites waking up to their call, they are beginning to see the light of YAHWEH unto them and will soon be restored to the Promised Land of Yisrayah.

Meanwhile, let's examine who the Yisray'lites are, and how their faith in YHWH is rooted in the Covenant He made with the fathers. Yisray'lites are known as covenant-keepers. They were given the Law and the Prophets; they were given the Ten Commandments and the Promises – including the gift of the Saviour and Messiah, and inheritance of the Land of Yisrayah described as flowing with milk and honey.

YISRAYAH'S SECOND EXODUS IS FAST APPROACHING

A brilliant light is already shining on the people of YHWH as they plan for the Second Exodus!

WHO ARE THE ISRAELITES?

Descendant of Abraham. It's expedient to understand the people whom the Creator of Heaven and Earth called to be His first chosen race to know Him and obey Him. He called them His firstfruit, firstborn, peculiar treasure, chosen people, set-apart nation, royal priesthood, and YAHWEH's own special possession. Yisrayah was chosen to learn His ways and to declare His praises. The hope of Yisrayah's restoration is being witnessed in the awareness of many across the world. They believe the light of deliverance is already beaming from on high. A brilliant light is already shining on the people of YHWH as they plan for the Second Exodus. The chosen people are beginning to see the light of deliverance. They now know His Name, keep His Shabbat, keep His Feast, call Him Father, and recognise that they are Yisrayah, an identity which they lost for two millennia and more. Apostle Peter declared this about Yisrayah:

"But you are a chosen people, a royal priesthood, a holy nation, Yahweh's special possession, that you may declare the praises of Him who called you out of darkness into His wonderful light" (1 Peter 2:9; see Exodus 19:5; Exodus 4:22; Amos 3:1-3; Hosea 11:1-2).

They are called Yisrayah (or Israel) – the descendants of Abraham, Isaac, and Yaaqob (Jacob).

Foreigners Can Become a Yisray'lite. In the Book of the Covenant a foreigner is also known as a Gentile. Yisray'lites are the chosen people of YHWH out of the Gentiles. A Yisrayah is a covenant-keeper who is called to serve, love, obey, and fear YAHWEH, the Father, and to keep His Torah Commandments. Today's Yisray'lites is anyone who has faith in Yahshua Mashiach and keeps the Covenant commandments of YAHWEH. You are a Yisray'lite provided you are obedient to your Creator and His instructions. It doesn't matter whether you are a descendant of Abraham, Isaac, Jacob, or not. What matters is to have faith in Him and to obey His Word (see Revelation 2:9; 3:9; Revelation 3:8, 10). The Gentiles who love righteousness, keep His Sabbath, and follow His Law are welcomed as Yisray'lite (Isaiah 56:6-8). Yisrayah are the people that were given the Torah, the Law, the two tablets of stone known as the Ten Commandments, and the Covenant. Initially, the Covenant was made with the Yisrayah, not with the Gentile Christianity or any religious body of this world. However, the citizenship of being a Yisrayah has been extended to the Gentiles if they are obedient. A Yisrayahlite has faith in YAHSHUA HaMashiach and the Saviour [not Jesus Christ of Christianity]. YAHWEH made a firm covenant with them, thus:

"You shall be to Me a kingdom of priests and a holy nation..." (Exod. 19:5-6; Exod. 4:22; Amos 3:1-3; Is. 56:4-6; Deut. 6:1-5; Rom. 3:2; Rom. 9:4-5; Jn. 14:15; Jn. 15:10; Rev. 14:12; Matt. 1:21; Luke 1:30-33).

If anyone born of Abraham rejects the COVENANT COMMANDMENTS or breaks them, he/she ceases to be part of the covenant family. If a child of YAHWEH violates the Covenant, he would be classified as a Gentile who does not obey the Law of YHWH. On the other hand, if a Gentile keeps the FATHER's Commandments and receives YAHSHUA the SAVIOUR and does those things that please YHWH, the individual will be grafted to the household of Yisrayah by virtue of being baptised in the Name of YAHSHUA HaMashiach, and he will be called a Yisray'lite (Acts 2:38; Jn. 4:10-15; 7:37-38; 15:10; Gal. 5:22-23).

THEREFORE, a Yisray'lite is a covenant-keeper. YHWH instructs His people never to harden their hearts when they hear His voice. They must believe in YAHSHUA (HaMashiach, or Messiah), given to them to save them from their sins and to restore them to their Land. He gives them the gift of Ruach HaKodesh (Holy Spirit) to continue in obedience to the Father's Commandments (Acts 2:38; Jn. 15:10; Gal. 5:22-23).

Worship of Gods of Nations. In the days of the fathers, they travelled from the land of Canaan to the land of

Egypt because of the famine that ravaged the place of their abode. Owing to providence, they were moved to go to Egypt, where they sojourned for 400 years under slavery, persecution, affliction, hard labour, torture, dehumanisation, pain, and death. These evils happened to them because they worshipped the 'gods' of Egypt instead of 'YAHWEH'. Fortunately for them, they received YHWH's divine intervention. He judged **all** the Gods of Egypt (Exodus 12:12). He delivered Yisrayah and brought them back into the Promised Land. However, notwithstanding YHWH's love and great deliverance, the Egyptian religious culture influenced Yisrayah's spiritual life that even in the wilderness, inspite of YHWH's redemption and leadership, they created a golden calf, a typical God they worshipped in Egypt, which is a clear example of idolatry that YHWH forbids (Exodus 32:1-4; Ezekiel 20:7-8).

Unfortunately, just as He predicted, they didn't keep the Covenant He made with them. Their disobedience led to the loss of their land and their scattering throughout the world to this day. Yisrayah are suffering the same fate they encountered in Egypt because they forsook and forgot YAHWEH, their FATHER, who called them, and worshipped foreign gods. They completely abandoned His Torah Covenant, and the consequences have been damning and disastrous.

The prophetic good news is that in these latter days, Yahweh will revisit them, and based on their repentance, He will restore them to Himself and return them the second time to the Promised Land of Israel. Meanwhile, let's probe a little into the Torah Covenant they broke and abandoned and how He intends to bring them back to their Land.

YHWH'S COVENANT WITH YISRAYAH

The children of Israel left Egypt on the first day of the Feast of Unleavened Bread and crossed through the Red Sea on the seventh day of the Feast. The journey through the wilderness meant that YHWH would instruct them to learn His Torah, thereby establishing a Father-sons-and-daughters relationship with them. In the Torah, they would learn His Truth, His Way, His Righteousness, Set-Apartness [holiness], etc., so that these would form the national ethos, culture, values, and doctrine of the people. In the wilderness of Mt. Sinai, YHWH made an everlasting Covenant with His people. If they OBEY Him, they will live and be His people forever. But if they disobey Him, they will perish, and the remnant will be scattered into the nations. Unfortunately, they did not truthfully obey Him. This led to their being scattered into nations. However, in the latter days, after they diligently repent, forsake their sins, and call upon Him, He will hear them, return to them, and show them favour again by restoring them back to their Land. This would mark their SECOND EXODUS back to the Land of Yisrayah (Deut. 30:1–20;

Isaiah 11:10–11; Ezek. 20:33–40; Matt. 24:29–32; Rom. 11:25–26).

CALL FOR A COVENANT WITH YISRAYAH

"On the third new moon (month) after the people of Yisrayah had gone out of the land of Egypt, on that day they came into the wilderness of Sinai. They set out from Rephidim and came into the wilderness of Sinai, and they encamped in the wilderness. There, Yisrayah encamped before the mountain, while Mosheh went up to YHWH. YHWH called to him out of the mountain, saying,

"Thus you shall say to the house of Yaacob, and tell the people of Yisrayah, 'You yourselves have seen what I did to the Mitzrayim (Egyptians), and how I bore you on eagles' wings and brought you to myself. Now therefore, if you will indeed obey my voice and keep my covenant, you shall be my treasured possession among all peoples, for all the earth is mine; and you shall be to me a kingdom of priests and a set-apart nation.' These are the words that you shall speak to the people of Yisrayah" (Exodus 19:5–6).

If Yisrayah would not keep the Covenant:

"I call heaven and earth to witness against you today, that you will soon utterly perish from the land that you are going over the Jordan to possess. You

will not live long in it, but will be utterly destroyed. And YHWH will scatter you among the peoples, and you will be left few in number among the nations where YHWH will drive you. And there you will serve gods of wood and stone, the work of human hands, that neither see, nor hear, nor eat, nor smell" (Deut. 4:26–28).

Yisrayah's Hardened Heart. Unfortunately, the people did not learn lessons from their first exodus experience in which they suffered so much in Egypt, as they forsook and forgot YHWH and His Covenant Way, which He made with the fathers. Even after the Covenant was made with them, they did not adhere to the agreement that would have guaranteed their perpetual occupation of the land they were about to enter. The rebellion of the people led to their being persecuted and murdered in millions, and consequently, their land was possessed by their enemies. The Scripture reveals that their enemies, who plundered and took over their lands, included various empires — for instance, the Assyrians, Babylonians, Greeks, and the Roman Empire. These were the Gentile nations predicted to plunder them if they forsook YHWH their Father and worship the God of the Gentiles.

Hint about Second Exodus after the First

The First Exodus suggested that Yisrayah would not be enslaved again into Gentile nations, provided they heeded the Covenant YAHWEH their FATHER made with them. This was one of the promises that heralded the first exodus. But there's more because of their rebellion! The people would entangle themselves with the Gods of the Gentiles, resulting in their destruction and remnants scattered into nations. Unfortunately, about 721 BCE, the Ten Tribes of Yisrayah (Israel) were removed from their land. After many years, the two tribes (Yehudah) were scattered into nations because of their unfaithfulness to YHWH. The biblical prophets speak of a Second Exodus to occur in the last days, where YHWH's people who have been scattered throughout the nations of the world will be set free from their spiritual, economic, and political enslavement, which is under the control of today's 'Babylon the Great'.

This book reveals more reasons why the whole house of Yisrayah was scattered into nations after they were promised in the Wilderness that they would not experience a second Egypt again [Exodus 14:13-14]. The Second Exodus of Yisrayah is YHWH's prophetic revelation that teaches Yisrayah's return from the nations by the power of their true SAVIOUR, YAHSHUA HAMASHIACH. The Second Exodus is one of YHWH's secrets revealed to diligent and dedicated Yisrayahlites that LOVE Him in these last days [Deut. 29:29; Deut. 30; Isaiah 11:10-16, etc.]. Second Exodus reveals the reasons YAH's people went into captivity the second time and worshipped the gods of nations as prophesied instead of YHWH. Second Exodus reveals that the Yisray'lites must serve their punishment in foreign lands and be restored after completing it. Second Exodus reveals YHWH's powerful visitation against nations that will be forced to release Yisrayah from captivity. Second Exodus describes in great detail how the movement is going to take place; more importantly, Second Exodus describes what a Yisrayahlite must be doing now to qualify for the Exodus – [e.g. return to the Covenant]. It's important that one understands the subject of the Second Exodus thoroughly since it affects one's physical and spiritual destiny.

What Second Exodus Reveals

Let's grab hints of the knowledge this book provides the reader before digging deep into Yisrayah's troubles and the restoration that would follow in the latter days. This book answers all the questions stated in Chapter 1, giving the reader a clearer picture of who Yisrayah is, and the Covenant they received and broke, plus the consequences that followed. The book provides a comprehensive guideline [though not exhaustive] on such topical issues as how to KNOW YHWH (1 Jn. 2:2-3); how to return to YHWH. The book reveals Christianity as a religion that preaches the replacement of Yisrayah as they live amongst the nations. The message of Yisrayah's replacement meant that the people had been rejected by YHWH and continued with Gentile Christianity. This concocted narrative was not supported in the Book of the Covenant. The book reveals end-time biblical prophecies, particularly affecting the return of Yisrayah. It will guide you to know how a Gentile covenant-keeper can be part of the journey back into the Promised Land. The book addresses rapture and what the promise of the Kingdom is all about. Indeed, most Christians have not read anything like this before. All they have heard in the days of safety is rapture into heaven, which is not even taught in the BOC. This book will help the reader to understand where he fits into end-time Bible prophecy! You need this book for your daily walk! To know YHWH, the Creator of heaven and earth, and to serve and worship Him as He commands, is to understand the Covenant He made with Yisrayah at Mt. Sinai, and His subsequent messages to the Prophets and Yahshua for His people. Lack of knowledge of the Covenant means the individual will not walk with YHWH; the person will live a Gentile life that does not follow His Covenant Way. Knowledge and obedience to the FATHER is the key for those who must be saved and restored into the Land of Yisrayah. The next chapter explains the Covenant and why every covenant-keeper needs to practice it.

CHAPTER 2:
Covenant

Keep the Covenant Commandments

Anyone who wants to be saved – Yisrayahlite or Gentile – should take these salient questions stated below seriously. One must be ready to answer them truthfully. Obedience to YHWH's Law proves one's love and fear of YAHWEH, which are the basis upon which those who would be saved shall receive His unmerited favour and salvation for the Promised Land and eternal Kingdom. These are frequently asked questions by teachers of the Covenant:

- Do you genuinely want to be a son or daughter of YHWH?
- Do you live a set-apart life based on His commandments?
- Do you love Him and fear Him as prescribed in the BOC?
- Do you serve and worship the FATHER in spirit and truth?
- Do you daily depend on Him for your life and blessings?
- Do you want to inherit the Land, even the Eternal Kingdom?

Response to the above queries is tied to Torah obedience, which demands that everyone keep the Covenant commandments. This means YHWH's people must keep His commandments as summarised in the Ten Commandments. The Ten Commandments are the summary of the Torah Covenant. The figure below captures Torah obedience criteria. It's all about hearing YHWH's Word. It means to reverence Him, which is the equivalent of having 'fear' of YAH. Fear of YHWH in the proper manner means to honour, respect, and worship YHWH as a FATHER. It encapsulates the 'love' of the FATHER, which in turn impacts the fruit of knowledge that enables the individual to 'lead', teach, guide, and direct others to YAHSHUA HAMASHIACH, who leads the lost souls back to the FATHER, as He gives them the eternal Kingdom. These Torah Obedience Criteria are what covenant-keepers need to obey YHWH's instructions to the end. Those who are obedient and faithful are promised life, prolonged life, prosperity, and success as they live their lives now and prepare for eternal life.

Figure 1

Torah Obedience Criteria (TOC)

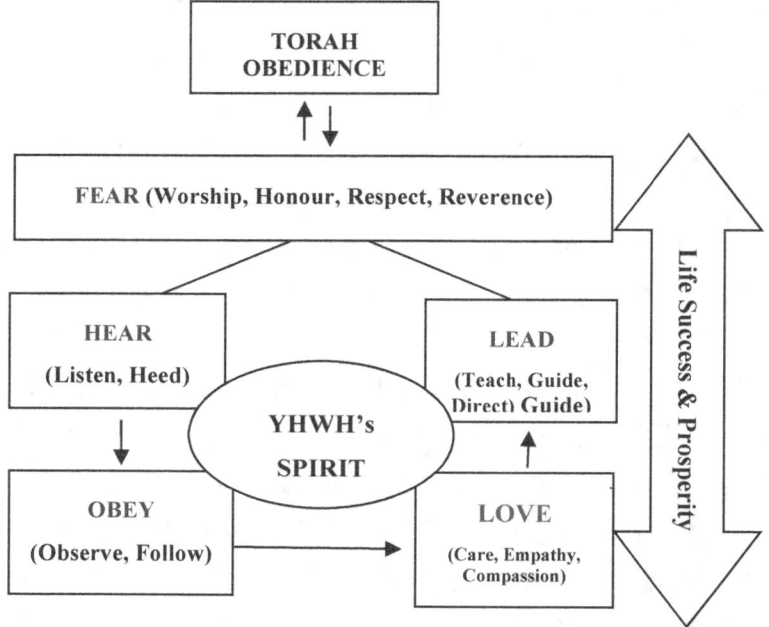

Key: Torah Instructional Framework

MEMBERS AND LEADERS USE THE FRAMEWORK

HERE ARE THE SECRETS:

YHWH's family members and leaders who are wise learn the five secrets of the Torah Instruction framework that open the door of obedience to YHWH's Word. The TOC are the compass of the Ten Commandments that enable parents, children, organisations, and their leaders to achieve success in life.

I. FEAR YHWH
II. HEAR HIS WORD
III. OBEY YHWH'S INSTRUCTIONS OR COMMANDS
IV. LOVE YHWH WITH ALL YOUR HEART (LOVE BRETHREN ALSO)
V. LEAD: TEACH, GUIDE, DIRECT – OTHERS TO HIM THROUGH YAHSHUA.

The five TOC frameworks (see Figure 1 above) provide everyone with the keys to unlock disobedience and free them to obey the Torah of YHWH. Once learnt, they are internalised and practised. Apart from individuals in the homes and assemblies, TOC is recommended to servant leaders because it may help them to navigate their behavioural attributes and the roles they play to achieve organisational performance. Torah instruction is the Creator's "WORD of SPIRIT" (WoS), which every obedient servant leader must know, observe, and possess for organisational efficiency and effectiveness (Matthew 6:63; Joshua 1:8 BOC). WoS is a secret code behind the influence and empowerment of the leader, enabling him to play his roles effectively. Obedience to YHWH, the Creator and Owner of human knowledge and understanding, inspires the individual's mind to receive the relevant wisdom required for goal performance. The WoS says: "You shall remember YHWH your FATHER, for it is He who gives you power to get wealth, that He may establish His covenant which

He swore to your fathers, as it is this day" (Deuteronomy 8:18). YHWH told Joshua:

"This Book of the Torah [Law] shall not depart from your mouth, but you shall meditate on it day and night, that you may observe to do according to all that is written in it. For then you will make your way prosperous, and then you will have good success" (Joshua 1:18).

TOC is a friendly force that enables people to hear the Word and obey it. It is the Spirit upon which life depends that activates the love characteristics, which in turn influence the person towards aspiring to good behavioural attributes to influence and motivate self, family members, or subordinates into performance. Leading others toward good behaviours is a task people must pursue to remain relevant to themselves, neighbours, and their Creator. To lead becomes easier when subordinates emulate the leader whose performance sets an example for others to follow. If one doesn't have the required behavioural characteristics, they would never perform optimally, whether at home or in a business setting. In an organisation, the combined leader's roles, approaches (styles), characteristics, and behaviours result in a repertoire of behavioural complexity that can enhance organisational performance. Possession of TOC enables both the leader and the subordinates to achieve the set goals and objectives of the business, barring business strategy and contingency factors. Researchers and authors have shown that effective leaders must have sound instructional tools and behavioural attributes that are instrumental to role performance. A TOC that produces sound behavioural attributes can make a tremendous positive impact on servant leaders who possess them. Research has shown that leaders achieve good success if they properly apply these behavioural complexities in their day-to-day activities. A father who is a leader in the house and an executive who is a leader in an organisation both seek to perform well consistently. YHWH provided the key obedience criteria as outlined in the passages mentioned below. The Covenant remains the 'agreement' where TOC is binding between the Creator and His subjects to obey. Obedience is the hallmark of good success (Josh. 1:8).

YAHWEH'S COVENANT DEMAND:

Exodus 19:5-6 NLT: "Now if you will obey ME and keep my COVENANT, you will be My own special treasure from among all the peoples on earth; for all the earth belongs to ME. And you will be my kingdom of priests, my set-apart nation.' This is the message you must give to the people of Yisrayah." [See 1 Peter 2:9-10.] Deuteronomy 4:39-40 NLT so, remember this and keep it firmly in mind: YHWH is YHWH both in heaven and on earth, and there is no other. If you obey all the decrees and commands I am giving you today, all will be well with you and your children. I am giving you these instructions so you will enjoy a long life in the land YHWH, your FATHER, is giving you for all time.

Deuteronomy 6:24-25 NKJV "YHWH commanded us to observe all these statutes, to fear YHWH our FATHER, for our good always, that He might preserve us alive, as it is this day. Then it will be righteousness for us if we are careful in observing all these commandments before YHWH our FATHER, as He has commanded us."

2 Corinthians 6:14-18 NLT "Don't team up with those who are unbelievers. How can righteousness be a partner with wickedness? How can light live with darkness? What harmony can there be between MESSIYAH and the devil? How can a believer be a partner with an unbeliever? And what union [alliance] can there be between YHWH's temple and idols? For we are the temple of the living YHWH. As YHWH said: I will live in them and walk among them. I will be their FATHER, and they will be my people. Therefore, come out from among unbelievers, and 'Separate yourselves from them,' says YHWH. Don't touch their filthy [unclean] things, and I will welcome you. And I will be your FATHER, and you will be my sons and daughters, says YAH SHADDAI". You may have heard that YHWH's Laws are cancelled. It's a lie! The Law is true; the Law is set apart; the Law is righteous and cannot be changed or removed until YAHSHUA returns and governs the earth with the Law (Rom. 7:12; see Isaiah

2:2-3). The Prophets, YAHSHUA HAMASHIACH, and the Disciples say the Law is not cancelled. YAHSHUA categorically stated that He did not come to cancel the Law or the Prophets but to accomplish His own part as provided in the BOC (Matt. 5:17, Exod. 3:15; Is. 53:1-12). He commands all to obey it (Matt. 5:19). He says, "If you love Me, keep My commandments." To love Him, you must hear His Word, fear Him, obey Him, and do all He commands you, as He also loves the FATHER and obeys His commandments. All these are summed up in the love of YHWH and the love of brethren. YAHSHUA HAMASHIACH instructs that to love is to keep His commandments.

If you love Me, keep My commandments (John 14:15). If you keep My commandments, you will remain in My love, even as I have kept My FATHER's commandments and remain in His love (John 15:10).

If a man loves Me, he will keep My Word. My FATHER will love him, and we will come to him and make our home with him. He who does not love Me does not keep My Words. The Word which you hear is not Mine, but the FATHER's who sent Me (John 14:23-24).

The only way to love the FATHER and the SON is to keep the TORAH (INSTRUCTION or LAW) as commanded by YHWH in the wilderness. YAHSHUA worked on behalf of the FATHER. The Word He taught was the FATHER's Word, not His. What's more! How do we know that we know Him? John the beloved wrote on how we KNOW HIM.

This is how we know that we know Him: if we keep His commandments. One who says, "I know Him," and doesn't keep His Commandments, is a liar, and the truth isn't in Him (1 John 2:2-4).

We are of YHWH. He who knows YHWH listens to us. He who is not of YHWH doesn't listen to us. By this we know the spirit of truth and the spirit of error (1 John 4:6).

Those who keep His Law are those who know Him and abide in Him. The only way His people know that they remain in Him always is by continuing to be obedient to His commandments. This is what pleases Him.

He who keeps His commandments remains in Him, and He in him. By this we know that He remains in us, by the Spirit which He gave us (1 John 3:24).

Equally, to love fellow brethren emanates from the love for YHWH and keeping His commandments. Many runaway from His commandments, but it's the KEY to obedience and eternal life. His commandments are not burdensome like the laws of men. His laws guide and direct one's mind to live a righteous life. Those who live an obedient life will receive His blessings instead of curses; they shall inherit the promised Land, the coming Kingdom, and eternal life. This is what the disobedient ancient fathers missed. Those who seek Him and the everlasting kingdom must love one another and keep YHWH's commandments, which are the evidence of His love. By this, we know that we love the children of YHWH when we love YHWH and keep His commandments. For this is loving YHWH: that we keep His commandments. His commandments are not grievous (1 John 5:2-3).

THE TEN COMMANDMENTS

In the above passages, the Prophets and YAHSHUA spoke from the depth of the FATHER's Commandments. Here are the Ten Commandments given to Yisrayah at Mt Sinai. Upon these commandments and others, YHWH drew the ears of mankind, that every soul must shama, i.e., hear, listen, as pointed out by Mosheh in Deuteronomy 6:3-4. YHWH commands that mankind should fear and serve YHWH ALONE: "You shall fear YHWH your FATHER; and you shall serve Him, and shall swear by His Name" [Deut. 6:13].

Exodus 20:1-17

YHWH spoke all these words, saying:

No. 1

² "I am Yahweh, your FATHER, who brought you out of the land of Egypt, out of the house of bondage.

No. 2

³ "You shall have no 'gods' before Me.

⁴ "You shall not make for yourselves an idol, nor any image of anything that is in the heavens above, or that is in the earth beneath, or that is in the water under the earth. ⁵ **You shall not bow down to them nor serve them, for I, YHWH your FATHER, am a jealous YHWH, visiting the iniquity of the fathers on the children to the third and fourth generation of those who hate Me, ⁶ and showing loving-kindness to thousands of those who love Me and keep My commandments.**

No. 3

⁷"You shall not misuse the name of YHWH your FATHER, for YHWH will not hold anyone guiltless who misuses his Name.

No. 4

⁸"Remember the Sabbath day, to keep it holy. ⁹ You shall labour six days and do all your work, ¹⁰ but the seventh day is a Sabbath to YHWH your FATHER. You shall not do any work on it, you, nor your son, nor your daughter, your male servant, nor your female servant,

nor your livestock, nor your stranger who is within your gates; ¹¹ for in six days YHWH made heaven and earth, the sea, and all that is in them, and rested the seventh day; therefore, YHWH blessed the Sabbath day and set it apart.

No. 5

[12] "Honour your father and your mother, that your days may be long in the land which YHWH your FATHER gives you.

No. 6

[13] "You shall not murder.

No. 7

[14] "You shall not commit adultery.

No. 8

[15] "You shall not steal.

No. 9

[16] "You shall not give false testimony against your neighbour.

No. 10

¹⁷ "You shall not covet your neighbour's house. You shall not covet your neighbour's wife, nor his male servant, nor his female servant, nor his ox, nor his donkey, nor anything that is your neighbour's."

The Ten Commandments summarise the Torah (Instruction, Law). It's meant to be written in one's heart and meditated upon day and night (Josh. 1:8). The Covenant Commandment is so very important that YHWH foretold that in the days that are coming, it will be renewed and written in men's hearts, instead of the Stone Tablets of old. Apostle Shaul wrote:

Hebrews 8:8-12: ⁸ "Behold, the days are coming," says YHWH, "that I will make a NEW COVENANT with the house of Yisrayah and with the house of Judah; ⁹ not according to the COVENANT that I made with their fathers in the day that I took them by the hand to lead them out of the land of Egypt; for they didn't continue in my covenant, and I disregarded them," says YHWH. ¹⁰ "For this is the COVENANT that I will make with the house of Yisrayah. After those days," says YHWH, "I will put my laws into their minds; I will also write them on their hearts. I will be their FATHER, and they will be my people. ¹¹ They will not teach every man his fellow citizen and every man his brother, saying, 'Know YHWH,' for all will know Me, from their least to their greatest. ¹² For I will be merciful to their unrighteousness. I will remember their sins and lawless deeds no more."

CHAPTER 3:
Law Of Love And Liberty Stumbling Block To Many

Torah Obedience Criteria (TOC) Rooted in the Ten Commandments

YAHSHUA summarises the Ten Commandments as "love for YAHWEH" and "love for neighbour" (Exodus 20:3-11, 12-17). YAHSHUA is the embodiment of the Law, the goal of the Law, and the stumbling block to many. He is the Word of YHWH made flesh. Anyone who rejects the Law, which is what YAHSHUA represents, will surely stumble and fall. Isaiah says that YAHSHUA shall be the stumbling block for Yisrayah: "And He shall be for a sanctuary; but for a stone of stumbling and for a rock of offence to both the houses of Israel, for a gin and for a snare to the inhabitants of Jerusalem" (Isaiah 8:14). Because of YAHSHUA, the Jewish Brothers stumbled and fell. They rejected His Word and, as a result, rejected Him and the FATHER (see Matt. 23:36-39). The Gentile Christians, like the Jews, are still busy telling themselves that the Law is cancelled, thereby stumbling and falling as the Jews did who did not receive Him. The Law and its obedience are the KEY to serving and worshipping the FATHER. The Torah Obedience Criteria underpins the nitty-gritty of the Law, enabling individuals or communities to learn it, obey it, and live by it. When YAHSHUA returns, people will not only learn the Law but will obey it and live by it as a way of life (Isaiah 2:2-3).

The Law, as enumerated in the previous chapter, is divided into two:

i. Love for YAHWEH with all your heart; ii. Love for neighbour as oneself. Love for YAHWEH with all your heart
ii. Love for neighbour as oneself

Moses summarised the first four laws as "love for YAHWEH" (Deuteronomy 6:5). YAHSHUA affirms that "Love for YAHWEH" is the "first and greatest commandment" (Matthew 22:38). To love YAHWEH is to fear Him, obey Him, love Him, and lead or teach others to know His Law and to do it. "The fear of YAHWEH is the beginning of wisdom, knowledge, and understanding" (Psalm 111:10a). Yahweh teaches His Law to those who fear Him and love Him. This is the reason it's called Torah Obedience Criteria (TOC), whereby an individual makes it mandatory for himself to learn and obey it. "The secret of YAHWEH is with those that fear Him, and He will show them His covenant" (Psalm 25:14). Furthermore: "…a good understanding has all they who do His commandments" (Psalm 111:10b). We ought to do His commandments, not despise them. Those who despise His wisdom and commandments are called "fools" (Proverbs 1:7). Until a repentant soul begins to fear YAHWEH and obey His commandments, no understanding of His WORD nor His GRACE will be given to him for true conversion.

Let's reiterate the demand of the Torah Obedience Criteria (TOC):

I. FEAR YHWH
II. HEAR YHWH
III. OBEY YHWH
IV. LOVE YHWH
V. LEAD OTHERS TO YAHSHUA

To observe these TOC avails YHWH's children the righteousness of YAHWEH, as well as guarantees their salvation and makes way for eternal life in the Kingdom (Deut. 6:25).

LAW OF LIBERTY AND ROYAL LAW

The Ten Commandments are the Law of Liberty and the Royal Law, which have been in existence since life began. The Law of Liberty is a law of freedom, a law that sets the captive free from bondage; it is a law which, if obeyed, liberates an individual whose faith is in Yahshua from the power of sin. The power of sin is equated to the house of bondage in Egypt. In this case, only YAHWEH has the power to liberate the captive. YAHWEH declared, "I am YAHWEH thy ELOHIM, which has brought thee out of the land of Egypt, out of the house of bondage" (Exodus 20:2). Similarly, Apostle James identifies the Royal Law as the Ten Commandments that must be fulfilled: "If you really fulfil the royal law according to the Scripture, 'You shall love your neighbour as yourself,' you do well; but if you show partiality, you commit sin and are convicted by the law as transgressors." (James 2:8-9). Isaiah says that YAHSHUA will judge the world with this law: "…and he will teach us of his ways, and we will walk in his paths: for out of Zion shall go forth the law, and the word of YAHWEH from Jerusalem, and He shall judge among the nations, and shall rebuke many people…" (Isaiah 2:3-4). The Ten Commandments covenant is briefly explained below. These laws are known as everlasting laws. The fathers were unable to obey them; they rejected and forsook them and worshipped the gods of the Gentiles. This resulted in their being scattered all over the world to this day. In these latter days, YAHWEH has planned to restore them back to their Land. This is called the SECOND EXODUS OF YISRAYAH, after the First Exodus from Egypt.

First Commandment Warning: "I AM YAHWEH YOUR FATHER WHO BROUGHT YOU OUT OF THE LAND OF EGYPT, OUT OF THE HOUSE OF BONDAGE" (Exodus 20:2). This commandment tells us His Sacred Name. In verse 3, He warns that the name of 'God' shall not be worshipped. "You shall have no Gods before Me" is a Covenant commandment that stops mankind from worshipping any creature, e.g., man, angel, carved images, or objects. To do so would attract punishment by death. If one serves and worships only YHWH, the individual shows love for Him. His Love is tied to His Name – YAHWEH – which He promptly declared to Yisrayah and wrote the same on the tablet of stone: "I AM YAHWEH your FATHER, who has brought thee out of the land of Egypt, out of the house of bondage" (Exodus 20:2). By His Mighty Name, Yisrayah was brought out from the bondage of Egypt. His name connotes POWER, AUTHORITY, AND STRENGTH. His Name is in the SON – YAHSHUA – in whom human SALVATION, FREEDOM, LIBERTY, and LIFE ETERNAL are domiciled and form an integral part of His Law. The command "You shall have no Gods[2] before Me" (verse 3) demands obedience from His people – because His Name is highly exalted above all other names. This is the first and the greatest commandment that many have either misunderstood or ignored. Here, our attention is drawn to the fact that YAHWEH is the Creator of heaven and earth, the very true YAHWEH – the Owner, Possessor, Sustainer, and Saviour of mankind. Any other 'thing' you love more than YAHWEH becomes an idol, e.g., father, mother, wife, children, leader, oneself, Baal, Mammon, etc. (Luke 14:26; Matthew 6:24). Mammon represents money, worldly

---

[2] Gods or gods [Elohim] are never to be worshipped. See the book: 'In the Book of Covenant Yahweh is not God' (2025), pages 11-15, YHWH alone is to be worshipped.

possessions, worldly wealth, and gifts of Satan (read Matthew 4:4-10; 19:17-22; Luke 4:4-12) in this present decaying "kingdom of the world and the glory" (Matthew 4:8-10). To embrace the world and its glory is to love mammon, and to love mammon is to worship Satan; therefore, you are warned never to love the world and its glory! The first commandment directs us to love and worship Yahweh only and never worship the names of idols. "***And in all things that I have said unto you be circumspect (careful): and make no mention of the name of gods, neither let it be heard out of thy mouth***" (Exodus 23:13). Worshipping Yahweh means totally surrendering one's life to Him alone (Matt. 4:10; Luke 4:8); it means worshipping Him in accordance with His own terms, e.g., following and worshipping Him on His blessed and sanctified Sabbath day [not Sunday] and feast days. Any worship that deviates from the seventh-day Sabbath is disobedience, and the penalty is death when Yahshua returns.

From Genesis to Revelation, YAHWEH identifies a particular 'SIGN' for HIS worship, i.e., the Sabbath. This SIGN is hinged on YAHWEH's chosen day for His worship, called the Seventh Day. The Sabbath day was revealed by YAHWEH and upheld by YAHSHUA MESSIAH (Genesis 2:2-3; Exodus 20:8-11; 31:13-17; Ezekiel 20:12, 20; Mark 2:27-28; Revelation 14:7-9). YAHSHUA says we must follow His example. Whose example do you follow? Are you following the Sunday worship tradition established by men? Doing the will of the Father, obeying His Word, and teaching His Word, including worshipping Him on the Sabbath day, were examples YAHSHUA and His apostles left for the Assembly. For instance, YAHSHUA never missed Sabbath day worship from birth till He ascended into heaven. "…As His custom was, He went into the synagogue on the Sabbath day and stood up to read…" (Luke 4:16). YAHSHUA was constantly in the Temple teaching and doing the will of the Father on the Sabbath days. YAHSHUA kept all the Father's Ten Commandments and commands us to do the same. "If you love Me, keep My commandments"; "If you keep My commandments, you shall abide in My love, even as I have kept My Father's commandments and abide in His love" (John 14:15; 15:10). Do you obey Him as He instructed?

Second Commandment Warning: "You shall not make for yourself a carved image" – this commandment follows the first above, thus identifying 'Who' to worship. It tells us how to worship YAHWEH, what dangers to avoid in our worship, and the continuing blessings or penalties that will come to us and our offspring if we worship idols. The phrase 'not' to 'make' directs the worshipper never to design any physical or spiritual object or image in the form of a picture – drawn, photographed, or carved by any means. This law demands that one should never think or imagine in one's heart any form of identifiable 'entity' in the likeness of anything, whether in the heavens, on earth, or beneath the earth. In particular, this law guards us from making a god out of anything and putting it in place of YAHWEH. No image, no intermediary, no picture, or physical object is required to approach or worship YAHWEH. Anything created in Yahweh's semblance is Baal or an idol. What is an idol? An idol is anything that takes Yahweh's place or replaces His Name, or that one loves beyond the love for YAHWEH. Yahweh warns His people never to substitute, replace, or exchange His NAME YAHWEH for Ba-al ['Lord'], which has its origin in Babylon. This is where the second law interlinks with the third law that warns worshippers never to make His Name vain. Yahweh knew that Yisrayah would change His Name and make it vain, thus prompting Him to query them: "…What iniquity have your fathers found in Me, that they are gone far from Me, and have walked after vanity, and are become vain? Hath a nation changed their mighty ones [gods], which are yet no mighty ones? But my people have changed their glory for that which doth not profit. Hast thou not procured this unto thyself, in that thou hast forsaken Yahweh, when He led thee by the way?" (Jeremiah 2:5, 11, 17). Indeed, Yahweh saw it coming! To what did Yisrayah change the name of Yahweh, their Father? The false prophets of Israel caused Yahweh's people "to forget [His] Name by their dreams which they tell every man to his neighbour, as their fathers have forgotten My Name for Ba-al"

(Jeremiah 23:26-27; also see Hosea 2:16-17; Malachi 2:2). When Yahweh eventually scattered Israel into the nations of the world because of their idol worship and forsaking His commandments, they left with the names of Baals and have continued to live with the names of Baals to this day. Following the substitution or exchange of Yahweh's set-apart Name for Baal [meaning: 'Lord'], today's Bibles in the same manner replaced or removed the NAME of Yahweh with 'the Lord' from Genesis to Revelation, causing humanity to forget YHWH's revered Name. Yahweh swore that none of those who have the names of Baals on their lips will enter into His kingdom because they are 'already cursed with a curse' (Malachi 2:2; Ezekiel 20:38; Hosea 2:16 17). The fathers served and worshipped the Lord God of the nations, thus bringing upon them the wrath of YHWH.

All through the Scriptures, YAHWEH kept warning mankind: "You shall not make idols[3] for yourselves, neither a carved image nor a sacred pillar… nor shall you set up an engraved stone…to bow down to it; for I am YAHWEH your FATHER" (Leviticus 26:1). When artwork or sculpture is used as a form of worship or an aid to worship, it becomes an idol. Why would an image be brought into churches, and why do the people pretend they do not worship it? That is the lie of the

---

[3] Idols are foreign Gods which Yisrayah are not permitted to worship. Authors describe gods, Gods, el, elohim, Elohim, Baal, as Gods of nations, alien to Yisrayah. Ref. 'Yahweh and the Gods and Goddesses of Canaan' (2002); 'A Handbook of Gods and Goddesses of the Ancient Near East…' (2021).

devil. Knowingly or unknowingly, people worship image(s). Images are worshipped; that is the reason they bring them into the congregation. These images can be in the form of a cross or a picture of a man (e.g., an effigy of 'Christ' depicted on wood or stone, known in Scripture as false images!). Yahweh says, "Make no mention of the name of gods, neither let it be heard out of thy mouth." Do you mention the name(s) of these gods depicted in images, objects, or pictures? If you say no, what about the name people call and praise in worship? Do you know that the consequences of disobeying YHWH are death? Yes, death!

What about money? Money is Satan's instrument of possessiveness for the pursuit of riches, wealth, lust, vain glory, fame, and recognition. The love of money is idolatry. Money is an image worshipped by many. It is an idol predominantly worshipped in these last days by the young and old. "The love of money is the root of all evil"; many pursue it and are ensnared in covetousness; thus, "they err from the faith, and pierce themselves through with many sorrows" (1 Timothy 6:10). Do we need money? Yes, we do, but through the leading of the Spirit of YAHSHUA that guides the heart not to be covetous and adulterous with money. He told us the first and most important thing to seek in life: "Seek first the kingdom of YHWH and His righteousness, and all these things shall be added unto you" (Matthew 6:33). Lack of absolute trust in YHWH and lack of contentment result in covetousness, stealing, and idolising money. Our priority is to seek to be admitted into YAHWEH's kingdom by way of His righteousness, which will guarantee our salvation and eternal life. Then "all these things" shall be added to you, which includes a fruitful family, money, wealth, joy, peace of mind, etc. Do not forget that YHWH is the owner and possessor of all things. All power belongs to Him, both in heaven and on earth. If anyone refuses the first and most important assignment for human life – to get sealed into His Spirit for righteousness – Satan, the head of mammon, will use his spirit and power to entangle the disobedient soul in damnable sin. Remember, anything you love beyond YHWH and His righteousness is idolatry – whether money, modern technologies, pleasure, parents, siblings, leaders, or even self (see Luke 14:26-27, 33; Matthew 16:24). Furthermore, remember that YAHSHUA is the Son of YAH and is Spirit (Hebrews 1:8; John 4:24; 2 Corinthians 3:17). Any picture or likeness of His person breaks this second warning. Pictures, crucifixes, crosses, and images of "Jesus" people carry completely describe Exodus Chapter 20:3 5, which is a rebellion against the Word of YHWH – that His people must not make images, objects, or pictures for worship. People who make images depicting "Jesus" simply submit to idol worship because the Book of Covenant warns against image worship. The worshippers give the false impression that they don't worship the image but the man "Jesus". What's the difference between a man and his name? The man is his name, and his name is him. People should stop deceiving themselves by exonerating themselves from idol worship because they are daily committing the same crime they are denying. There are not two Messiahs. YAHSHUA is the true Messiah! Who is the "Jesus" Gentile Messiah? No man can capture the image of YAHSHUA MESSIAH, because He is the promised Seed all the way from Adam, and finally, He was born a Hebrew from the lineage of Abraham. He is the EMMANUYAH – "YHWH with us" (Matthew 1:23); He is also the Spirit of YHWH (2 Corinthians 3:17). Compare Revelation 1:12-18 with Revelation 19:11-16. Both reveal YAHSHUA MESSIAH in His majesty, but in different forms and shapes. In these, none of His images or pictures are seen or kept anywhere for worship. Similarly, none of the pictures of the FATHER are seen anywhere for worship. The FATHER is worshipped by His Name, YAHWH, alone! (Matt. 4:10; Luke 4:8).

Again, as explained earlier, you shall not call any man 'Father', for only YHWH in heaven is your FATHER; you shall not call any human being 'Rabbi', for only YAHSHUA MESSIAH is your 'Rabbi' (Matthew 23:9, 10; also see Jeremiah 3:19; John 20:17). Do not call your church leader 'Father', for we are all brethren – "he that is greatest among you shall be your servant" (verse 11). Love YHWH and worship Him; love YAHSHUA and worship Him as our FATHER instructed (Heb. 1:6; Ps.

97:7). All angels and men are commanded to worship Him. As you "honour the Son, so also honour the Father", and they will come and live in you and give you eternal life (John 5:23, 24; John 14:21, 23). If you refuse to abide by the warnings offered to serve and worship YAHWEH, His wrath will be revealed and the consequences will be terrible. Obey and worship YAHSHUA MESSIAH as you honour the Father. Again, listen to YAHSHUA: "That all men should honour the Son, even as they honour the Father. He that honoureth not the Son honoureth not the Father which hath sent Him." (John 5:23). Any attempt to make an image of YAHSHUA is dishonouring Him and the Father because both are One (John 10:30).

Third Commandment Warning: "You shall not take the name of YAHWEH your FATHER in vain..." – This law closely follows the second commandment discussed above, which guards people from making idols out of anything. YAHWEH wants us to recognise and honour His name, His office, and His position as the great sovereign Creator and Ruler of the universe. We are commanded to call on the name of YAHWEH in spirit and in truth, not in vain (worthless or ruin). His name is sacred, holy, and powerful. He tells us never to take His NAME in vain [replace, substitute, or ruin: read Jeremiah 2:11-13, 17, 26-29, 31-32; 3:7-25; 7:8-34; 8:1-12, 15 22; 9:1-26; 10:1-25; 11:1, 23; 12:1-17; 23:27]. Despite Yahweh's warning not to REPLACE or

SUBSTITUTE His NAME for IDOLS, Israel and Judah disobeyed Him and made idols [Baal] of nations their YHWH. As a result of their failure to keep to His Word, the people of Yahweh were scattered all over the world, to this day. The true Yisrayah and Judah who keep His Commandments will return as one nation [ISRAEL] when Yahshua returns to this Earth to rule and reign over it.

YAHWEH's Form and Attributes: The Name of YAHWEH reveals His attributes – e.g., Salvation, Eternal Father, Eternal Life, All-Powerful Creator – who shows by His works that He is the Creator of Heaven and Earth, Sustainer, and Supreme Judge of the world. YAHWEH is His SALVATION Name declared to Yisrayah upon which they were delivered from Egypt (Exodus 3:15; 14:13-31); and also, YAHWEH is His SALVATION Name that this present age must CALL on for their SALVATION as mankind heads into great tribulation and the wrath of Yahweh (Joel 2:32; Psalm 9:10; Psalm 91:14; Acts 4:12). No other name is given to those who have FAITH in Him for their Salvation – except the NAME OF YAHWEH, from which the Name of His Son, YAHSHUA [SAVIOUR], is given, Who is to Save His people from their sins (Matthew 1:21; Acts 4:12; John 17:6, 11, 22). He is sent to prepare them for salvation and will deliver them during the great tribulation and wrath that is coming upon the Earth. The short form of Yahweh is YAH (see Psalm 68:4 in the

NKJV proper translation). Remember, our Father gave His Son, Yahshua, power and authority to create, to judge all things, and to SAVE His people from their sins and to deliver them from the oncoming trouble on the Earth. The relationship between the Father and the Son as one family is clearly documented in the BOC, where it is explained that the Father gave the WORD, YAHSHUA MESSIAH, the authority to create and judge all things. YAHSHUA will: "Bring to an end the violence of the wicked and make the righteous secure – You, the righteous One who probes minds and hearts" (Psalm 7:9). Our YHWH has a title name, called "Father". The Patriarchs knew YHWH by His title – Father – and by His Name – Yahweh. His name was called by the fathers even in the days of Adam. YHWH's Name was called at the time of Seth (Gen. 4:26). The BOC revealed that Abraham built an altar for YAHWEH in many places. Although the Elohim Source Writers (Elohoist)[4] claimed that YHWH did not reveal His Name to the patriarchs, they knew Him as 'El Shaddai' (Exodus 6:3). This claim contradicts the BOC, which tells us that the patriarchs called upon the Name of YAHWEH and worshipped Him accordingly. The 'Elohoists' who changed the true Name of YAHWEH to 'El' or 'Elohim' gave the impression that YHWH only revealed His Name to the children of the patriarch in the

---

[4] Elohoist began replacement of the Sacred Name, **YHWH**, to El, Elohim, which YHWH hates. Elohoist introduced 'religions and idol names' to replace Yahwist original scripts. Ref: 'In the Book of Covenant Yahweh Is Not God' (2025), pages 149-'43 [describes religions and idol names]

wilderness, and not to the fathers. According to Exodus 20:3-5, 'Elohim' belongs to the titles credited to images of gods, which the people of Yahweh were warned not to worship. The Hebrew Strong's Dictionary alludes to 'Elohim' as rulers, judges, gods, and angels, as well as God. Isaiah 42:8 and 48:11 insist that the Name of YHWH must be worshipped and should not be shared with carved images or idols.

The Name of YHWH connotes His SALVATION POWER to His people. Note that the Father's name and His title are not the same. His Name is extremely powerful and potent and depicts the exact purpose of its use more than His title. At times, His title FATHER is shortened to YAH and used as part of longer titles: YAH Almighty – meaning, YAHWEH Almighty (Genesis 49:24); Yah-Elyon – meaning, YHWH Most High (Deuteronomy 26:19); Yah Roi – meaning, YHWH Who Sees (Genesis 16:13), etc. For further reading on YAH's title, request our Book[5]: *In the Book of Covenant Yahweh is not God*. The name most commonly translated "YAHWEH" in the Old Testament is translated from the Hebrew letters YHWH, sometimes rendered YAHWEH or YAHVEH (Genesis 21:33). The original Hebrew word means 'the Eternal' or 'Self-Existent One'. The Hebrew word incorrectly rendered as "Jehovah" in some translations shows YAHWEH's

---

[5] In the Book of Covenant Yahweh Is Not God (2025), pages 41-51 [reveals the difference between YHWH's Name and titles]

character as the Ever-living YAHWEH and is used to show His everlasting office in a covenant relationship with mankind whom He created. His name should be revered because it stands for the One Who is the source of All Powers, All Might, and All Authority, and these are connected with His attributes – His Power, His Eternal Existence, His Mercy, His Faithfulness, His Wisdom, His Righteousness, His Love, and His Unchangeable nature. Also, YHWH's title and His office must be respected, as we call on His Powerful SALVATION Name – YAHWEH – for worship, honour, adoration, praise, glory, and reverence.

Notice that personal names of His people can include the name of Yahweh: e.g., Dan'yah (Yah Is My Judge); Nathanayah (Gift of Yah); Samuyah (Heard by Yah); Elijah (Yi'yah Is Yahweh); and Ariyah (Lioness of Yah). Names of places can contain the shortened form of YHWH: e.g., Beth'yah (House of Yah); Jezre'yah (Yah Will Sow); Yisrayah (Prince of Yah), etc. Wrong Use of His Name: Every day, people profane YAHWEH's name, either by swearing or damning the very name of our Creator and our YHWH. The key to understanding what YAHWEH means was given to us by our YAHSHUA HAMASHIACH in His Sermon on the Mount about 'Swearing' (Matthew 5:33-37). Man is created in the likeness of YHWH. The breath of YHWH is in mankind. In the Genesis account of creation, the breath of YHWH gave man – "life" – and he became a living soul; and that life is in YAHSHUA HAMASHIACH. John records: "In Him was life; and the life was the light of men" (John 1:4). When we curse, abuse, insult, and malign somebody – e.g., saying, "You fool," "Racca," "Stupid," or "Idiot" – we are in that sense invoking a curse not only against the individual but also cursing and damning the indwelling Spirit of YAHSHUA inside the person – because His Spirit is in the person. Human beings are created in YHWH's likeness. Therefore, care must be taken not to damn, abuse, or malign anybody because the Spirit of YHWH is resident in human beings. Remember, the body of believers is the temple of YHWH. What about cursing people and even invoking the "Set-apart Spirit" to consume our perceived human enemies with 'fire', 'thunder', and other forms of adjectives used in prayer, such as 'YHWH: kill, strike, destroy, punish, overthrow, disgrace ...you'?

YAHSHUA's sermon on 'murder' must be taken seriously (Matthew 5:21 26). To use any of the above expressions is trifling, and it showcases that one is ignorant of the very Creator and Faithful FATHER who is calling mankind to return to Himself. This is the reason YAHSHUA died. By invoking murderous adjectives, they are asking YHWH to do something that is contrary to His nature and something that He has never intended to do. However, He kills those who live in disobedience. YHWH is not judging, damning, or condemning anybody, at least for now! But His judgement of destruction is coming swiftly against the wicked. He gives all mankind equal opportunity to repent, after which His judgement will take place. YAHSHUA does not damn people in the way many seem to invoke His Name (although not Him but 'Jesus' of the Christian religion) to harm or kill others! This idea emanates from the spirit of the devil. YAHSHUA came to save sinners, not to destroy them. YHWH will deprive no one of eternal life, except those who refuse to obey Him, or those who wilfully reject His way, His law, and His commandments. He says, "On this one will I look: on him who is poor and of a contrite spirit, and who trembles at My Word" (Isaiah 66:2).

The Bible provides a clear example of how Yahshua rejected bidding 'fire from heaven' to consume a perceived human enemy. YAHSHUA cautioned James and John for asking for fire from heaven to destroy the people of Samaria because they did not allow them to enter their city to prepare for YAHSHUA's journey to Jerusalem. YAHSHUA rejected their prayers because they did not meet the will of the Father. Their motives came from the spirit of the devil. The Bible records:

"When his disciples, James and John, saw this, they said, 'Sovereign Yah, do you want us to command fire to come down from the sky and destroy them, just as Elijah did?'" But Yahshua turned and rebuked them, "You don't know of what kind of spirit you are. For the

Son of Man didn't come to destroy men's lives, but to save them" (Luke 9:54-56).

The passage tells us exactly the work of Yahshua. He came to save the lost. Each time we are praying against the death of those whom we perceive as hating us, or our enemies, we do so without knowledge, and wrongly too, because the spirit of the devil is at work. Through such unwarranted prayers, our FATHER is attacked and insulted. YAHWEH does not respond to prayers targeted at destroying His Covenant people who are under His treaty and who possess His Spirit. They are special people He created in His likeness. Our common enemy is Satan the devil and his fallen angels. When we are confronted by the enemy, our prayers should be directed to YAHWEH to deal with the devil and his agents, not to destroy our fellow human beings. You don't have the right to destroy any life either, because you cannot create one. The one you intend to kill today may be the one in whom the Father is working to carry the gospel across the world. Your fellow human being whom you target to destroy may be one YAH appointed to help you tomorrow, even to be of immense help to you in the future. Covenant-keepers are their brothers' keepers. Be careful with the type of prayer you say!

Swearing by YAHWEH's Name: In Matthew 5:33-37 YAHSHUA taught not to swear in YAHWEH's name at all because swearing can invoke lies. Lies can defame, malign, damn, and damage the name of YAHWEH, which bears His nature and character. The name of YAHWEH is sacred and set apart and must be reverenced. His name must be feared. We call and praise Him in His Name. YAHSHUA says, "But I say to you, do not swear at all: neither by heaven, for it is YAHWEH's throne; nor by the earth, for it is His footstool; nor by Jerusalem, for it is the city of the great King" (verses 34-35). Do not invoke the name of YAHWEH to back up your oath because His Name is sanctified and above all creatures. Live an upright life! Let your 'yes' be yes, and 'no' be 'no'; in that way, your word should always be true.

Father, Reverend and YAHWEH: Do not usurp the name of the Father; also do not usurp the 'Reverend' title of the Father; and never usurp the name of YAHSHUA, nor His title – 'HaMashiach'. As remarked earlier, we are commanded by HaMashiach: "And call no man your Father upon the earth: for One is your Father, which is in heaven. Neither be ye called Mashiach, for One is your Mashiach, even MESSIAH." (Matthew 23:9, 10; also see Jeremiah 3:19; John 20:17). Unfortunately, many today violate His warning. They quickly explain it away, saying they call 'Father' or 'Daddy' as a way of respect and a mark of loyalty to their religious leaders. We are not called into religion but into a life of Covenant and eternal life! We are people of the Kingdom of Yahweh. We should not do what the religious people of the world are doing. Whom must we obey, honour, respect, or show our loyalty to? Religious leaders or Yahshua HaMashiach? Religious leaders take you to traditions or commandments of men, instead of commandments of Yahweh. Yahshua cited an example to the Jewish leaders in which they were breaking one of the spiritual laws of the Father that concerns honouring their parents (see Exodus 20:12; 21:17; Leviticus 20:9; Proverbs 28:24). He taught that keeping the commandments of the Father is the way to go (Matthew 15:1-14; 5:19; 19:17-22; Luke 11:38; Mark 7:6-13). There is flagrant abuse of His commandments in religious churches that parade themselves as saints, yet they teach men to continue to rebel against MESSIAH's clear teaching on obedience to the LAW (Matthew 5:19).

YAHWEH the Father is our only spiritual FATHER, no other! YAHSHUA is our only Mashiach and Saviour, no other! Usurping the name that belongs to the Father or the Son is an outright challenge and disobedience to His third commandment. It is blasphemous and an abomination to bear the title due only to the FATHER in Heaven and His Son – Yahshua. We are only permitted to use "father" for our human parents as indicated in the fifth commandment (Exod. 20:12). Some have argued that the Bible allows the use of "father" for religious leaders. They claim that Apostle Shaul called Timothy and Titus 'son'. Did Shaul usurp YAH's position? Did he use 'son' as a perpetual name? Did the brethren call him 'father' continually, as leaders of today's churches do? Did Apostle Shaul permit the use of "father" and "son" as a religious authority? Was the nomenclature "father" used on the apostles to replace their names as we have today – in such names as "Reverend", "Father", "Father-in-the-Lord", and "Daddy G.O."? Get it clear! YAHSHUA spoke to the twelve apostles, and all of them heard Him and obeyed His command! There is no place in the Scripture that any of those twelve apostles disobeyed this command. Refusing to abide by the simple instruction YAHSHUA gave to His Assembly is rejection of His authority and rebellion against the FATHER! The title of 'Reverend' applies to YAHWEH alone. The Bible is clear on this:"He sent redemption unto his people: He hath commanded his covenant forever: Holy and Reverend is His name" (Psalm 111:9). YAHWEH's Name is Set Apart and must be Revered – His Name must be respected, honoured, and worshipped. No human mortal is worthy of His title. Those who usurp YAHWEH's title – 'Reverend', 'Father' – have succeeded in making their congregations worship them. The implication is that they present themselves as 'gods' to be worshipped, thus making themselves 'idols'[6], like their father Satan the devil, whom the Bible calls the 'god of this world'! In case they are ignorant of this, they need to repent quickly because they are breaking the second commandment that requires no

---

[6] Arikibe (2025), explains Idols: meaning of idols and idolatry explained in the book: 'In the Book of Covenant Yahweh is not God', 2025, page 10, 21-30.

one to make an idol! People are to fear and worship YHWH in spirit and truth!! May YAH grant you the willing heart to listen and obey His WILL and LAW!!! To understand how the Third Commandment has been broken, refer to the book, 'Babylon Is Fallen'[7] and 'Yahshua's Greatest Commandments'[8]. YAH's Name must be known, respected, feared, trusted, and prayed to. He answers prayers based on His Name (Psalm 9:10; 91:14). His Name shall be in a worshipper's heart as He sees every heart and guides it; else, one may be serving and calling 'another', and His curse may destroy the person (Malachi 2:2; Deuteronomy 27:26; see John 4:22). It is compulsory that we know Him if we truly love Him!

Fourth Commandment: "Remember the Sabbath day, to keep it holy…" – This commandment is tied to the first, second, and third commandments, thus completing what YAHSHUA described as love for YHWH, which is "the first and greatest[9] commandment" (Matthew 22:38; Mark 12:29-30). This is also depicted in the first section of the Decalogue, which deals with man's relationship with YHWH.

As mentioned earlier, the fourth commandment existed before the Ten Commandments were given. Genesis

---

[7] Arikibe (2019) Babylon is fallen! *Come out of her my people,*

[8] Arikibe (2019) Yahshua's Greatest Commandments, Laws of Love and Liberty Revealed

[9] Arikibe (2019) Yahshua's Greatest Commandments, Laws of Love and Liberty Revealed

Chapter 2:1-3 reveals it existed before any law. Noah, Abraham, and Eber (Hebrew) knew and worshipped YAH on the Shabbat day. Descendants of Abraham kept Shabbat, particularly after it was given to them in the wilderness. YAHWEH used this commandment to test the obedience of Yisrayah (Exodus 16).

Why is the fourth commandment the most controversial of all the ten? It is the commandment that defines the ownership of heaven and earth. It defines who the Creator is. It is a SIGN and AUTHORITY of YHWH's creation. Satan has been making claims as the Creator and Owner of Heaven and Earth. Satan has been luring mankind to believe him and worship him as the god of this world that created heaven and earth. By using his lies and deception, he has succeeded in deceiving many that he is 'God'.

No wonder billions of humanity worship "God", the creature, instead of YAHWEH, the Creator of heaven and earth. The fourth commandment, which commands men to REST and WORSHIP YHWH, makes Satan mad. The Shabbat day of rest undermines Satan's agenda of hiding himself as one to be worshipped. As he could not base his sign and authority on the Creator, Satan deceived mankind into rejecting the Sabbath day so that they would worship him on the first day – Sunday. Sunday is Satan's mark or sign for worship.

Fourth Commandment has been a TEST commandment for those who obey YAHWEH and WORSHIP Him (Revelation 14:7-9). In Exodus 16:4, YAHWEH used it to "prove" or test His people to know "whether they will walk in My law or not." YAHWEH intentionally built the Sabbath law into the Ten Commandments to ascertain those who will obey His law. As such, from Genesis to Revelation, the Sabbath day is magnified and made honourable by YAHSHUA HAMASHIACH so that no one will have an excuse for dishonouring it.

It is in this commandment that YAHSHUA identified Himself as the SUPREME AUTHORITY of Sabbath. He commands people to keep the Shabbat day as provided in the BOC. Why do Christians forbid Shabbat day? Many of them believe that Shabbat day was changed on the day the Messiah rose from the dead. This is a massive fraudulent lie! Where is it written that the sacred day of rest should be changed to another day? Nowhere! If it is not written in the Covenant Law to inform people of the change, that means the change is fabricated and must be rejected for the sake of obedience to YHWH's instruction.

In Genesis, the Bible records that YHWH ended creation [work] on the Sabbath day, resting on that day (Genesis 2:2-3). The plain meaning of Mark 2:27-28 is that YAHSHUA is the Creator of the seventh-day Sabbath, and as the Supreme Authority of Sabbath, mankind should worship the FATHER of creation on His appointed day of rest. The disobedient "Churchianity" of today finds this truth hard to comprehend.

This commandment was most magnified and honoured by YAHSHUA, even as He renewed other laws in Matthew Chapters 5, 6, and 7. It is the lengthiest and most detailed of all the commandments in Exodus 20:8-11, Deuteronomy 5:7-21, and Exodus 31:13-17 (see Ezekiel 20:12, 20; Isaiah 56:2, 4, 6; Isaiah 58:13-14). Yet it is the most misunderstood, disliked, and condemned by mainstream Christians, who assume that the Sabbath day has been nailed to the 'cross', or cancelled, or replaced by Sunday worship. This is simply Satan's agenda!

It is the Law men debate and reject the most; it is the Law they readily tear asunder and try to separate from the rest of the commandments. It is the law most hated by people. It is the Law: Satan attacks more than others. Indeed, Satan blinds people's hearts so that they will not worship their Creator on His Sabbath day. Speaking through Isaiah, YHWH was explicit on the Shabbat commandment:

"Blessed is the man who does this, and the son of man who holds it fast, who keeps the Sabbath without profaning it and keeps his hand from doing any evil. For YHWH says, "To the eunuchs who keep My Sabbaths, and choose the things that please Me and hold fast to

My Covenant: I will give them in My house and within My walls a memorial and a name better than of sons and of daughters. I will give them an everlasting name that will not be cut off. Also, the foreigners who join themselves to YHWH, to serve Him, and to love YHWH's Name, to be His servants, everyone who keeps the Sabbath from profaning it, and holds fast my covenant..." (Is. 56:4, 6).

In the above passage, both a Yisrayahlite and a Gentile who observe the Sabbath and keep the Covenant without profaning them belong to YHWH. Conversely, any Yisrayah or Gentile who rejects the Sabbath and keeps the day of his own choice does not belong to YHWH. It's as simple as that. Once someone refuses to obey His commandments, the fellow ostracises himself from YHWH's Family.

Furthermore, those who rebel against YHWH's Sabbath day of rest do not ask themselves the question, 'Why did the fourth commandment start with the word "Remember"?' YAHSHUA, who knows the heart of mankind, knew that they would find excuses to disobey it. He knew that others would forget it and wish it away! Yet others would think that it is cancelled. No wonder YAHSHUA told the Jews: "Think not that I come to destroy the law, or the prophets..." (Matthew 5:17). In this same verse, YAHSHUA clearly told them, "I am not come to destroy the Law, but to fulfil it."

By 'fulfil', it means He came to accomplish His own assigned work of human salvation, as appointed to Him (the 'Seed') from the beginning (Genesis 3:15; Genesis 22:18; Matt. 1:21; Luke 1:30-33). Many did not understand Him, and in their ignorance, they deduced that the Law was cancelled. How can the Sabbath Law be cancelled when YAHSHUA told you to keep the Law as He also kept it (Matt. 5:19; John 14:15; John 15:10, etc.)?

YAHSHUA was categorically clear that none of the Ten Commandments has been destroyed. He unequivocally stated in Matthew 5:19 that anyone who destroys the Law will be dealt with. Anyone who destroys it or refuses to obey it is lawless; that person will not enter the Kingdom of YHWH (Matthew 7:21-23; 5:19). Those who keep the Law will have access into the Kingdom (Matt. 5:20). YHWH did not mince words on His verdict against those who reject His Shabbat. In Exodus 31:13-15, YAHWEH commands Mosheh to speak to His people:

"Speak also to the children of Yisrayah, saying, 'Most certainly you shall keep My Sabbaths, for it is a sign between Me and you throughout your generations, that you may know that I am YHWH who sanctifies you. You shall keep the Sabbath, therefore, for it is set apart (holy) to you. Everyone who profanes it shall surely be put to death; for whoever does any work therein, that soul shall be cut off from among his people. Six days shall work be done, but the seventh day is a Sabbath of solemn rest, set apart to YHWH. Whoever does any work on the Sabbath day shall surely be put to death.'?"

In the above passage, and following Isaiah 56:2, 4, 6, whosoever, whether Yisrayahlite or Gentile, who profanes or blasphemes the Sabbath day, that person shall DIE! Provided such an individual was called, and he/she rejects the invitation, the fellow will face the death sentence. Like other Covenant Feasts, the Sabbath is a law that no one can cancel; even the commandments of men cannot remove it. It's a perpetual law. YHWH commands it shall be kept in all generations. It's an everlasting Covenant (Exodus 31:13; Isaiah 24:5-6).

The Sabbath day belongs to YAHWEH as part of His Covenant, and His Covenant cannot be broken. The Sabbath covenant was renewed by YAHSHUA, and He vowed it has not been destroyed. YAHSHUA, the Maker and the Creator of the Sabbath, sincerely kept the Sabbath day. In Mark 2:27-28, He did not say that the Sabbath was made for only the Jews or Israelites, but for man – for all mankind. In other words, YAHSHUA MESSIAH, the Supreme Authority of the Sabbath, claims the authority as the Maker of the Sabbath (see Luke 4:16). And in the same manner, He invites all mankind to keep the Sabbath as He did. All the four synoptic Gospels reveal that YAHSHUA kept the Sabbath as His custom.

The BOC declared that YAHSHUA created all things – "all things were made through Him; and without Him nothing was made that was made" (John 1:1-3; Ephesians 3:9; Hebrews 1:2). So He has authority over Shabbat. He created all the days, from first to sixth, and told mankind to work in them, but after He created the seventh day, He blessed it and sanctified it and rested in it. Thus, He gave mankind the six days to do all their work, but:

"The seventh day is the Sabbath of YAHWEH your FATHER. In it you shall do no work: you, nor your son, nor your daughter, nor your male servant, nor your female servant, nor your cattle, nor your stranger who is within your gates. For in six days YAHWEH made the heavens and the earth, the sea, and all that is in them, and rested the seventh day. Therefore, YAHWEH blessed the Sabbath day and hallowed it" (Exodus 20:8-11).

YAHWEH is so magnanimous, kind, and loving that He spared man a day of rest. Yet His people reject it! Of all the seven days, He took only one day as His day of rest and a day that we should worship Him, yet men query the favour of YAHWEH and His love. They challenge MESSIAH on His authority to create that day and to own it. This is mankind's covetousness – usurping YAHWEH's authority, YAHWEH's reserved resting day, and rejecting to abide by His instruction. Thus, rejecting His love and invitation to worship Him on His Sabbath day, marked as a SIGN of His covenant between Him and His people. Whoever is disobeying the fourth commandment is outrightly telling YAHWEH: 'You are not the Creator'; 'You are not the Maker of Sabbath'; 'You are not the Creator of heaven and earth'; 'You are not supposed to command me to worship You on the Sabbath day'; 'You are not my Saviour and Salvation'; 'You are not my Father'; 'I do not belong to You'. Read Exodus 31:13-17 again to understand the reasons adduced for Sabbath day, because anyone who says 'NO' to Sabbath day is doomed to die.

YAHWEH says Sabbath shall be the SIGN between Him and His people. The only way to know that we belong to the Living YAHWEH is to submit to His prescribed Sabbath day of worship and reverence and honour Him. In Ezekiel 20:12-20, YAHWEH lamented that His people polluted His Sabbath day, and as a result, He wanted to destroy them. Surely, He did destroy many of them in the wilderness because of their disobedience. I believe that sets an example of what will befall people during the great tribulation days. YAHSHUA said He will destroy those who wilfully disobey Him on His return (Revelation 11:18). YAHWEH commands in Isaiah:

"Keep the Sabbath day holy. Don't pursue your own interests on that day, but enjoy the Sabbath and speak of it with delight as YAHWEH's holy day. Honour the Sabbath in everything you do on that day, and don't follow your own designs or talk idly.

Then YAHWEH will be your delight. I will give you great honour and satisfy you with the inheritance I promised to your ancestor Jacob. I, YAHWEH, have spoken!" (Isaiah 58:13-14, NLT).

YAHWEH kept the seventh day of the week holy. He blessed it and sanctified it. It is the only day amongst others that is BLESSED and SANCTIFIED. We should not pursue our own interests (work) on the holy day of Sabbath. STOP polluting the holy Sabbath day. Stop following those who changed Sabbath day rest to Sunday rest. This is the falling away Apostle Shaul talked about (2 Thessalonians 2:3). We are to enjoy the Sabbath day: praising Him, worshipping Him, reverencing Him, honouring Him, and praying to Him on His day of rest. He created the Sabbath day for His own glory. The twenty-four elders fall down before Him and worship Him, saying:

"Worthy are you, our YHWH and FATHER, the Sanctified One, to receive the glory, the honour, and the power, for You created all things, and because of Your pleasure they existed and were created!" (Revelation 4:11).

Blessings for Keeping Shabbat: Yes, YHWH deserves glory due unto Him, honour, and worship on His Sabbath day, which He created for His glory. Do not deny Him the glory, honour, and worship due to Him, so that you may get your blessings. The Sabbath day possesses huge blessings in it, with the promises YAHWEH made to those who keep it. He promised to "give you great honour and satisfy you with the inheritance I promised to your ancestor Jacob" (verse 14). Meaning that our lives and days on earth will be blessed, and as we enter into the promised Kingdom of YAHWEH, His blessings will follow us. In this He stamped His Name and Authority: "I, YAHWEH, have spoken!" (verse 14). Let us follow YAHSHUA's example, whose custom it was to keep the seventh-day Sabbath as a holy convocation (Luke 4:16; Leviticus 23:3).

YAHWEH is so magnanimous, kind, and loving that He spared man a day of rest. Yet His people reject it! Of all the seven days, He took only one day as His day of rest and a day that we should worship Him. Yet men query the favour of YAHWEH and His love. They challenge MESSIAH on His authority to create that day and to own it. This is mankind's covetousness – usurping YAHWEH's authority, YAHWEH's reserved resting day, and rejecting to abide by His instruction. Thus, rejecting His love and invitation to worship Him on His Sabbath day was marked as a SIGN of His covenant between Him and His people. Whoever is disobeying the fourth commandment is outrightly telling YAHWEH, 'You are not the Creator'; 'You are not the Maker of Sabbath'; 'You are not the Creator of heaven and earth'; 'You are not supposed to command me to worship You on the Sabbath day'; 'You are not my Saviour and Salvation';

'You are not my Father'; 'I do not belong to You.' Read Exodus 31:13-17 again to understand the reasons adduced for Sabbath day, because anyone who says 'NO' to Sabbath day is doomed to die.

YAHWEH says the Sabbath shall be the SIGN between Him and His people. The only way to know that we belong to the Living YAHWEH is to submit to His prescribed Sabbath day of worship, reverence, and honour to Him. In Ezekiel 20:12-20, YAHWEH lamented that His people polluted His Sabbath day, and as a result, He wanted to destroy them. Sure, He did destroy many of them in the wilderness because of their disobedience. I believe that sets an example of what will befall people during the great tribulation days. YAHSHUA said He will destroy those who wilfully disobey Him on His return (Revelation 11:18). YAHWEH commands in Isaiah:

"Keep the Sabbath day holy. Don't pursue your own interests on that day, but enjoy the Sabbath and speak of it with delight as YAHWEH's holy day. Honour the Sabbath in everything you do on that day, and don't follow your own designs or talk idly. Then YAHWEH will be your delight. I will give you great honour and satisfy you with the inheritance I promised to your ancestor Jacob. I, YAHWEH, have spoken!" (Isaiah 58:13-14, NLT).

YAHWEH kept the seventh day of the week holy. He blessed it and sanctified it. It is the only day among others that is BLESSED and SANCTIFIED. We should not pursue our own interests (work) on the holy day of Sabbath. STOP polluting the holy Sabbath day. Stop following those who changed the Sabbath day of rest to Sunday rest. This is the falling away apostle Shaul talked about (2 Thessalonians 2:3). We are to enjoy the Sabbath day: praising Him, worshipping Him, reverencing Him, honouring Him, and praying to Him on His day of rest. He created the Sabbath day for His own glory. The twenty-four elders fall down before Him and worship Him, saying:

"Worthy are you, our YHWH and FATHER, the Sanctified One, to receive the glory, the honour, and the power, for You created all things, and because of your pleasure they existed and were created!" (Revelation 4:11).

Blessings for Keeping Shabbat: Yes, YHWH deserves glory due unto Him, honour, and worship on His Sabbath day, which He created for His glory. Do not deny Him the glory, honour, and worship due to Him, so that you may receive your blessings. The Sabbath day possesses huge blessings in it with the promises YAHWEH made to those who keep it. He promised to "give you great honour and satisfy you with the inheritance I promised to your ancestor Jacob" (verse 14). This means that our lives and days on earth will be blessed, and as we enter into the promised Kingdom of YAHWEH, His blessings will follow us. In this He stamped His Name and Authority: "I, YAHWEH, have spoken!" (Verse 14). Let us follow YAHSHUA's example, whose custom it was to keep the seventh-day Sabbath as a holy convocation (Luke 4:16; Leviticus 23:3).

Biblical evidence points to the seventh day as YAHWEH's true Sabbath day to honour, worship, and adore the Father and the Son. As MESSIAH did, it is a day for preaching, expounding the Scriptures, and even healing the sick, diseased, maimed, and the dying, as He commanded (Matthew 10:8). Learn to keep the Sabbath and not to pollute it with Sunday worship. Neither the Father nor YAHSHUA ever commanded the keeping of the first day – Sunday – as a day of rest. If you obey Him, your life will be blessed on this earth and in His coming Kingdom. If you disobey Him, curses will follow. Yahshua's seven letters to His Assemblies in Revelation Chapters 2 and 3 clearly warn against breaking any of these laws, which those Assemblies were breaking and were being asked to repent. Do not reject His Sabbath call to rest and worship on His Sabbath day, because the Sabbath day is YAHWEH'S day [not the Lord's day as wrongly taught]; whereas Sunday is founded on tradition or the commandment of men as instituted by Satan for man to worship him, the Sabbath is clearly Yahweh's (see the booklet 'Babylon is Fallen' on our website: www.livingyahweh.com)¹⁰. Obey and avoid His wrath and receive your blessings! May you be blessed as you keep YAHSHUA's word of patience (Revelation 3:10), which includes His Sabbath day!

LAW OF LOVE

Satan has succeeded in teaching mankind that the Ten Commandments, which is the Law of Love, have been cancelled. Satan does this so that YHWH will abhor the disobedient person. Satan wants YHWH to do away with people who hate His Law. In removing YHWH's moral law, Satan eliminates "love", which the commandment offers. However, Yahshua asserts that the Ten Commandments Law is not cancelled nor destroyed; neither is it nailed at the stake, as Churchianity claims. The false teachers preach that the Law is cancelled so that they can avail themselves of the opportunity to continue to disobey YAHSHUA's clear commandments. If mankind were obeying YAHWEH's Laws, they would never have been sinning against Him and their neighbours, and life would not have been brutish. Evil would not have dwelt with human beings; there would have been peace in the homes, towns,

---

¹⁰ Babylon is Fallen, and Yahshua's Greatest Commandment – provide in-depth knowledge on Shabbat keeping.

cities, nations, and peoples; there would have been peace and tranquillity all over the world.

Fifth Commandment – Exodus 20:12

"Honour your father and your mother, that your days may be long upon the land which YAHWEH your FATHER is giving you."

Obedience and respect for father and mother are demanded: the primary focus of the fifth Commandment is to honour father and mother and listen to and obey them, which is an integral part of the Torah that demands respect for biological parents, elders, authorities, etc. People who obey this rule are truly the children of the Most High, provided they also keep the other commandments. They are called children of YAH because they exhibit His characteristics of righteousness. This Law showcases a series of commandments that define proper relationships with others. The Ten Commandments are the standard of conduct people must keep. Their consequences on individuals, families, groups, communities, societies, and nations are clearly documented in the BOC. If children obey the fifth Commandment, the overwhelming blessings pronounced on it flow from YHWH to the parents down to the offspring. Any individual or group — including the nation — that keeps this law reaps the benefits of strong family relationships ordained by YHWH.

Unfortunately, today, respect for fathers, mothers, the elderly, and seniors among people is gone. YHWH meant that families should live in peace and harmony, and by extension, family cohesion would positively impact society and the nation, thus making the world a peaceful place to live. Disobedience to the fifth Commandment has led to divisions and acrimony in families, societies, and countries. This is a rebellion against YHWH, which in effect damages the Earth He created for His glory and mankind's habitation, joy, and peace. Yes! A rebellion at the highest level. Apart from individual rebelliousness, leaders worldwide have rebelled and trodden down the commandments of YHWH, thereby trodden down peace in families, communities, nations, and the world. These leaders have succeeded in teaching traditions or commandments of men instead of the Commandments of YHWH, thereby leading people away from the love of the FATHER. Yahshua charged the leaders of His Assembly:

"Why do ye also transgress the commandment of YHWH by your tradition? For YAH commanded, saying, HONOUR THY FATHER AND MOTHER: AND HE THAT CURSETH FATHER OR MOTHER, LET HIM DIE THE DEATH. But ye say, 'whosoever shall say to his father or his mother, "It is a gift, by whatsoever thou mightest be profited by me," and honour not his father or his mother, he shall be free.'

Thus have ye made the commandment of YHWH of none effect by your tradition" (Matthew 15:3-6; also see Exodus 20:12; Exodus 21:17; Deuteronomy 4:21).

The Jewish rabbinic leaders had taught the people that ritual laws of washing of hands and feet and their supposed right to adjust even the fifth Commandment to suit their whims and caprices were more important than observing YHWH's commandments, which urge the people to honour and respect fathers and mothers. According to scholarship, such washings are common among the eastern nations. Adam Clarke's Commentary states: "This sort of washing was, and still continues to be, an act of religion in the eastern countries and was likely borrowed by Mohammed from the Jews. The rabbinic Jewish doctrine is: 'If a man neglects the washing, he shall be eradicated from this world.' Bathing is an indispensable prerequisite to the first meal of the day among the Hindus, and washing the hands and the feet is equally so before the evening meal." Messiah Yahshua condemns this kind of doctrine that makes such laws obligatory or equal to Yahweh's Law (Heb. Torah) [also see Mark 7:1-23 and Colossians 2:20-22].

These leaders were told that setting aside Yahweh's laws and yet turning to worship Him is hypocrisy. He told them that "in vain they do worship Me, teaching for doctrines the commandments of men" (Matthew 15:9).

Disobedience to the Law of Yahweh renders one's worship vain [worthless, ruin, or without effect]. This is exactly what today's religious leaders have done to His NAME, the Shabbat Day of Rest, and Feasts, making them worthless by replacing them with their traditions and commandments. The most painful of their disobedience is the removal and replacement of His Sacred Name — YAHWEH — with the names 'Elohim' and 'Baal', translated as 'God' and 'the Lord' respectively, as contained in English Bibles. This is what YHWH forbids. Yahshua called them blind guides, who will surely be exterminated with those they lead (Deut. 8:19-20). He further reminded them that setting aside Yahweh's Law in place of human commandments attracts the death penalty.

Yahshua directs that keeping the fifth Commandment, plus others, and following Him [i.e. to have faith in Him], perfects one for salvation and eternal life, as well as makes way for the promised eternal inheritance — the Kingdom of Yahweh (Matthew 19:18-21; Heb. 9:15). Those who keep and obey the first five commandments show LOVE to the FATHER and SON. YAHSHUA reveals that these five commandments are tied into one greatest commandment of the Law. When someone loves YHWH and YAHSHUA with his heart, it means the individual is accomplishing those first five commandments that belong to YHWH. YAHSHUA said, "You shall love YHWH your FATHER with all your heart, with all your soul, and with all your mind. This is the first and great commandment" (Matt. 22:37-38; see Exodus 20:2-12; Deut. 6:5; 10:12; 30:6). Obedience to the commandments defines love for YHWH, and love for brethren is reflected in the sixth–tenth commandments. John the Beloved summarises it thus: "By this we know that we love the children of YAH when we love and keep His commandments. For this is the love of YAH, that we keep His commandments. And His commandments are not burdensome" (1 Jn. 5:2-3; Jn. 14:15; Matt. 11:30; 23:4). This is what YAHSHUA meant when He said, "If you love Me, keep My commandments" (Jn. 14:15). Let's continue with the love of the children of YAH, i.e., love of the brethren.

Sixth Commandment – Exodus 20:13

"You shall not murder."

This commandment deals with murder: Life is a precious gift from YAHWEH; therefore, He instructs, "You shall not murder." This sixth commandment teaches the preservation of the sanctity of life. Who is the life-giver? YAHWEH is the life-giver! Who possesses the authority to take human life? Who has the right to make that decision? Life is YAHWEH's breath. You have no right to take your life or another person's life, because life is YAHWEH's breath. You cannot create life; only YAHWEH can kill and make alive! It took Him His breath to create life. If any life must be destroyed, YAHWEH must sanction it. Only YAHWEH has the power and authority over life because He is the source of life. You are not to deliberately kill — premeditatedly or kill in the anger of the moment. Sanctity of life would have been maintained and preserved if mankind had heeded the sixth commandment. People would not have hated one another to the point of taking their life. People would not have been murdering or slaughtering one another in the name of wars and conflicts. It is the failure to keep this law that has left the earth in chaos today, and it is getting worse by the day. According to YAHSHUA, hatred, anger, and wars would increase and finally escalate to the point that humanity would nearly wipe itself out before He returns. But for His timely intervention, a remnant will survive. YAHSHUA taught men to stop abusing the law of murder. Mankind should refrain from anger, which is one of the characteristics of the devil that leads to murder. Anger stirs the heart to commit murder (Matthew 5:21-26). Strife, quarrel, and hatred are co-contributors to murder. In recent times, Satan has released a spirit of hatred and anger, and divisions and crises are already heralding the world. Obey the teaching of Yahshua on the Law of murder! Stop the murder of an unborn innocent baby! Stop the murder of a father, mother, brother, sister, relative, or neighbour, no matter how evil you think they may have been or what they may have committed against you. Murder can be through hurtful verbal words; it can be with a weapon.

Any means that can lead to the destruction of human life must be avoided! Yahshua teaches that "all who take the sword will perish by the sword" (Matthew 26:52). Murder goes against the TOC of LOVE. Murder truncates the commandment to love one another. Love disappears in the presence of murder. YHWH forbids murder! Murder negates the principle of life – that is, 'live and let live'.

The penalty for killing one another is huge: *"Whosoever sheds the blood of man, by man shall his blood be shed; for in His own image YHWH has made mankind" (Genesis 9:6)*. Again, "Whoever strikes and kills a man must surely be put to death" (Exodus 21:12). Furthermore, "If anyone is destined for captivity, into captivity he will go; if anyone is to die by the sword, by the sword he must be killed. Here is a call for the perseverance and faith of the saints" (Revelation 13:10). Those who take others captive or kill them shall die in the same manner and even face the second death because of disobedience to the Law. The love of another person does not permit murder. Where there is love, evil cannot thrive; murder cannot breathe; enmity is put away. We are not even allowed to hate our enemies, let alone murder them. We are to pray for our enemies, feed them, and forgive them. Our King and High Priest commands us: "Love your enemies, bless them that curse you, do good to them that hate you, and pray for them which despitefully use you and persecute you: that ye may be the children of your FATHER which is in heaven…" (Matthew 5:44-45). Yahshua adds, "For if ye forgive men their trespasses, your heavenly FATHER will also forgive you: But if ye forgive not men their trespasses, neither will your FATHER forgive your trespasses" (Matthew 6:14-15; also see Mark 11:26). Believers, watch out! The sixth commandment is like the seventh, which states that the children of YAH should not commit adultery. Committing adultery is an act of one killing himself or herself before the Creator. It's, first and foremost, a self-inflicted destruction. If a Covenant-keeper messes oneself up with adultery or fornication, the Spirit of YAH withdraws from the person. To cause the Spirit of YAH to walk away is the beginning of the death of the saint and a loss of the Kingdom. Let's explore the BOC to uncover what the seventh commandment teaches.

Seventh Commandment – Exodus 20:14

"You shall not commit adultery."

This commandment deals with adultery, fornication, and all forms of sexual immorality. The seventh law is given to protect marital relationships and also to ensure that those who are not married live a set-apart life. It deals with the whole sphere of unfaithfulness, lust, and betrayal in relationships. Unless the natural desires that attract members of the opposite sex are channelled exclusively toward a loving marriage relationship, the temptation to engage in sexual immorality can easily overpower one's spiritual 'self-control', which is one of the fruits of the Spirit. Furthermore, be careful because adultery can also be committed from the heart. The thought process of the heart encourages the 'eyes' to look lustfully at the opposite sex.

"You have heard that it was said to those of old, 'You shall not commit adultery.' But I say to you, that whosoever looketh on a woman to lust after her hath committed adultery with her already in his heart" (Matthew 5:27-28).

In saying this, Yahshua emphasised that adultery was essentially a thing of the heart. This weakness is the focus of the seventh commandment. Originally, YAHWEH created a man and a woman to be together, and He divinely joined them to meet the needs of each other. This law authorises the marriage relationship and establishes it as the foundation of the family, which in turn stands as the foundation and the most important building block of society. Marriage is meant for two unmarried persons of the opposite sex – joined together – to create their own family apart from their parents. Only then should they "become one flesh" by physically uniting in a sexual relationship. YAHSHUA makes it clear that YAHWEH, from the beginning, intended that marriage should be a monogamous and permanent relationship (Matthew 19:3-6).

The consequence of violating the marital law is huge. The social and personal harm brought by sexual immorality is so pervasive that it defies our ability to quantify its toll in human suffering. Most people simply refuse to contemplate its staggering consequences. If people obey YAHSHUA on this commandment, they will not commit adultery or fornication. YAHSHUA took time to teach that adultery and fornication must be stopped because they are unholy behaviours, which destroy the individual's body. Also, indulging in sexual immorality blocks the Ruach HaKodesh (Holy Spirit) from living in the life of the person. Yahshua taught that committing adultery or fornication begins with a lustful look. Therefore, "Whosoever looks on a woman (or man) to lust after her has committed adultery with her (or him) already in his (or her) heart." Adultery (extra-marital sex with a married person) or fornication (unmarried persons having sexual intercourse) is sinful and punishable by death.

Yahshua also taught that couples should not divorce and get remarried to another when they are still alive. "It hath been said, 'WHOSOEVER SHALL PUT AWAY HIS WIFE, LET HIM GIVE HER A WRITING OF DIVORCEMENT.' But I say unto you, that whosoever shall put away his wife, saving for the cause of fornication, causeth her to commit adultery: and whosoever shall marry her that is divorced committeth adultery" (Matthew 5:31-32; also see Deuteronomy

24:1-4; Matthew 1:18; Luke 16:18; Romans 7:2-3). The clause 'saving for the cause of fornication' has been a subject of debate amongst scholars. Some consider it to be an insertion or addition and not the Word of Yahshua. In Matthew 19, Yahshua made it plain:

"And He answered and said unto them, 'Have ye not read that he which made them at the beginning made them male and female...?'"FOR THIS CAUSE SHALL A MAN LEAVE FATHER AND MOTHER, AND SHALL CLEAVE TO HIS WIFE: AND THEY TWAIN SHALL BE ONE FLESH? Wherefore they are no more twain, but one flesh. What therefore Elohim hath joined together, let not man put asunder" (Matthew 19:5-6; Genesis 2:24; 5:2; Mark 10:6).

The Bible asserts 'no remarriage'. YAHWEH avows, "I hate divorce!" says YAHWEH, the FATHER of Israel. "To divorce your wife is to overwhelm her with cruelty," says YAHWEH of Heaven's Armies. "So, guard your heart; do not be unfaithful to your wife" (Malachi 2:16). The verdict of no divorce on a man equally applies to the woman. If they divorce or separate, no remarriage should be consecrated until death takes one of them. The argument here is not accommodating anyone who indulges in extra-marital sex, adultery, fornication, cohabiting, etc. If, perhaps, the breaking of this law occurs, any of the parties can separate or divorce but would not marry until death takes its course.

Failure to comply with the keeping of the seventh commandment results in adultery, and no fornicator, sexually perverse, or immoral person shall enter the Kingdom of YHWH. The Scripture queries, "Do you not know that the wicked will not inherit the Kingdom of YHWH? Do not be deceived: neither the sexually immoral, nor idolaters, nor adulterers, nor men who submit to or perform homosexual acts, nor thieves, nor the greedy, nor drunkards, nor verbal abusers, nor swindlers will inherit the Kingdom of YHWH" (1 Corinthians 6:9-10).

YHWH says that the penalty for breaking His Law is death, including men who have sex with men (homosexuality) and women who have sex with women (lesbianism), and even those who have sex with animals (bestiality). These are considered abominations in the sight of YAHWEH. You must never have a sexual relationship with your neighbour's wife because you will defile yourself with her (Leviticus 18:20). The BOC states that if a man is found lying with another man's wife, both the man who slept with her and the woman must die (Deuteronomy 22:22). This law still stands today – because there's nowhere that it was abolished. Those who break this law and commit all sorts of immoral wickedness are also categorised as destroyers of the earth (Revelation 11:18). Apostle Paul commands the Assembly:

"Now I am writing you not to associate with anyone who claims to be a brother but is sexually immoral or greedy, an idolater or a verbal abuser, a drunkard or a swindler. With such a man do not even eat" (1 Corinthians 5:11).

Apostle Paul adds: "Flee from sexual immorality. Every other sin a man can commit is outside his body, but he who sins sexually sins against his own body" (1 Corinthians 6:18).

To avoid sexual immorality and other vices, keep away from **"Bad company that corrupts good character"** (1 Corinthians 15:33). The BOC reiterates: **"For of this you can be sure: No immoral, impure, or greedy person (or an idolater) has any inheritance in the kingdom of MASHIACH and YHWH"** (Ephesians 5:5). We are advised: **"Put to death, therefore, the components of your earthly nature: sexual immorality, impurity, lust, evil desires, and greed, which is idolatry"** (Colossians 3:5). Did you hear that? Sexual immorality is inclusive in the list of idolatry – the worship of idols.

Notice,

"Now we know that the law is good, if one uses it lawfully, understanding this: that the law is not laid down for the just but for the lawless and disobedient, for the wicked and sinners, for the unrighteous and profane, for those who strike their

fathers and mothers, for murderers, for the sexually immoral, for homosexuals, for slave traders and liars and perjurers, and for anyone else who is averse to sound teaching [doctrine] that conforms to the gospel concerning the glory of the blessed Elohim, which He entrusted to me" (1 Timothy 1:8-12).

Apostle Shaul (Paul) writes that the Law is good because it tells sinners not to commit abominable things mentioned above. It restricts people from violating the LOVE of YAHWEH and the LOVE we ought to have for one another. It is the mirror that helps everyone to remove all the above evils and wickedness.

Based on the evil of breaking the LAW, including the seventh Commandment, Apostle Shaul wrote:

"The wrath of YHWH is being revealed from heaven against all the unrighteousness and wickedness of people, who suppress the truth by their wickedness, since what may be known about YHWH is plain to them, because YHWH has made it plain to them. For since the creation of the world Yahweh's invisible qualities — His eternal power and divine nature — have been clearly seen, being understood from what has been made, so that people are without excuse. For although they knew YHWH, they neither glorified Him as YHWH nor gave thanks to Him, but their thinking became futile and their foolish hearts

were darkened. Although they claimed to be wise, they became fools and exchanged the glory of the immortal YHWH for images made to look like a mortal human being and birds and animals and reptiles. Therefore, YHWH gave them over in the sinful desires of their hearts to sexual impurity for the degrading of their bodies with one another. They exchanged the truth about YHWH for a lie, and worshiped and served created things rather than the Creator — who is forever praised. Amen.

Because of this, Yahweh gave them over to shameful lusts. Even their women exchanged natural sexual relations for unnatural ones. In the same way, the men also abandoned natural relations with women and were inflamed with lust for one another. Men committed shameful acts with other men, and received in themselves the due penalty for their error. Furthermore, just as they did not think it worthwhile to retain the knowledge of YHWH, so YHWH gave them over to a depraved mind, so that they do what ought not to be done. They have become filled with every kind of wickedness, evil, greed, and depravity. They are full of envy, murder, strife, deceit, and malice. They are gossips, slanderers, YAH-haters, insolent, arrogant, and boastful; they invent ways of doing evil; they disobey their parents; they have no understanding, no fidelity, no love, no mercy. Although they know

YHWH's righteous decree that those who do such things deserve death, they not only continue to do these very things but also approve of those who practice them" (Romans 1:24-32).

Therefore, **"Little children, let no one deceive you: The one who practices righteousness is righteous, just as Messiah is righteous"** (1 John 3:7). Everyone who professes to follow Yahshua must not be named after the above wicked behaviours. Put to death all the above components of earthly nature, which destroy YAHWEH'S LOVE and the love of the brethren, and in the end, deny people access into the Kingdom of YHWH. The seventh commandment has ties with the eighth, as it forbids brethren from stealing what belongs to one another. Let's open the BOC to closely examine this sacred Law of interest.

Eighth Commandment – Exodus 20:15

You shall not steal."

The law of this commandment is expanded in Ephesians 4:28:

"Let him who stole steal no longer, but rather let him labour, working with his hands what is good, that he may have something to give him who has need."

This commandment covers three areas of honest living: pursuit of decent wealth, pursuit of productivity to make honest gain, and pursuit of an honest goal for purposes of meeting the needs of the needy. The prophetic message of Malachi 3 strictly warns that we should not steal or rob YHWH of His tithes and offerings (read Malachi 3:8-9). Stealing what belongs to YHWH is robbery, and those who perpetuate the act of robbery in His Assembly are "cursed with a curse", and no robber will enter the Kingdom of YHWH [Malachi 3:8-9; Revelation 22:15; 1 Corinthians 6:9-10; Galatians 5:19-21].

Steal: "You shall not steal" teaches, amongst others, that we should "practice giving rather than getting by fraudulent means." This law safeguards everyone's right to legitimately acquire and own property. We need to understand and apply true values to life. At the heart of this commandment is love. Love of YAHWEH defeats the desire to steal. YAHWEH wants your right to own and keep your valuables honoured and protected. If we love our neighbours, we shall not steal their belongings. Also, if we love YAHWEH, we shall not rob Him of His tithes and offerings (Malachi 3:8). If most preachers are not robbers amassing indescribable wealth, how come they are competing with the top millionaires and billionaires of this world? In the process of acquiring wealth to become multi-millionaires, they cheat and deny people their legitimate means of livelihood. Most pastors are ranked among the top richest people in the world. Do not get it wrong! There is nothing wrong with being rich, but if riches or wealth come by stealing what belongs to others, such a person is a thief, and no thief will enter the kingdom of YAHWEH. The tithes and offerings of the people disappear into the pockets of these fake men. The commonwealth of worshippers, such as schools and charitable businesses opened to support the fellowship or assembly, is confiscated by the leader(s) as personal property.

Both YAHSHUA and the Apostles taught that Assembly members who are rich should distribute their wealth for the benefit of others (1 Timothy 6:18). Today, given the Word of YAHSHUA MESSIAH, we look in astonishment at how leaders of Churchianity establish colleges, universities, industries, and commercial aeroplanes, yet the member-contributors cannot send their children to such institutions or benefit from such business ventures due to high tuition fees (in the case of academic institutions). The zeal in amassing wealth amongst pastors betrays YAHSHUA'S injunction about serving 'mammon'. How can a single pastor acquire fleets of jets all in the name of shuttling the world for evangelism? If the Assembly has an aircraft to facilitate the work of ministers, that can be understood. But a leader acquiring two, three, or more aeroplanes in the name of preaching the gospel shows covetousness and stealing. Such a leader ends up using the name of the Assembly to float an air transport business at the expense of the poor people sweating to pay tithes and offerings meant to facilitate the work of YHWH on Earth. Again, this is utter covetousness, the core breaking of the eighth and the tenth commandments, which forbid stealing and covetousness. Such a leader is not only a thief and a covetous person but also an idolater, and no idolater will enter the Kingdom. **"For you may be sure of this, that everyone who is ... covetous (i.e., an idolater) has no inheritance in the Kingdom of Messiah and YHWH"** (Ephesians 5:5; also see Revelation 22:15; 1 Corinthians 6:9-10; Galatians 5:19-21).

It is crazy to see what is happening in Churchianity, Messianic ways, and most other religions, where leaders parade themselves with so much affluence in jets, cars, lands, housing estates, and all sorts of businesses. If they are not using them for commercial purposes that would benefit the poor amongst them and the less privileged ones, what are they using them for? Are they called to run businesses with jets, lands, houses, and the import and export of goods and services? Can one leader use two, three, or even four jets at the same time to crisscross nations to preach the good news? Wouldn't one be sufficient? These people are businessmen, not preachers! They are thieves, not shepherds of the people. They rob Yahweh and the people of what belongs to them. Going by the standard of YAHSHUA and the Apostles, whom we follow as examples, one can never, as a full-time minister, run a full-time worldly business because there's no time to spare for other activities. The work of the ministry is huge. It's understood that pastors or evangelists called into the sanctified ministry of Yahshua can sometimes work [outside their ministry] to make a living or complement it, but it's obvious that such engagement may NOT be on a full-time scale. True ministers do not work for covetous reasons; they do not work for personal enrichment; they do not work to become billionaires or to be famous globally.

The fame of ministers is endowed by YHWH, who promotes them through what they do for Him, as in the case of Yahshua HaMashiach, Moses, Aaron, Joshua, Gideon, Samuel, etc. These men were rich in faith and in the work of the FATHER. Our Master did not allow His disciples to carry out advertisements of Himself, even when He healed the sick (read Isaiah 42). He tried as much as possible to maintain a low profile, despite being the King and High Priest of the Earth. The FATHER wrote of Yahshua:

"Behold My Servant [Yahshua], whom I uphold; mine elect, in whom My soul delights; I have put My Spirit upon Him: He shall bring forth judgement to the Gentiles. He shall not cry, nor lift up, nor cause His voice to be heard in the street" (Isaiah 42:1-2).

Yahshua fulfilled this prophecy of a low profile (read Matthew 12:17-19). He never accepted nor pursued the glory and fame of this world, even when He was invited to do so by Satan (read Matthew 4:8-10). He was never covetous, nor sought the wellbeing of His own at the expense of others. You can never fully express the demand of the ministry with full-time secular work. In doing so, one consumes the other, and the pastor may end up giving the people garbage because he has no time to pray and to seek the face of YHWH and the Holy Spirit for direction. Who is the 'Messiah' people are following today? Is YAHSHUA their Messiah? No, no, not at all! Indeed, their Messiah is 'Jesus', the Messiah that does not obey the commandments of the FATHER, YHWH. Our HaMashiach YAHSHUA obeyed the FATHER's commandments and abided in His love (John 15:10). He set the example which every covenant-keeper must follow.

Full-Time Work and the Work of the Ministry: Immediately after Yahshua commenced His Earthly Ministry, He resigned from His full-time carpentry work. He led by example! None of the disciples nor apostles, whose examples are followed today, were businesspeople or full-time secular workers [they may occasionally do part-time work to augment, but not full-time]. These key officers in the Ministry of YAHSHUA resigned from their secular or professional works. When Apostle Peter attempted to go back into the 'fishing' business, YAHSHUA STOPPED him. YAHSHUA called out all His disciples who were into various full-time businesses before they could join Him in His kingdom work. When Apostle Shaul [Paul] was called, he resigned from his full-time legal practice. One like Shaul supported his daily living with a 'menial' job – e.g., tent-making. If the false ministers of today followed the examples of our YAHSHUA MESSIAH and His Apostles, they would not steal people's monies, possessions, etc., in the name of preaching the gospel. Preaching the gospel does not make room for anyone to amass wealth. False pastors and deceivers in the false assemblies are seriously competing with greedy politicians and businessmen. They go on embezzling what belongs to the people, all in the name of deceptive prosperity messages they preach – just to deceive those who do not read the Book of Covenant (Bible)

If politicians were honest in their services to the people, suffering would have been curtailed or stopped; wealth would have been fairly distributed, and the less privileged people in the society would have had something to eat. Politicians covet what belongs to many. This is getting worse across the world. If businesspeople were sincere, prices of goods and services would not skyrocket every day. Just look at the greed that thrives during their worldly feasts called 'Easter' and 'Christmas' [these are not commanded by YHWH], not to mention those during Muslim and other religious festivals. If greed was not part of enrichment at the expense of the poor, people would have lived joyfully and happily without over-labouring themselves to make ends meet. If stealing were not made the order of the day, the poor in the society would have had enough to eat and drink; the widows would have had helpers for their provisions; sicknesses and diseases would have been minimised – because people would get the best medical care; life would have been good to everybody; everybody would have had enough for his or her daily bread. Because most heartless pastors, politicians, and wicked leaders steal what belongs to the people for their selfish enrichment, the people are impoverished. This behaviour renders the eighth commandment handicapped; stealing destroys an individual, a community, and a nation. It undermines the law of equal opportunity; it does not accommodate sharing the commonwealth of the people. It breeds greed and covetousness. The wrath of YHWH awaits the thieves, including those who eat YHWH's tithes and offerings. In these latter days of great tribulation and wrath of YAH, His anger will be poured down against the wicked in a way that never happened before upon the evil people of the world. Yahweh vows to descend upon these vultures that eat up His people. He calls them insects, termites, locusts, cankerworms, and destroyers, and He promised to deal with all the locusts, caterpillars, and cankerworms that destroy His people, as the world tumbles into great tribulation and His wrath.

Breaking the eighth law that commands His people not to steal will result in the disobedient being cast into eternal fire, where they would not find life again. This law appears to be silent, but it screams before our ears and eyes every day. Let's be warned and desist from saying "NO!" to YHWH's commandments! Furthermore, the ninth law is like the eighth law. Let's carefully peruse through the BOC and learn from it.

Ninth Commandment – Exodus 20:16

"You shall not bear false witness against your neighbour."

Bearing False Witness: *'You shall not bear false witness against your neighbour'* is the ninth commandment that establishes 'TRUTH as a Way of Life'. The commandment is saying, "Don't tell lies!" The commandment reminds us that we must NEVER do anything with falsehood or lies. How important is truth? To fully appreciate the ninth commandment, with its prohibition of lying, we must realise how important truth is to YAHWEH. YAHSHUA took time to teach how to avoid falsehood and to say the truth always (Matthew chapter 5:33-42). He warns His Assembly that their "No" should be "No", and "Yes" should be "Yes". This commandment establishes YAHWEH's LOVE amongst people if they keep and obey it. It depicts YAHSHUA'S character, and, as such, if His Assembly loves Him, they must keep these LOVELY characters, which He gave them as His "new commandment" (John 13:34). If His people love Him, they should keep the whole of His commandments as He kept the FATHER's commandments and abode in His love (John 14:15; 15:10). If the words of YAHSHUA are heeded, people will not be standing to bear false witness against their neighbours. Swearing and lying to deceive would have been eliminated, and societies would have been pleasant to live in if the people of YHWH were to obey His Word; court cases would not have been like trading companies, where people seize every opportunity to outsmart one another and, in some cases, tell lies so as to take advantage of the other, coveting what belongs to another. Innocent people would not have been jailed or killed on flimsy excuses. It's either you obey Yahweh's Law and live or disobey it and die. The choice is yours!

Purpose and Meaning of the Ninth Commandment

What do the Scriptures tell us about Yahweh, His WORD, and TRUTH? "Every word of YHWH is pure: He is a shield unto them that put their trust in Him" (Proverbs 30:5). Daniel refers to YHWH's Word as "the Scripture of Truth" (10:21). Yahshua said of YHWH the FATHER, **"Your Word is truth"** (John 17:17). The Scripture tells us that "YHWH is not a man, that he should lie" (Numbers 23:19). "The Word of YHWH is right, and all His works are done in truth" (Psalms 33:4) because He is "YHWH of truth" (Deuteronomy 32:4), and "His truth endureth to all generations" (Psalms 100:5). Truth has no end because YHWH is truth, and the Word He speaks is truth. Whereas the world lives in lies, you are not to join them. As the Source of Truth, YHWH requires His people to speak the truth always, because those who will inherit the Kingdom are those "…whose walk is blameless and who does what is righteous, who speaks the truth from his heart and has no slander on his tongue, who does his neighbour no wrong and casts no slur on his fellow-man… who keeps his oath even when it hurts" (Psalms 15:1-3).

Yahshua and the Truth: Truth will be restored as a universal way of life when YAHSHUA HAMASHIACH returns to establish His Kingdom on Earth. **"Thus says YAHWEH: I am returned unto Zion, and will dwell in the midst of Yerusalem; and Yerusalem shall be called a city of truth; and the mountain of YAHWEH of hosts is the holy mountain"** (Zechariah 8:3). The Book of Psalms 85 further reveals how the truth and righteousness must reign in the land of Yisrayah when Yahshua returns: **"Surely His salvation is nigh them that fear Him; that glory may dwell in our land. Mercy and truth are met together; righteousness and peace have kissed each other. Truth shall spring out of the earth, and righteousness shall look down from heaven. Yes, YAHWEH shall give that which is good, and our land shall yield her increase. Righteousness shall go before Him and shall set us**

in the way of His steps" (Psalms 85:9-13). From Yahshua's throne in Yerusalem, He will insist that all of mankind must follow His Law, and people will accept, believe, and speak in the truth of YHWH (Isaiah 2:2-4). Yahshua's character was and is a perfect reflection of the character of our heavenly FATHER, YHWH of truth. He said, **"I am the Way, the Truth, and the Life. No one comes to the FATHER except through Me"** (John 14:6). Therefore, we must **"speak the truth in love, that we may grow up into Him in all things, which is the Head, even Messiah"** (Ephesians 4:15). Servants of Yahshua Messiah must be consistent in speaking the truth, demonstrating the sincerity of our love for others. We must accept and obey the commandments and teachings of YHWH that guide us into "the way of truth". We are appealed to: **"Only fear YHWH, and serve Him in truth with all your heart: for consider how great things He has done for you"** (1 Samuel 12:24; Psalms 119:30, 151, 160).

Lies of Yisrayah Yesterday and Today: In ancient Yisrayah and today's world, truth has always been scarce. Today, it's difficult to know who is telling the truth. It's getting worse as we progress into the future. Many try to balance the risk of being caught against the perceived benefits of lying. You see this more amongst individuals and businesses that display their wonderful creativity, camouflaging deceit in their advertised products with a view to luring people to buy. In today's businesses, we can spot individuals, small and medium businesses, and big companies using deception in a sophisticated way, designed so that they will not attract lawsuits. Isaiah vividly described today's world:

"None calleth for justice, nor any pleadeth for truth: they trust in vanity, and speak lies; they conceive mischief, and bring forth iniquity" (Isaiah 59:4). The nation of Israel was described thus: ***"But you shall say unto them, 'This is a nation that obeys not the voice of YAHWEH their FATHER, nor receives correction: truth has perished, and is cut off from their mouth"*** *(Jeremiah 7:28).*

The BIG question is: Do you tell lies? Or is telling lies offensive to you? These questions are crucial, and require only you to truthfully answer them yourself, because everyone will surely give account of his or her work to Yahweh when Yahshua returns. Temptations to lie never cease. They are always with us. Lying is such a quick and effortless way to gain an advantage over others. It appears to offer easy and swift escape from embarrassment, fear, guilt, or chastisement. But the Bible says, "Lying lips are an abomination to YAHWEH, but they that deal truly are His delight" (Proverbs 12:22). Notice that TRUTH belongs to Yahweh and lies belong to Satan the devil – **"a liar and the father of lies"** (John 8:44). Satan is the deceiver of the whole world (Revelation 12:9), and it is too easy for people to follow his example in dealings with others, especially when lying is so commonly practised all around us.

Tenth Commandment – Exodus 20:17

"You shall not covet your neighbour's house; you shall not covet your neighbour's wife, nor his male servant, nor his female servant, nor his ox, nor his donkey, nor anything that is your neighbour's."

Covetousness: What about covetousness, the mother of greed? *"You shall not covet"* is the tenth commandment that teaches true righteousness that comes from the heart. This last commandment forbids coveting, cheating, greed, and insatiability. In Matthew 19, the young rich ruler left sorrowful because he was covetous. He loved material possessions to the point that he could not sell those things that had become his stumbling block to entering into the Kingdom. He was steadily breaking the tenth commandment. Covetousness will surely STOP many at the gate of the Kingdom. Covetousness is an earthly nature that enrols people to long for things that legitimately belong to another. The greedy lots go the way of covetousness, and they get suffocated. Covetousness is an immoral longing for something that is not rightfully ours.

The teaching of the Tenth Commandment – covetousness – is aimed directly at the heart and mind of every human being. In prohibiting covetousness, it defines not so much what we must do but how we should think. The law of covetousness asks us to look deep within ourselves to see what we are on the inside. It teaches that covetousness is an affront to equitable distribution of wealth. The rich few covet what belongs to the people and deny them their valuables and property. Covetousness is the mother of greed and avarice. It promotes idolatry. Today, the idol called 'covetousness' has paralysed the worldly Churches and, by extension, is eating into the Messianic Assemblies, which the Bible calls the pillar of truth. It is absolutely hard today for members of Christian churches to tell the truth about money, simply because of greed. Unfortunately, the people of the Covenant are emulating them instead of separating themselves from their unrighteous behaviours. Because of the appetite to covet, people lie at will, betray one another, and grab other people's possessions. Covetous people borrow and do not pay. Covetous people take away land, houses, wives, servants (male or female), and businesses that belong to another, thereby destroying the love that ought to exist between neighbours. The Tenth Commandment was given in order to destroy covetousness, but many do not pay attention to this vital law of life. It's a sin to disobey YHWH's Law. The consequence of breaking the Tenth Commandment is being followed by a curse and death (Deuteronomy 27:26).

Covetousness portends selfishness – always thinking of oneself first. It thinks of what to get instead of what to give. YHWH denounces the lifestyle of greed. We should not think about self alone. We must quit seeking only our individual interests. Covetousness is a selfish approach to a destructive life, and selfishness is the root of the transgressions of YHWH's Commandments. Apostle James cautions thus:

"But every man is tempted when he is drawn away by his own lust and enticed. Then when lust has conceived, it bringeth forth sin: and sin, when it is finished, bringeth forth death" (James 1:14-15).

James notes how dangerous out-of-control desires can be.

"From whence come wars and fighting among you? Come they not hence, even of your lusts that war in your members? You lust, and have not: you kill, and desire to have, and cannot obtain: you fight and war, yet you have not, because you ask not" (James 4:1-2).

Covetousness is akin to lust. Paul wrote that we have "conducted ourselves in the lusts of our flesh, fulfilling the desire of the flesh and of the mind" (Ephesians 2:3). We've always allowed our desires to rule our behaviour; in that way, we have all sinned (Romans 3:10, 23).

The Sin of Covetousness is Death: Brethren, breaking any one of the Ten Commandments is evil, an abomination, and a curse that attracts the punishment of death. Covetousness has always cursed humanity. Both the rulers and the ruled are found covetous. The prophets were more profound against covetousness. Jeremiah wrote:

"But thine eyes and thine heart are not but for your covetousness, and for shedding innocent blood, and for oppression, and for violence, to do it" (Jeremiah 22:17).

The problem of covetousness was not limited to the kings. Jeremiah adds:

"For from the least of them even unto the greatest of them, everyone is given to covetousness; and from the prophet even unto the priest, everyone deals falsely" (Jeremiah 6:13).

YAHWEH warns that His people must desist from covetousness, otherwise its outcome will be destructive:

"And they covet fields and take them by violence; and houses and take them away: so they oppress a man and his house, even a man and his heritage. Therefore thus saith YAHWEH: Behold, against this family do I devise an evil, from which you shall not remove your necks..." (Micah 2:2-3).

Because every law broken must be visited with YAHWEH'S wrath and fury, those who understand the danger of breaking His law should run and never look back.

Latter Days' Covetousness: In this day, covetousness has been the order of the day – ushering in perilous times. People want to be famous; people want to have money at all costs, even money that belongs to others; people want to be heard; people want to be noticed; people want to receive honour and glory so that they can show off. But we were duly warned about unwarranted covetousness and its consequences of loving this dying world. We were told that judgement will follow the wicked who do not live in accordance with the way of YAHWEH. Apostle Paul wrote:

"This know also, that in the last days perilous times shall come. For men shall be lovers of their own selves, covetous, boasters, proud, blasphemers, disobedient to parents, unthankful, unholy, without natural affection, trucebreakers, false accusers, incontinent, fierce, despisers of those that are good, traitors, heady, high-minded, lovers of pleasures more than lovers of YAHWEH, having a form of godliness, but denying the power thereof: from such turn away" (2 Timothy 3:1-5).

This is a vividly accurate description of our world. This is a clear warning pertaining to these last days. When you encounter people whose lifestyles are patterned after the above description, run away. Do not associate with them, or else they will corrupt you. Apostle Paul wrote:

"Let your conversation be without covetousness; and be content with such things as you have: for he has said, 'I will never leave you nor forsake you'" (Hebrews 13:5).

In other words:

"We brought nothing into this world, and it is certain we can carry nothing out. And having food and raiment, let us be therewith content. But they that will be rich fall into temptation and a snare, and into many foolish and hurtful lusts, which drown men in destruction and perdition. For the love of money is the root of all evil: which while some coveted after, they have erred from the faith and pierced themselves through with many sorrows" (1 Timothy 6:7-10).

The greed of these latter days is immense. Some people have taken it as a way of life and feel you cannot live life without being covetous or stealing what belongs to others. They believe that one must covet other people's possessions to be wealthy. Who said that? Listen to what the Spirit spoke through Apostle Shaul:

"Walk in the Spirit, and you shall not fulfil the lust of the flesh. For the flesh lusteth against the Spirit, and the Spirit against the flesh: and these are contrary to one another: so that you cannot do the things that you would" (Galatians 5:16-17).

However, the Set-apart Spirit gives you the fruit and enables you to obey YHWH's Commandments that keep one out of sin (Acts 2:38; Galatians 5:22-23). The Christians that preach and teach from the same Bible that the Hebraic Yisrayah use teach that 'faith and grace' alone bestow righteousness and salvation and make a way to the kingdom. This is a half-truth. They intentionally leave out OBEDIENCE TO YAHWEH'S TORAH COMMANDMENTS AND THE PROPHETS, WHICH YAHSHUA HAMASHIACH TAUGHT THAT THEY ARE NOT CANCELLED (Matt. 5:17, 18-19). Adam, after he repented, kept the commandments; Noah kept the commandments; Abraham and the patriarchs kept the commandments; Moses and the rest of Yisrayah returning from Egypt kept the commandments (where they violated them, many perished). Yahshua kept the commandments; the disciples and the apostles kept the commandments – and showed us examples of keeping them. Who then cancelled or removed it from the BOC (or Bible)? Who was commanded to preach the removal of the Law of YAHWEH from the BOC? None! It's a lie from the pit of hell. It was fabricated to deceive unsuspecting covenant-keepers. Open your eyes, open your heart, and open your mind to love YHWH, your FATHER, who gave you the law and says it's set apart or sanctified, and "the commandment is set apart and just and good" to keep and obey (Rom. 7:12; Rom. 3:2; Rom. 9:4-5). YAHSHUA says, "If you love Me, keep My commandments" (Jn. 14:15).

IF WE KEEP THE COMMANDMENTS OF THE FATHER AND FOLLOW YAHSHUA ALL THE DAYS OF OUR LIVES, WE SHALL DO WELL AND NO PUNISHMENT SHALL BE METED OUT AGAINST US; NO WRATH OF YAHWEH SHALL VISIT AND OVERTAKE US; BUT IF WE FAIL AND LIVE IN DISOBEDIENCE, CURSES AND PUNISHMENT OF DEATH AWAIT THE PERSON.

TO BE FOREWARNED IS TO BE FOREARMED!

TAKE HEED THAT NO MAN DECEIVES YOU!!

OBEY THE COMMANDMENTS TODAY, AND LIVE!!!

LOVE OF YAHWEH, WILL OF YAHWEH, AND THE WORD OF YAHWEH

YAHWEH IS SALVATION

The first five of the Ten Commandments are Laws of liberty or royal laws that YAHSHUA summarised and called the first and greatest commandment, depicted as "**love for YAHWEH**". The last five of the Ten Commandments are the same as the "Law of Liberty" or "Royal Law" and are described by YAHSHUA as "Love for Neighbour". Do not forget that the fifth commandment captures both ends of love's definition for YAHWEH and brethren, as shown above. Indeed, the first five commandments reveal YAHWEH as "I AM", the Eternal, the Self-Existing Father, the Unchangeable Father, the very Creator of the Heavens and Earth, the Creator of mankind, and the Liberator of Hebrew Yisray'lites from the bondage of Egypt (Exodus 20:1-2; Exodus 3:14; John 8:58). He is YAHWEH, our SALVATION. The commandments were given to establish love between Him and His people and to commit His people to love themselves. The commandments are all about love. These commandments teach us to "Love YAHWEH" and to "Love our neighbours", which fulfils doing the WILL of the FATHER (Matthew 7:21). Given the failure of men to obey His commandments, Yahshua queried, "Why do you call me 'Rabbi, Rabbi' and do not do what I say?" (Luke 6:46). People are quick to call Him without obedience to His instructions. What He commands must be done. It's the primary obligation of every covenant keeper. It's the Father's instruction to those that seek His Kingdom and eternal life. No lip service, no eye service, no gainsaying, no rhetoric. YHWH's commandments are His Law. His Law is summed up in the Ten Commandments. The Ten Commandments are the moral or spiritual law. They were written by the finger of YHWH on durable tablets of stone, meant to be kept from generation to generation, though they were later renewed and called the Renewed Covenant (Matthew 26:26-28; see Jeremiah 31:31-33). YHWH bound Himself with His People in the Renewed Covenant as a perpetual contract with His people. The Covenant was renewed with the BLOOD of YAHSHUA to open the door of salvation to those who would obey Him and return to YHWH for eternal inheritance. He gave the obedient His Spirit required for bearing righteous fruit. The Spirit was also given to fulfil YHWH's promise for a new heart and a new spirit which would take away the hardness and stony heart from His people. Ezekiel 36:26-32 declares:

"I will give you a new heart and put a new spirit within you; I will take the heart of stone out of your flesh and give you a heart of flesh. I will put My Spirit

within you and cause you to walk in My statutes, and you will keep My judgements and do them. Then you shall dwell in the land that I gave to your fathers; you shall be My people, and I will be your FATHER. I will deliver you from all your uncleannesses. I will call for the grain and multiply it, and bring no famine upon you. And I will multiply the fruit of your trees and the increase of your fields, so that you need never again bear the reproach of famine among the nations. Then you will remember your evil ways and your deeds that were not good, and you will loathe yourselves in your own sight for your iniquities and your abominations. Not for your sake do I do this," says YAH ALMIGHTY, "let it be known to you. Be ashamed and confounded for your own ways, O house of Israel!"

The reason for the giving of the Set-apart Spirit is to spiritually recreate the heart to conform to the obedience of YHWH's statutes, judgements, and laws so that His people will obey Him and be blessed. Obedience to His laws ushers in blessings, but disobedience invokes curses (Leviticus 26; Deuteronomy 28). In His opening speech in Exodus 20:1, the "I" speaking with tremendous power and authority quite evidently showcases YHWH as the Great Creator and Owner of the heavens and earth. Before He appeared to Yisrayah on Mount Sinai, where He announced His LAW to His people, Yisrayah, there were powerful thunderings, lightning, a thick cloud, the sound of a trumpet, and fire that heralded His presence, "so that all the people who were in the camp trembled… and the whole mountain quaked greatly" (Exodus 19:16, 18). He demonstrated His awesome power, majesty, and glory! He overwhelmingly draws our attention to Himself so that we shall have no god before Him. He came down powerfully so that our hearts, souls, and minds would submit to His reverence and worship.

YAHSHUA said that the greatest commandment is to love YHWH with all your heart, and with all your soul, and with all your mind. Many have fallen into the mistake that the Word of the Father and the Word of the Son are two different doctrines. No! That is the devil's plot to deceive people. In fact, there are no two doctrines. It has always been one doctrine of the Father from Genesis to Revelation. The prophets preached it, Yahshua preached it, and the apostles passed it on. The words, or "doctrine", that YAHSHUA taught were from the Father and not His own (John 7:16). He further said,

"If anyone loves Me, he will keep My Word; and My Father will love him, and We will come to him and make Our home with him. He who does not love Me does not keep My Words; and the Word which you hear is not Mine but the Father's who sent Me" (John 14:23-24).

Indeed, anyone who rejects the Old Testament teaching or the New Testament teaching rejects the Father, and that means hatred toward Yahshua instead of love for Him.

"He who has My commandments and keeps them, it is he who loves Me. And he who loves Me will be loved by My Father, and I will love him and manifest Myself to him" (John 14:21).

We clearly notice here that Yahshua, more than anything else, preached obedience to the Father's Commandments [Ten Commandments] throughout His Earthly Ministry. The foregoing demonstrates that the Ten Commandments are love, the will, and the unchangeable word of the Father. Anyone who does not keep them does not know Him, nor love Him. Moses sums it up thus:

"Now therefore hearken, O Yisrayah, unto the statutes and unto the judgements, which I teach you to do, that you may live, and go in and possess the land which Yahweh of your fathers gives you. You shall not add unto the word which I command you, neither shall you diminish aught from it, that you may keep the commandments of Yahweh your Father which I command you" [Deuteronomy 4:1-2; also see Deuteronomy 12:32; Proverbs 30:6; Matthew 15:6; Mark 7:8-9; Galatians 3:15; Revelation 22:18-19].

Hear the FATHER'S Word and obey it. Do not add to it, nor subtract from it. This is the Father's call to OBEDIENCE.

MAGNIFICATION OF THE LAW BY YAHSHUA

Let's get the Oneness of the Father and YAHSHUA clear before we progress further. YAHSHUA said, "*I and My Father are One*" (John 10:30). Both Father and Son share common characteristics and identity. The Father and the Son relationship is beyond human comprehension, as both are tied into one SPIRIT – Power. Remember that the Father commits to the SON, YAHSHUA, authority and power to create and to judge all things. YAHSHUA came to magnify and to make the Words (laws) of the Father honourable. He also authenticated the message of the prophets as given to them by the Father to mankind. The Law and Words which YAHSHUA preached are the same Word the Father gave the prophets; and if anyone preaches not in accordance with "To the law and to the testimony: if they speak not according to this word, it is because there is no light in them." (Isaiah 8:20). Yahshua was busy preaching the Law and upholding the testimonies of the prophets that were based on the Law. Apostle John captures it more clearly: "If there come any unto you, and bring not this doctrine, receive him not into your house, neither bid him YAH's speed" (2 John 1:10). Verse 9 states: "Whosoever transgresses and abides not in the doctrine of HaMashiach has not YHWH. He that abides in the doctrine of HaMashiach, he has both the Father and the Son." John further states:

"Hereby we do KNOW that we KNOW Him, if we KEEP HIS COMMANDMENTS. He that says, "I KNOW Him," and keeps not His commandments, is a LIAR, and the TRUTH is not in him" (1 John 2:3-4).

In other words, whosoever does not keep YHWH's Law does not know Him; such a person is a liar; he or she does not follow the true Father and Messiah. According to Apostle John, keepers of YHWH's commandments should not welcome those who rebel against His commandments in their houses because they transgress (break) YHWH's law. Christians think that the Father's doctrine is different from what Yahshua HaMashiach preached. Although one is not surprised, because the "Jesus" they call the Messiah is different **from** the true Hebrew Yisrayahlite HaMashiach. The Bible asserts that the Word of YAHSHUA is the Word of the Father. No difference! The Father commits everything to YAHSHUA Messiah, including judgement. The judgement of the Father is the judgement of YAHSHUA.

"For the Father judges no man, but has committed all judgement unto the Son: that all men should honour the Son, even as they honour the Father. He that honours not the Son honours not the Father which hath sent Him..." (John 5:22-24).

Our salvation and everlasting life depend on honouring the Father and Yahshua and obeying their words. For this reason, Yahshua said, "Man shall not live by bread alone, but by every WORD that proceeds out of the mouth of YHWH" (Matthew 4:4). The Word of the Father and the Word of YAHSHUA are the same. Yahshua did not come to teach a different doctrine but that of the Father.

Many people erroneously think that the Father's Word belongs to the Old Testament, while those of Yahshua belong to the New Testament. No! Not at all! Yahshua said, "If a man **loves** Me, he will keep My Words, and My Father will love him, and we will come unto him and make our abode with him. He that loves Me not keeps not My sayings: and the word which ye hear is not mine, but the Father's which sent Me." (John 14:23, 24). Exactly, the Word we hear from Yahshua is not His. It is the Father's Word, which we heard from the beginning (2 John 1:5-6).

The only way we can claim to love YHWH is by keeping His commandments: "For this is the love of YHWH, that we keep His commandments, and His commandments are not burdensome" (1 John 5:3). Therefore, when YAHSHUA said, "If you love Me, keep My commandments," He was simply calling on covenant-keepers to keep the Father's Commandments of "love" (John 14:15). Yahshua has no doctrine of His own but that of the Father (John 7:16-17). This is the reason He upheld the Law and the Prophets (Matthew 5:17). He had to magnify the Law and make it honourable as the Father commanded Him (see Isaiah 42:21). Our Father commands that whosoever will not hearken to His Words, which He (Yahshua) shall speak in the Father's name, He, the Father, will require it of the person (Deuteronomy 18:18-19). What is written from Genesis through the Books of the Prophets are all acknowledged by Yahshua HaMashiach as the Father's Word, even up to the Book of Revelation, where Yahshua finally declared that we should worship Him. Thus, referring to YHWH's Sabbath worship ordained in Genesis chapter 2:2-3 and given to us as a law in Exodus 20:1-17 and declared in Exodus 31:13-17 as a sign that:

(1) He is the true Creator of Heaven and Earth;

(2) He is our YHWH, and we are His children that belong to Him. Anyone who refuses to worship YHWH on His Sabbath Day must be worshipping the beast on the 'sun-god' day [Sunday] of Satan. YAHWEH did not mince words in warning His people in the Books of Revelation, chapters 13 and 14, and Exodus, chapter 31:13-17, where He repeatedly warned that anyone who rejects the Sabbath day worship must face eternal death.

THE WILL OF THE FATHER

What is the will of the Father?

It's not enough to pretend to know His Name without knowledge of His will. Some call Him HaMashiach yet refuse to do what He instructs them to do **(Lk. 6:46-48)**. Yahshua HaMashiach revealed that "Not everyone who says to Me, 'Rabbi, Rabbi,' shall enter the kingdom of Yahweh, but he who does the will of My Father in heaven. The will of the Father is to DO whatsoever He commands. Many will say to Me in that day, 'Rabbi, Rabbi, have we not prophesied in Your Name, cast out demons in Your Name, and done many wonders in Your Name?' And then I will declare to them, 'I never knew you; depart from Me, you who practise lawlessness.'" **(Matthew 7:21-23).** The will of the Father is to practise His Law. Lawlessness is rebellion against His Law, and the result is hardness of heart and breaking of the everlasting Covenant, which leads to anarchy, disorder, violence, destruction, murder, and death, etc. All those who live without His Law are classified as destroyers of the Earth, and they will partake in the second death **(Revelation 11:18).** In Revelation 14:6, with a loud voice, YAHSHUA instructs: "Fear YAHWEH and give glory to Him, for the hour of His judgement has come; and WORSHIP Him who made Heaven and Earth, the sea and springs of water." "If anyone worships the beast and his image and receives his mark on his forehead or on his hand, he himself shall also drink of the wine of the wrath of YAHWEH..." **(verses 9-10)**. Is worshipping and calling on His Sacred Name His will? Definitely! Is observing the Sabbath one of His laws to keep? Yes, of course! Is keeping the annual feasts part of His commandments to the faithful? Absolutely! Why then do people refuse to obey these instructions? Why did they leave His Sacred Name and call Him names of the Gentile Gods, which He forbids? Why did they choose an alternative 'day' – Sunday worship? Is it not **an** act of disrespect, disobedience, and abomination not to do His will?

The Command to "do": Yahshua came to teach mankind not only to listen but also to do whatever the Father's Law requires from His people **(Deut. 10:12-13; 6:5; Jer. 7:22-28; Eccl. 12:13; Micah 6:8; Isaiah 1:10-17; Matt. 5:19; 7:24-27; Luke 6:46-49, etc.).** Instead of hearing and doing the will of the Father, they turned against His Word and chastised the prophets who taught them; they found fault with Yahshua HaMashiach and gave an excuse to murder Him; in the end, they claimed the Law had been nailed to the 'cross' so that they would continue to disrespect and disobey the Father even more. Soon after Yahshua ascended into Heaven, the majority of the believers wandered away and embraced the religions of this world that abhor YAH's teachings. They followed the beastly power, choosing the path of abomination – worshipping idols, which YAH forbade and hates (read Revelation Chapters 2, 3, and 4). Ever since, they have continued to call on the 'Elohim' of this world, their father, instead of YHWH, who called them. Refusal to obey the Law of

YAH is the height of human rebellion against his Creator. Despite the vigorous reorientation Yahshua carried out to redirect them and to bring them to YAH during His earthly ministry, His efforts were trodden down by the leaders that ought to have guided the people out of the worship of 'the Lord God' of this world (John 8:12-44; 2 Cor. 4:4; see Ezekiel 8 and 9).

When Yahshua could no longer bear the resistance of the priests, scribes, Pharisees, and Sadducees of His days, He had to reveal to them that **the one** they called their 'father' was indeed Satan the devil, an adversary of YHWH **(John 8:44; Rev. 12:9)**. Does that sound like a surprise to you? Yahshua HaMashiach taught them in the Temple that He is the Supreme Authority of the Shabbat **(Mark 2:27-28)**. According to the Scriptures, the Sabbath is a seventh day of rest and will NEVER be changed nor cancelled, no matter how people may twist it to suit their rebellious hearts. Unfortunately, many do not know that a death sentence awaits those who refuse to honour YAH's Shabbat Day of rest **(Exodus 31:14-15)**. The Renewed Covenant Book declared that Yahshua HaMashiach kept the annual festivals, including the Shabbat. In those days, He taught them on the Shabbat days as written in the Law **(Exodus 31:14-15; Ezek. 20:12, 20; see Luke 4:16; Mark 2:27-28; Acts 17:2; Matt. 12:1-14)**. Although, before Yahshua HaMashiach came, they had altered the Torah, adding and subtracting from it. This prompted the warning to remind them that no one should add to or subtract from the Law:

"You must not add to or subtract from what I command you, so that you may keep the commandments of YHWH your Father that I am giving you. Do not add to what I command you, and do not subtract from it, but keep the commands of YHWH your Father that I give you." (Deut. 4:2)

Death awaits those who deliberately choose to ignore the Shabbat Law and refuse to recognise and observe it as YHWH's Own Set-apart Day of rest. YHWH warns:

"**Speak also to the children of Yisrayah, saying, 'Most certainly you shall keep my Sabbaths; for it is a sign between me and you throughout your generations, that you may know that I am YHWH who sanctifies you. You shall keep the Sabbath, therefore, for it is set apart to you. Everyone who profanes it shall surely be put to death; for whoever does any work therein, that soul shall be cut off from among his people. Six days shall work be done, but the seventh day is a Sabbath of solemn rest, set apart to YHWH. Whoever does any work on the Sabbath day shall surely be put to death.'** (Exodus 31:13-15)

Most people argue that any day one chooses to worship is okay! These **sets** of people believe their 'messiah' rose on the first day; as a result, the 'day' of YAH's rest was changed from the Sabbath Day to the first day, Sunday. Unfortunately, they can't **prove** from the BOC or Bible where YHWH changed the Law of the Sabbath Day of rest to Sunday. YHWH never changed any of His Laws through the Prophets or Yahshua HaMashiach, except that Yahshua restored, magnified, and made those they removed honourable **(see Isaiah 42:21; see Matthew Chapters 5, 6, and 7)**. He commanded them to keep them because He did not come to cancel them but to restore and magnify them. Where the Law of Priestly Animal Sacrifices was stopped, it was clearly stated in both the First and Second Covenants. YHWH would be accused of destroying His Covenant if He had removed any without documenting it in His Book of Covenant. People would have accused Him **of** breaking the Law and hiding it from them. Yahshua made it clear that He did not come to destroy or change the Law and the Prophets **(Matt. 5:17-19)**. In the excerpts below, Yahshua describes those who hear the words of the FATHER and do them as those who would escape the coming troubles of this world and, in the end, enter His everlasting Kingdom. Those who add or subtract shall perish, but they did so to lead many away from the truth. Indeed, those who choose the path of disobedience shall perish. He is returning soon to execute **judgement** on death.

I testify to everyone who hears the words of the prophecy of this book: if anyone adds to them, YHWH will add to him the plagues which are written in this book. If anyone takes away from the words of the book of this prophecy, YHWH will take away his part from the tree of life, and out of the set-apart city (Yerusalem), which are written in this book. He (Yahshua) who testifies these things says, "Yes, I am coming soon." HalleluYah! Yes, come, Yahshua HaMashiach! Revelation 22:18-20

Judgement day awaits those who refuse and reject the Father's will. In Matthew Chapter 7, verses 21-23, the false teachers and false pastors declared that they did miracles, signs, and wonders in the Name of Yahshua HaMashiach. But He denied them because it was obvious they called on the name of the Gentile religious messiah. What the fathers did is the same thing the children in different religions are doing today. They hide His Name in the religious titles they are calling. For instance, the Christians hid His name, YHWH, in "Lord God", and the name of Yahshua HaMashiach in "Jesus Christ". The Muslims call Him Allah. The Book of Covenant was rewritten in what are today called the Bible and the Koran. Is this not what Yahshua meant in Matthew Chapter 7:21-23, that He doesn't know them because they were lawbreakers? He repeated **the** same in Luke 6:46-49, where He gave an in-depth description of their disobedient character and revealed the consequence of their action. It's apparent that though they know the truth, they refuse to do His will. Yahshua said:

"Why do you call me 'Rabbi, Rabbi' and don't do the things which I say? Everyone who comes to Me and hears My words and does them, I will show you who he is like. He is like a man building a house who dug and went deep and laid a foundation on the rock. When a flood arose, the stream broke against that house and could not shake it, because it was **founded** on the rock. But he who hears and doesn't do is like a man who built a house on the earth without a foundation, against which the stream broke, and immediately it fell; and the ruin of that house was great." **Luke 6:46-49**

The name of Yahshua is the rock on which the faith of every covenant-keeper is entrenched. No other name can stand **the** flood and **judgement** that is coming. If one builds on another foundation that does not follow YAH's TOC, the individual will never withstand the already announced trial, great tribulation, and the wrath of YHWH that will come upon the children of disobedience.

To ensure that the TOC gets into the ears and hearts of people, Matthew repeated Yahshua's warning:

"Everyone, therefore, who hears these words of mine and does them, I will liken him to a wise man

who built his house on the rock. The rain came down, the floods came, and the wind blew and beat on that house; and it didn't fall, for it was founded on the rock. But everyone who hears these words of Mine and doesn't do them will be like a foolish man who built his house on the sand. The rain came down, the floods came, and the winds blew and beat on that house; and it fell — and its fall was great." **Matthew 7:24-27**

Instead of listening to Yahshua's Word (hearing and obeying), they **criticised** Him for undermining the observance of the Sabbath Law, as if He came to destroy it. Ridiculous, isn't it! As they denied Him then, generations after generations, people follow the same path of disobedience **as** the fathers. Why not obey YAHWEH's commandments and live? Those who partake in Sunday worship instead of Sabbath worship will surely face Him when He returns to judge the obedient and the disobedient **(Revelation 14:7-11; Revelation 11:18)**. What's the Law all about?

Law Like a Mirror Depicts Action:

The Ten Commandments **are the** perfect Law of Liberty, the Law of Freedom **(James 1:23-25)**, which commands **OBEDIENCE** and **LOYALTY to YAHWEH**. **The** Law is described as a mirror, which draws one into action. Whosoever looks into it and continues to examine himself or herself in it, without abandoning it, that "man shall be blessed in his deed". It is the Law of **'DOING'**. This law of doing depicts **ACTION.** Keeping the Law is doing His WILL; doing His will is effective and meaningful when His fruit of FAITH is combined with **ACTION** to achieve good works. Apostle James affirms that faith without works is dead. Faith in **the** MESSIAH goes with works – 'doing'. In Revelation Chapters 2 and 3, YAHSHUA remarked in each of the seven Assemblies, 'I know your works' – this was repeated seven times in the course of admonishing His Assembly. Also, in the whole of the gospels, YAHSHUA emphasised that our faith in Him is very important for our righteousness. **In other words**, faith and works go together in doing **the** good work of the FATHER. Good work can only be achieved **if** faith is applied; else, nothing happens. In today's Churchianity, some display works only, and others preach faith without works. According to the Scriptures, works and faith in **the** MESSIAH are prerequisites for righteousness, as exemplified in the case of Abraham and Rahab **(James 2:23, 25).** What then are the works? And what type of works does the Scripture describe? **Ecclesiastes** 12:13 provides the answer:

"Fear YAHWEH, and keep His commandments: for this is the whole duty of man."

Work is duty; duty is responsibility. YAHSHUA taught that it is the responsibility of every man to 'do', 'keep', and 'obey' the FATHER's commandments, for it is the first work. Indeed! The works YAHSHUA meant **are** keeping the commandments — because it is the 'whole duty of man'. Keeping the commandments must accompany faith in **the** MESSIAH YAHSHUA. YAHSHUA directed the young rich ruler to add faith to his work; then he would be perfect, but the man left in sorrow because his heart was in his possessions **(Matthew 19:17-21)**. Thus, righteousness can only be realised by combining works with faith in YAHSHUA (following YAHSHUA). These are what Yahshua meant by doing the will of the Father. Anyone who prepares for the Second Exodus must think on these things — hearing, obeying, and doing the commandments of the Father. Without obedience, the individual may lose his crown of righteousness. The **BOC** says that righteousness is rooted in obedience **to** YHWH's commandments **(Deut. 6:25; Deut. 10:12-13)**.

LAW LIKE A MIRROR REVEALS SIN IN HUMANITY

Apostle James taught that the Law is like a mirror that reveals who the children of YAH are. When the Law is kept, it reveals human nature. It reveals the sin in the person. From the revelation of the law, action is taken to remove the sin. Professor Veith asks, "When **you look in the mirror in the morning and see that something must be done with yourself before you dare step outside, do you feel angry at the mirror for revealing this information to you? Do you feel that the mirror is the enemy?"** He concluded that many think the mirror (in this case, the **LAW**) is the enemy. This is exactly the approach that many take with YAHWEH's moral law. Many think the law should be thrown away. This was also the thinking of the fathers of old. It was the same law we are taught today; the fathers also received it, but they rejected it, and many of them perished (Heb. 4:1-11). The fathers, though they knew the law, kept hiding the truth until it was too late for them. Because they did not want their sins to be revealed, they kept looking for excuses and sometimes outright antagonism.

The law that James describes as a mirror is *the perfect law of liberty. It has not been destroyed and cannot be removed until YAHSHUA returns and uses it to reign on earth (Isaiah 2:2-4).* Many hate this law and preach that it has been destroyed, cancelled, or nailed to the stake. Why? It is because it reveals their sins, which they do not want exposed. Others feel that the moral law belongs to the sacrificial or ceremonial laws that have been done away with. Yet others think the law was meant for the tribal Yisrayah, not them, the Gentiles. Unfortunately, they do not distinguish which law the Bible is referring to when it talks about the law, particularly from the writings of Apostle Shaul. We know that the sacrificial and ceremonial laws were done away with at the tree because YAHSHUA'S BLOOD liberates all covenant-keepers from the power of sin.

In the foregoing, Apostle James speaks about the Ten Commandments Law. He called it the **ROYAL LAW** and quotes the second greatest commandment taught by MESSIAH in Matthew 22:39: **"If ye fulfil the Royal Law according to the scripture, 'Thou shalt love thy neighbour as thyself,' ye shall do well."** In order to clarify that James was referring to the Ten Commandments as the Royal Law, he adds: **"For whosoever shall keep the whole law, and yet offend in one point, he is guilty of all. For he that said, 'Do not commit adultery,' said also, 'Do not kill.' Now if thou commit no adultery, yet if thou kill, thou art become a transgressor of the law"** (verse 11 KJV). The transgressor of the law is a commandment breaker. Thus, James references YAHSHUA's call to **DO** and **TEACH** the Commandments of the Father (Matthew 5:19).

YAHSHUA and Apostle James see the Ten Commandments in particular as a bundle or a unit. If one part of the unit is broken, the rest are broken, and the breaker is guilty of them all. Isaiah prophesied that:

"It shall come to pass in the last days" that **YAHWEH's law shall flow from Jerusalem, the mountain of YAHWEH, to teach nations His ways,** and peoples will **"walk in His paths: for out of Zion shall go forth the law, and the Word of YAHWEH from Jerusalem. And He shall judge among the**

nations, and shall rebuke many people..." (Isaiah 2:2-4).

THE ROYAL LAW AND SIN

We all have broken YAHWEH'S Law. **"For all have sinned, and come short of the glory of YHWH."** (Romans 3:23; Revelation 13:3, **4**). **"For the wages of sin is death"** (Romans 6:23). Everybody is guilty and under obligation to pay the penalty for transgressing YAHWEH'S Law. The penalty is death. This is being under the law. The blood sacrifices were performed in the Old Testament era to temporarily atone for sin. Unfortunately, those sacrificial ceremonies were not meant to permanently blot out sin, for the blood of animals cannot cleanse sin. We thank YAHSHUA, who took our death penalty and paid the price for us, as long as we accept His sacrifice. That is what the Scripture says: **"For sin shall not have dominion over you: for ye are not under the law, but under grace."** (Romans 6:23).

Notice, being under 'grace' means that once one accepts His sacrifice and does His will, he receives pardon for the committed sins and gets deliverance from the death penalty; the individual is released from the bondage of sin. The power of sin that caged mankind like iron is broken by the power in the BLOOD of YAHSHUA, which no man could have delivered himself from. Therefore, the unmerited favour of YAHSHUA

MESSIAH is meant to free the sinner from sin. This is not all for Favour! The grace of YAHSHUA is His Spirit that bears fruit in us – this is called the fruit of the Holy Spirit. The fruit now empowers us to obey the law we were not able to keep because of the weakness of the flesh (read Galatians 5:19-21 and 22-23). Without the fruit of the Spirit, no one can obey the royal law of YAHWEH. Forgiveness of our sins and receiving His Spirit's fruit provide us abundance of grace that equips us to obey YAHWEH'S LAW.

HOW CAN KEEPING YAHWEH'S LAW GIVE FREEDOM?

According to James 1:23-25, YAHWEH'S LAW is a mirror. The Book of Torah, or Law, reveals unrighteousness in men. It reveals the chains of sin Satan wrapped around humanity, who bows to him. It gives instruction on how to flee from sin and get cleansed through the Name and blood of YAHSHUA so that one returns to the FATHER, whose standard is righteousness. The law itself does nothing more to remedy sin than a mirror can wash a dirty face. However, the individual needs to follow its guidance and depend on the cleansing BLOOD of YAHSHUA HAMASHIACH to wash away the sins. Once this guideline is accepted, something else happens. As the individual receives YAHSHUA, immersed in the water in His Name, His BLOOD cleanses the sinful nature, while His SPIRIT works to renew the heart and the spirit, as promised in the New Covenant (Ezekiel 36:26 and Jeremiah 31:31-33; Matthew 26:28; 1 Corinthians 11:25). Therefore, by reason of YAHSHUA's favour, the Spirit's fruit is released to the immersed person to continue on the path of obedience to His law (Galatians 5:22-23). At this stage, the person is set free from the 'second death' sentence that awaits every unrepentant sinner. The fruit of the Spirit is the enabler for keeping the Law of YAHWEH. It is for this purpose that YAHSHUA went to the stake to save the souls that are lost. If, after the sacrifice of YAHSHUA in cleansing the individual, he/she returns to sin – to continue breaking the Law – that would be reckoned an act of **treading** underfoot the love and favour of the Son of YAHWEH and counting His Blood of the Covenant as nothing. Thus, keeping the law of YAHWEH and having faith in YAHSHUA HAMASHIACH gives freedom from sin and facilitates one's way into YAH's kingdom. This great work of deliverance and salvation is available to all those who would repent, forsake their sins, and immerse themselves in the Name of YAHSHUA.

Obedience – the ability to submit, observe, and respect YAHWEH's Law – must never be overlooked; otherwise, one will be like the person who looks at himself in the mirror and quickly forgets how he appears. By keeping the Law and having faith in YAHSHUA, one is set free from sin and bestowed with the righteousness of YAHWEH. Keeping the Law is an indication of doing the will of the FATHER. This way, the person proves to YAHWEH that he/she now walks with Him and follows the path of His obedience and perfection, i.e., righteousness (see Genesis 17:1; Deut. 6:25).

Many folks argue that the Law has been done away with. If this were true, sin also would have been done away with, and there would have been no need for His favour. The Spirit of YAH's favour deals with issues of sin, provided one remains obedient to Him. The Bible says that those who preach that the royal law is cancelled are enemies of HAMASHIACH, and they do not know Him; there is no truth in them; they are liars (1 John 2:3-4). Apostle Shaul says that anyone breaking YAHWEH'S Law after the BLOOD of YAHSHUA has been shed for the remission of sins will be severely punished for making the sacrifice of HAMASHIACH unworthy; the person has **"trodden underfoot the Son of YAHWEH, and counted the BLOOD of the Covenant, with which he was sanctified, an unrighteous thing, and has insulted the Spirit of favour."** Such an individual is a rebel and will suffer death (Hebrews 10:28, **29**). YAHWEH will recompense the person with destruction when He shall judge His people. **"It is a fearful thing to fall into the hands of the living YHWH."** (verses **30–31**). To be forewarned is to be forearmed! Therefore, choose to keep and obey His Commandments – worship Him by His Name, set apart His Sabbath day of rest, and keep His annual Feasts instead of Christmas, Easter, etc. These are His core commandments that anyone who loves YAHSHUA HAMASHIACH should not ignore. For **"man shall not live by bread alone, but by every word that proceeds from the mouth of YHWH."** The Torah law, royal law, law of liberty, spiritual law, and the Ten Commandments are all part of YAHWEH's Covenant that proceeds from His mouth, which must be obeyed (Matthew 4:4; Luke 4:4). If you must be saved, stop following religions, human traditions, traditions of elders, or commandments of men which override YAH's commandments! Stop indulging human interpretation of the Word of YAH and reading your own meaning into His Word with a view to interpreting it to **suit** your delight.

OBEDIENT ARE THE OVERCOMERS

We are called to live life of obedience to overcome Satan, sin, flesh and the world of iniquity. Being freed from sin by His favour, we are expected to live a life uprightness and righteousness. YAHSHUA HAMASHIACH sets people free from carnal nature, which is a nature enticed by sin. YAHSHUA gives His divine nature via His Set-apart Spirit's fruit to obey the FATHER's Word. The Spirit enables covenant-keepers to see the beauty of YAHSHUA's character enshrined in His set-apart laws, which empowers the individual to walk by it. YAHWEH's law reveals His character and love. If anyone submits to it, the person will be free from burden of sin, and the individual shall take after His character. By the abundance of favour obtainable in the Spirit of Yahshua, one is set free from the bonds of sin. Based on having faith in Him, power to overcome addictions and tendencies to do wrong are dealt with. The person becomes overcomer. YAHSHUA came to set the captives [sinners] free from the bondage of sin (Luke 4:18). Satan has been the captor of humanity since the fall of Adam and Eve.

YAHSHUA's letter to the seven Assemblies warns the lawbreakers to REPENT, or He will plunge them and their children into great tribulation (Revelation 2:22-23). He announced that Philadelphia Assembly "kept the Word of My patience" [i.e. Commandments], as a result, YAHSHUA said: "I also will keep thee from the hour of temptation, which shall come upon all the world, to try them that dwell upon the earth." (Revelation 3:10). YAHSHUA will protect His Assembly that keep His Word during the great tribulation (see Zephaniah 2:2-3; also, Revelation 3:8,10; 12:6,14). The doers and keepers of His Word are the overcomers. Following YAHSHUA's invitation to worship YHWH and live, those who disobey His call will be destroyed (Rev. 14:10-11).

OVERCOMERS ARE PROMISED ETERNAL LIFE

Those who kept His commandments and have faith in Him (verse 12) shall be saved. YAHSHUA highly commended Philadelphia Assembly as an exemplary congregation that kept His Word (Revelation 3:8,10), meaning that they kept the FATHER's commandments and overcame by their obedience. The Bible says that those who overcome will enter everlasting life. To have life and freedom is to truly follow Him and obey His Laws (Deuteronomy 4:1; Revelation 14:12). Notice, that His Law [Torah] is His Word made flesh, which has spirit and life, and we must eat from the Word to live (John 6:54-56; 6:63). Obedience draws us to Him and equips us with His righteousness (Deut. 6:25); obedience to His moral law frees us from condemnation. Whereas disobedience separates us from Him and leads to destruction. The promises of YAHWEH to those who overcome are beyond comprehension. For instance, some of the promises in Revelation Chapters 2 and 3 bear testimonies:

Religion is not of YAHWEH butwill I give to eat of the tree of life, which is in the midst of the paradise of YHWH... (Revelation 2:7);

He that overcomes, shall not be hurt of the second death... (verse 11);

To him that overcomes, will I give to eat of the hidden manna, and will give him a white stone, and in the stone a new name written... (verse 17);

And he that overcomes, and keep my works unto the end, to him will I give power over the nations... (verse 26);

And I will give him the morning star... (verse 28);

He that overcomes, the same shall be clothed in white raiment; and I will not blot out his name out of the book of life, but I will confess his name before my Father, and before his angels... (3:5);

To him that overcomes will I grant to sit with me in my throne, even as I also overcame, and am set down with my Father in His throne (3:21).

By obeying YAH's perfect law of liberty, one is free to receive all the gifts YAHWEH promised those who love Him and keep His commandments. As a flower turns to the sun and allows its rays to beautify it, so when we turn to YAHSHUA, we allow His character to beautify our character. His beautiful law of liberty has set us free from the bondage of sin and death and offers promises that last for eternity! Thus, *"Blessed is he that reads, and they that hear the words of this prophecy, and keep those things which are written therein: for the time is at hand"* (Revelation 1:3; see Luke 11:28; 8:21; Revelation 22:7). *Let us hear the conclusion of the whole matter: Fear Yahweh and keep His commandments: for this is the whole duty of man. For Yahweh shall bring every work into judgement, with every secret thing, whether it be good, or whether it be evil."* (Ecclesiastics 12:13-14; see Matthew 10:26).

The forgoing portrays the Law of Love for Yahweh, which demands that we must obey it completely. The second is like it – the Law of Love for our neighbours. The Ten Commandments explained above summarises the Torah, which hinge on LOVE for YAHWEH and NEIGHBOUR. YHWH expects the covenant-keepers to observe and obey all these commandments, statutes, judgements, laws, as given in the Torah for individual's righteousness and salvation (Deut. 6:1-5,24-25). Those who endures to the end shall inherit eternal life in the Kingdom of Yahweh, which Yahshua shall return and establish.

The entire Law is enshrined in the everlasting covenant YHWH made with humanity, which everyone that does the will of the FATHER must keep. There are various covenants through ages. The next Chapter gives clarity on Covenants from Adam to Yahshua HaMashiach – the Mediator of the Renewed Covenant

CHAPTER 4:
The Covenants
YHWH'S COVENANTS

EVERLASTING COVENANT

"The earth also is defiled under the inhabitants thereof: because they have transgressed the laws, changed the ordinance, broken the <u>everlasting covenant</u>. Therefore, hath the curse devoured the earth, and they that dwell therein are desolate: therefore, the inhabitants of the earth are burned, and few men left" Isaiah 24:5-6.

INTRODUCTION

Do you believe in the Covenant of your CREATOR, YHWH? Or is your faith aligned with the world Religions? Do you know that the Bible is the BOOK OF COVENANT given to the Hebrew Yisrayahlites? Do you know that there is a massive difference between the

Covenant Way and Religious Way? Covenant and Religion are two distinct paths to salvation and damnation. Covenant is YHWH's Way for salvation and eternal life. Covenant as Agreement demands obedience to YHWH's instructions. In other words, to belong to the family[11] of YHWH, every covenant-keeper must be obedient to YHWH's commandments. The Covenant is invitation to obey YAHWEH's Commandments and be perfect (Ex. 19:5,6). Christianity as religion mimics the Covenant but dilutes it with traditions and commandments of men. The same applies to other religions of this world. The TORAH as contained in the Book of Covenant is the WORD of YAHWEH made flesh. YAHSHUA the SAVIOUR is that WORD made flesh (Jn. 1:1-2, 14; Rev. 19:13). He taught the Torah enshrined in the Covenant so that the keepers shall return to the FATHER [Jn. 14:6].

---

[11] Abraham was taught the 'Covenant' by YHWH so that he and his descendants shall live an obedient life and be perfect and serve YAHWEH alone. "*When Abram was ninety-nine years old, YHWH appeared to Abram and said to him, "I am YAHWEH Almighty. Walk before Me and be perfect" (BOC), Gen. 17:1.* Before Abram's call, it's reported that he worshipped 'Moon God' in Babylon. He may not have completely discarded 'God' worship, thus prompting YAHWEH to teach him His perfect way, which is based on **OBEDIENCE.** To be **perfect** is to be **righteous**, and the latter is learnt from obedience to YAH's Word (Deut. 6:25). The Covenant obedience was sealed with '**circumcision of the foreskin**' on every male child born in the family of Abraham as a mark of belonging to YAH's Family (Gen. 17:10-14). Any "uncircumcised man child" who is not circumcised breaks YHWH's covenant and will be cut off from the family of Yisrayah. This covenant marks the elimination of idol worship amongst the children of Abraham. Joshua warns that YAH's worshippers must never serve Elohim or God as the Gentiles do (see Joshua 24:14-15). The **Covenant Way** is the path we are called to follow. We are not to follow religions which worship God(s). The Circumcision Covenant is known as Abrahamic Covenant way (Gen. 17:14). This Covenant points to YAHSHUA as the Way, the Truth, and the Life (Jn. 14:6).

Religion is not of YAHWEH but was authored by Satan to deceive mankind to join him in his continuous rebellion against the Creator, YHWH. In doing so, he deceived all mankind to worship him as 'God'. Do you know that the Covenant Book is the 'Oracle of YAHWEH' given to Yisrayah at Mt Sinai to guide their life? (Exodus 19-20; 24:7; Rom. 3:1-3; Rom. 9:4). The first five books of the Covenant [Genesis, Exodus, Leviticus, Numbers and Deuteronomy] are called "Torah". "Torah" is a Hebrew word for "instruction", commonly called "law". Do you know that the TEN COMMANDMENTS are the summary of the LAW? It is summarised as LOVE: "Love for YAHWEH" and "love for the neighbour" (Exod. 20:1-17; Matt. 22:36-39). "*On these two hang the Law and the prophets*" (Matt. 22:40). Notice, YAHSHUA said, "*I did not come to destroy the LAW and the PROPHETS...*" (Matt. 5:17). Do you know that as a believer, you are bound to keep the LAW of Covenants? Why then do men reject the Law of Covenant, having heard it was not cancelled? YAHSHUA said, "*If you LOVE Me, keep My commandments*" (John 14:15). Do people know that anyone who continues to reject the Covenant of YHWH will die eternal death? Unfortunately, many do not know because religions taught them the opposite, that the law is cancelled. No! It's not true (see Matt. 5:17). Let's examine the Covenant and the consequences for disobeying it.

HISTORICAL PERSPECTIVE OF THE COVENANT

First Covenant

ADAM

ADAM & EVE IN THE FIRST COVENANT

The Bible is a covenant book that states the contract relationship between the Creator, YAHWEH, and His people. Every human being that will enter His Kingdom must keep His Covenant. The Covenant (or "Agreement") was first made between YAHWEH and Adam in the Garden of Eden as an INSTRUCTION (or LAW). Adam and Eve were to live forever if they kept the Covenant. Conversely, they would die if they broke it (Gen. 2:16-17). The Covenant Book says, "The wages of sin is death, but the gift of Yahweh is eternal life through Yahshua HaMashiach our Saviour" (Rom. 6:23). Unfortunately, the couple listened to Satan the deceiver and broke the everlasting Covenant, thus imputing death to mankind (Gen. 3:16-19). Adam's disobedience marked the beginning of sin on the earth. As a result of disobedience, death came, and man was to return to the dust from which he was made.

YHWH created the heavens and the earth and instituted a Covenant or Agreement with His creature as a "WAY" to serve HIM. All His words, instructions, laws, ordinances, commandments, and judgements to mankind are bound in the Covenant so that they will continue to do those things that would please HIM. To fear Him and obey His commandments are the main duties of mankind. Therefore, the WORD of YHWH is the "WAY" all human beings are mandated to serve and follow HIM. Rejecting or walking away from HIS WORD is a sin. To commit sin is to separate oneself from HIM, and the result is eternal death. Sin is defined as the transgression of the law.

1 John 3:4

"Whosoever commits sin also transgresses the law, for sin is the transgression of the Torah [Instruction or Law]."

HOW IT ALL BEGAN

Genesis is called the Book of Beginnings, which revealed the CREATOR, YHWH [not 'God' or 'Lord' as read in today's Bibles].YHWH created the heavens and the earth and all things in them. There is a massive difference between YHWH and God. The entire Book of the Covenant reveals this truth. Originally, angels and mankind were created as gods (Ps. 8:5; 82:6; Jn. 10:34-36). Then, Satan, the adversary of YAH, and his fallen angels hijacked the title for themselves. The fallen angels constitute the family of gods, of which Satan is their head. Satan bears the title in the Gentile Bibles – "God" or "LORD" (whether written in small letters or capital letters, all refer to Satan as the God or Prince of this world). Read: 2 Cor. 4:4; Jn. 8:44; Jn. 12:31; Jn. 14:30; Jn. 16:11). Although his title varies across religions of the world, Satan is the founder of worldly religions, and he has false messianic titles in them, as well as false human messiahs that profess his ways. YAHSHUA warns that believers must take heed so that they may not be deceived by MANY messiahs in the last days. "And YAHSHUA answered and said to them, 'Take heed that no one deceives you. For many will come in My Name [title-name – Messiyah], saying, 'I am the Messiyah,' and will deceive many.'" (Matt. 24:4-5). The Scriptures warn that children of YHWH should separate themselves from worldly religions, else they would be ensnared and entangled and share in their sins and plagues that will befall them (2 Corinthians 6:17; Romans 16:17; Rev. 18:4, etc.). The number one goal of the gods is to cause deception in the minds of believers so that they will believe a LIE and follow false doctrines.

ADAM BROKE THE COVENANT.

Genesis2:16-17

"And YHWH commanded the Man [Adam], saying, *'Of every tree of the Garden you may freely eat;*[17] **but of the tree of the knowledge of good and evil you**

*shall not eat, **for in the** day that you eat of it you shall surely die."'*

The warning is about good and evil. Both are the proverbial trees that men may easily eat, and they contradict each other. Knowledge of one tends to overshadow the other. Adam was prohibited from eating from the knowledge of evil. YHWH, the Creator, wanted Adam to follow the way of good, i.e., the righteousness of YHWH. But Satan, the adversary, wanted Adam to disobey the Creator, to follow the way of evil, i.e. unrighteousness. YHWH gave Adam a firm instruction never to break or transgress His Covenant. He must never submit himself to the fallen angels or the mighty ones [Elohim or God]. Unfortunately, he was outsmarted by the enemy, and he fell. Later, a similar commandment was handed to Noah, Abraham, and Yisrayah. Today, Yahshua Hamashiach instructs us to heed to the commandments of YHWH, to follow after His righteous way by keeping His commandments, "If you love Me, keep My commandments" (John 14:15; see Exodus 20:1-17; Matthew 26:26-28; Hebrews 8:6; Hebrews 9:15). The Commandments are the LOVE of YHWH. In other words, to keep the Commandments is to love YHWH, even one's neighbour [Exod. 19:5-6; Matt. 22:37-40; Jn. 14:15; Jn. 15:10]. The Covenant to Adam explains the relationship that exists between YHWH, the FATHER and His people, sons, and daughters created in His Own likeness. Obedience to

His Covenant commandments was to offer a return to the way of righteousness, blessings, and eternal life throughout generations. At the same time, disobedience meant that the person remains on the way of unrighteousness, which leads to a curse and perpetual death. Thus, YHWH explained to Adam that disobedience to His Covenant instructions would result in human suffering and death. YHWH offered Adam a RIGHTEOUS or GOOD way of life as food that was based on abiding by His WORD. Similarly, the Second Adam, Yahshua HaMashiach, described the Word as His 'flesh' and 'blood', the covenant-keepers must eat to be alive [see John 6:53-54, 63]. The same instruction given to Adam is what's handed to us today (Hebrews 4:1-2). Adam was not to know the EVIL way of life that leads to death, nor submit to it. YHWH's instruction was explicit, as it is today. Unfortunately, Adam and Eve submitted to the voice of the slippery and subtle serpent, thus bringing about the fall of all mankind. Below is the first covenant that began with the first human parents.

COVENANT WITH ADAM & EVE

Before long, Adam and Eve disobeyed YHWH's Word. How? They listened to a deceiver described as a "serpent", an allegory of a liar, an adversary of YHWH, that stands for deception, lies, and the devil [John 8:44]; he was known as that fallen angel, formerly Lucifer in heaven; he was one of the cherubim that stood in the presence of YHWH; he rebelled against the WORD of YHWH and vowed to unseat HIM from His throne in heaven. Eventually, he was cast down. On earth, he successfully deceived mankind and assumed the head of the family of fallen angels. YAHSHUA identified the devil as Satan (Gen. 3:1; Jn. 8:44; 2 Cor. 4:4; Jn. 12:31; Jn. 14:30; Jn. 16:11). The first Covenant was clear about who the serpent, the devil, was:

Genesis3:1

"The serpent was the shrewdest [cunning] of all the wild animals YHWH had made. One day he asked the woman, 'Did YHWH really say you must not eat the fruit from any of the trees in the garden?'"

Following the attention Eve gave to the serpent, she opened up to the enemy and was deceived by the cunning devil, who tricked her into believing a LIE that she would not "die" and that they would be like "gods." Unfortunately, she did not know that the adversary was being untruthful to her. They were blinded to the understanding that they were being moved from their glorious and exalted position as YHWH's son and daughter that were bestowed with the earth for inheritance. The plot was to deny them the kingdom of the earth and to remove all the blessings bestowed upon them. They would die, and they would never be like the "God" — Satan and his fallen angels — they were deceived to cross over to become. Rather, their fall ensnared them into iniquity, rebellion, and all manner of lawlessness that continued to provoke YHWH to anger until they were destroyed.

*Genesis 3 [NLT]*4

"You won't die!" the serpent replied to the woman. 5 "YHWH knows that your eyes will be opened as soon as you eat it, and you will be like God [KJV: 'be as gods'], knowing both good and evil." 6 The woman was convinced. She saw that the tree was beautiful, and its fruit looked delicious, and she wanted the wisdom it would give her [desire of the flesh]. So, she took some of the fruit and ate it. Then she gave some to her husband, who was with her, and he ate it, too. 7 At that moment their eyes were opened, and they suddenly felt shame at their nakedness. So, they sewed fig leaves together to cover themselves."

Why did Eve believe the lies? Given what we know from the Scriptures about constantly living with the instruction of YHWH, Eve may have spiritually walked away from the commanded WORD of YHWH (Gen. 2:16-17). Although she could physically recall it, the Spirit of truth had left her because of her own fleshly desire and willpower to do as she pleased, to follow whatever counsel she fancied, provided it convinced and satisfied her craving. To this, the adversary was happy. Anytime the flesh overrides the Spirit of truth, one's fall becomes obvious. Unknown to Eve and Adam, the plot of Satan was based on DECEPTION, LIES, and DECEIT to cause them to rebel against their FATHER'S WORD so that they would forgo the earth given them for their habitation, and also, they would be subjected to the worship of Satan, their new God. Satan's carefully planned downfall of man was to eventually lead to the demise and extermination of mankind from the earth.

CONSEQUENCES

YHWH pronounced a death sentence on Adam and Eve because they didn't heed His commandments. Although deliverance had been worked out, those who persist in their sinful ways will not escape second death, i.e., eternal death. Similarly, in the New Covenant, YAHSHUA warns that His followers must "take *heed that no one deceives you. For many will come in My Name [title-name – Messiah], saying, "I am the Messiah, and will deceive many*" [Matt. 24:4-5]. Deception leads to sin, and sin to curses, suffering and eternal death. After their fall, YHWH pronounced a curse that would lead to death upon them:

Genesis 3:19

"By the sweat of your brow will you have food to eat until you return to the ground from which you were made. For you were made from dust, and to dust you will return."

Ezekiel 18:4

"Behold, all souls are mine; the soul of the father as well as the soul of the son is mine: the soul who sins shall die."

Ezekiel 18:20

"The soul who sins shall die. The son shall not suffer for the iniquity of the father, nor the father suffer for the iniquity of the son. The righteousness of the righteous shall be upon himself, and the wickedness of the wicked shall be upon himself."

Romans 6:23

"For the wages of sin is death, but the free gift of YHWH is eternal life in Hamashiach Yashua, our Saviour."

SALVATION & RESTORATION - PROMISED

Genesis 3:15

"And I will cause hostility between you and the woman, and between your offspring and her offspring. He will strike your head, and you will strike his heel."

However, the first man, Adam, was created a righteous man for the perfect will of the FATHER; man at creation was a work in progress in the hands of YHWH, and he was not lost in the PLAN of the FATHER, who knew the plot of the enemy before the foundation of the earth was laid. YHWH knew Satan's evil heart desired to overthrow man; He therefore made adequate arrangements to rescue mankind through His masterplan, which was in "the SEED of the woman" – YAHSHUA HAMASHIACH [Gen. 3:15; Gen. 22:18; Gal. 3:16]. Besides, YHWH so loved man that He gave His YAHSHUA, His only SON that anyone who believes in Him and His work of salvation and has faith in HIM shall not perish but have everlasting life.

John 3:16

"For YHWH so loved the world that he gave his only Son, that whoever believes in Him should not perish but have eternal life.

Romans 10:13

For "everyone who calls on the name of YAHSHUA HAMASHIACH will be saved." [See Joel 2:32]

In YHWH's infinite mercy, and following His masterplan before the foundation of the earth was laid to save man, a clause in Genesis 3:15 points to how YHWH will save and restore mankind through the SEED of the woman. Redemption of man has begun with the shedding of the BLOOD OF YAHSHUA [Satan strikes His heel]. Satan will pay the price of his deception, lies and deceit with which he contrived to bring sin, curses and death upon man. Thus, Satan will be destroyed [Gen. 3:15b] at the return of YAHSHUA, for total freedom, redemption, salvation, and restoration of humanity on the earth created for his perpetual habitation.

CHAPTER 5:
Second Covenant
NOAH

NOAH – AND RENEWED COVENANT

COVENANT is a continuous contractual AGREEMENT that showcases the relationship between YHWH and His people. This covenant stipulates how Noah and his descendants should live their lives to not get into the corruption of sin. After the flood, Noah and his descendants continued with YHWH's Covenant. In Noah and his descendants, YAHWEH renewed the Covenant He made with Adam. The sign of the Covenant between Yahweh and Noah is the rainbow. As mentioned above, living a life outside YAHWEH'S Covenant Law gives rise to sin – iniquity, hatred, violence, corruption, murder, and death. The Covenant Book reveals that soon after the fall of man, violence and murder took over the earth. HATRED reigned, and LOVE disappeared! The generation of Adam could not be saved because evil beguiled it. There was inhumanity among men, just like what is happening today. The laws of men make no provision for the true love of YAHWEH. Not even in man's religion can one obtain love. Human laws, whether religious or secular, are designed for selfishness, covetousness, greed, and hatred. Those laws are used to intimidate and incarcerate those they hate. Human laws are the opposite of YAHWEH'S Law designed for LOVE. As a result of the obnoxious laws of men that breed SIN – evil, wickedness, violence, and bloodshed in the earth – YAHWEH called out the righteous Noah and his family; He saved them from the flood that destroyed their world.

RAINBOW DEPICTS YAHWEH'S COVENANT WITH NOAH

Immediately after the flood, YAHWEH deliberately made a Covenant with Noah and his generations – that if they continue to keep His Covenant, they would live – but if they rebel, death would follow them, as before the flood. After Noah had made a sacrifice to YHWH in appreciation of his deliverance with his family, YHWH was delighted with his offerings, resulting in the establishment of a rainbow as a mark or token of His covenant with him that He would not destroy the earth again with water. This covenant was not a pledge that in the end, YHWH would not destroy the earth and the wicked again. After the millennium reign of YAHSHUA, the decayed earth and the wicked will be destroyed with fire, and the face of heaven and earth will once again be renewed with a New Heaven and a New Earth.

The reason YAHWEH renewed the Covenant with Noah was to ensure that mankind lives a righteous life devoid of the sin, evil, and wickedness that had bedevilled his world. YHWH has always preached RIGHTEOUSNESS to mankind. Through the Covenant, Yahweh has been working out ways to preserve an obedient people who will inherit the earth forever. Obedience to YAHWEH'S Covenant inspires love, joy, peace, and harmony on the earth. YAHWEH promised Noah that the flood disaster will not occur again, but if mankind continues in sin, the consequence will be death by fire (Genesis 8:20–9:17; Isaiah 24:5–6; Psalm 75:2–3; 2 Peter 3:11–12).

As time went on, and unfortunately, some of the offspring of Noah, not Nimrod, broke the everlasting Covenant, resulting in the dispersal of mankind and ensuing devastation of the earth (Gen. 11:8; Isaiah 24:1–6). Disobedience against the Word of YAHWEH has been the problem of humanity in living happily on the earth. The earth would be peaceful and joyous if mankind were to follow the instructions of their Creator. Violation of YAHWEH'S Law through the institution of human laws has brought so much misery, calamity, and decay to the world. Mankind does not have the level of intelligence to govern themselves, except if they follow the Creator's instructions. We should not forget that the intention of YAHWEH in each covenant is to preserve a righteous people that will inhabit and inherit the planet earth (Psalm 37:9, 11, 29, 34; Matt. 5:5; Rev. 5:10). Today, obedience is required from mankind to save the earth and its inhabitants from impending disaster (Isaiah 24:5–6). Repentance is needed from everyone! Not rebellion!! Not rejection of the Torah of love given to save us.

Human religions, instituted by the act of Satan, preach that the law has been cancelled and 'nailed to the cross'. Again, this is Satan's deception, a lie from the pit of hell. His lie is meant to keep humanity in permanent, perpetual imprisonment of sin and eternal destruction. There is no single portion of the Covenant Book that suggests the law was cancelled; rather, mankind was told that the Covenant Law is a perpetual love of YHWH for His people, which provides them with the right character, attitude, and behaviour to fit into the world created to showcase the righteousness of YHWH. The Law is to be kept and obeyed (Gen. 19:5; Eccl. 12:13; Matt. 5:19). The only way to show love to Him is to keep His commandments (Jn. 14:15). The only way to do His WILL is to keep His Commandments (read Matt. 7:21–23). The only way to PLEASE the FATHER is to keep His Commandments and do them [1 Kings 2:3; Lev. 22:31]. Below are the covenant demands as received by the descendants of Abraham after the exit of Noah.

KEEP THE COMMANDMENTS

Deuteronomy 6:1-2

"Now this is the commandment, the statutes and the judgments which YHWH your FATHER has commanded me to teach you, that you might <u>do them</u> in the land where you are going over to possess it, so that you and your son and your grandson might fear YHWH your FATHER, to keep all His statutes and His commandments which I command you, all the days of your life, and that your days may be prolonged."

Deuteronomy 6:17

"You should diligently keep the commandments of YHWH your FATHER, and His testimonies and His statutes which He has commanded you."

Deuteronomy 7:11

"Therefore, you shall keep the commandment and the statutes and the judgments which I am commanding you today, to do them."

Deuteronomy 8:1

"All the commandments that I am commanding you today you shall be careful to do, that you may live and multiply, and go in and possess the land which YHWH swore to give to your forefathers."

Joshua 1:7

"Only be strong and very courageous; be careful to do according to all the law which Moshe My servant commanded you; do not turn from it to the right or to the left, so that you may have success wherever you go."

Joshua 22:5

"Only be very careful to observe the commandment and the law which Moshe the servant of YHWH commanded you, to love YHWH your FATHER and walk in all His ways and keep His commandments and hold fast to Him and serve Him with all your heart and with all your soul."

Joshua 23:6

"Be very firm, then, to <u>keep and do all that is written in the book of the law</u> of Moshe, so that you may not turn aside from it to the right hand or to the left."

1 Kings 2:3

"Keep the charge of YHWH your FATHER, to walk in His ways, to keep His statutes, His commandments, His ordinances, and His testimonies, according to what is written in the Law of Moshe, that you may succeed in all that you do and wherever you turn."

1 Kings 3:14

"If you walk in My ways, keeping My statutes and commandments, as your father David walked, then I will prolong your days."

1 Kings 8:61

"Let your heart therefore be wholly devoted to YHWH your FATHER, to walk in His statutes and to keep His commandments, as at this day."

Psalm 119:2

"How blessed are those who observe His testimonies, who seek Him with all their heart."

Proverbs 10:8

"The wise of heart will receive commands, but a babbling fool will be ruined."

Luke 11:28

But He said, "On the contrary, blessed are those who hear the word of YHWH and observe it."

1 Timothy 6:14

"That you keep the commandment without stain or reproach until the appearing of our MASTER YAHSHUA MESSIYAH."

1 John 5:3

"For this is the love of YHWH that we keep His commandments; and His commandments are not burdensome."

James 1:22

"But prove yourselves <u>doers of the Word</u>, and not merely hearers who delude themselves."

It's deliberate to list the above and many more in all portions of the Scriptures that commands us to do, keep and obey the WORDs of our FATHER. These are clear instructions to obey His Covenant, if we must live and inherit the earth. Eternity is for those who live in obedience.

CHAPTER 6:
Third Covenant
ABRAHAM

YHWH never relented in fulfilling His promise to save mankind from destruction. After the people in the days of Adam and Noah failed to walk in the Covenant Way of YHWH, ABBA YAH didn't relent. He continued to search for a seed that would eventually live a righteous life and inherit the earth. At this period of human history filled with evil, YHWH found Abraham and renewed His Covenant with him. He asked Abraham and his descendants to follow Him and be blameless (Gen. 12:1-3; Gen. 17:1). Unfortunately, the weakness of mankind to keep the everlasting Covenant continues to strengthen sin in the world. However, YAHWEH persisted in seeking the human race that would obey and keep His laws, commandments, statutes, and judgements as stated in His Covenant that is good and righteous.

In order to preserve life on the earth, YAHWEH called Abraham and his seed to obey Him. He promised to bless Abraham and his SEED and the LAND (Kingdom) He would eventually settle them in, if only they'll keep His Covenant. How did Abraham fare? Abraham heeded YAH's summon to follow Him and be blameless. The sign or token of obedience to His WORD began with circumcision of the foreskin of flesh (Gen. 17:7-14). Any male that fails to get circumcised will be cut off from the family of Yisrayah. The circumcision of the FORESKIN, which was a sign of OBEDIENCE to YHWH, is likened to the RAINBOW sign that marks obedience. Furthermore, the Covenant Book records, "That Abraham obeyed My voice and kept My charge, My commandments, My statutes, and My laws" (Gen. 26:5). As enumerated above, the ABRAHAMIC COVENANT for OBEDIENCE TO YHWH'S WORD was signed and sealed with Circumcision (Gen. Chapter 17). Every circumcised child of YHWH must live in obedience to His Word. It is a perpetual mark of following YHWH. Meanwhile, the children were to sojourn in Egypt for 400 years, and they would return to possess the promised LAND, provided they remain obedient.

CHAPTER 7:
Fourth Covenant
Descendants of Abraham

YISRAYAH – THE DESCENDANTS OF ABRAHAM

The Book of Exodus presents the renewed Covenant with the descendants of Abraham, known as Yisrayah (Exodus 19: 20:1-17; 6:4). The Torah and the Ten Commandments discussed above were because of the covenant sealed with Yisrayah when they were returning from Egypt after 400 years and thirty years of sojourn in a foreign land. Some writers argue that the patriarchs did not know Yahweh prior to this covenant (Exodus 6:3). But the previous covenants discussed above, from Adam to Abraham, speak otherwise. To these returnees, a fresh Covenant was required at Mt Sinai because many of them had forsaken the everlasting Covenant in Egypt, where they served and worshipped Gentile gods and idols of wood and stone. While in Egypt, they lost their relationship with YHWH as they served the gods of Egypt. They were held captive by the Egyptians ostensibly for walking away from the true YHWH who called them. They had to cry to Him for deliverance and restoration. In the ensuing preparation for their exodus back to their land, they were to spend 40 years in the wilderness to learn the COVENANT WAY of YHWH. In order to realign them with their FATHER, there had to be a renewed Covenant before they entered the PROMISED LAND (Kingdom of Yisrayah); and that was done in the wilderness at Mt. Sinai, where they received the COVENANT BOOK called TORAH, summarised in two Stone Tablets as "TEN COMMANDMENTS" discussed above (Exodus 20:1-17; Deuteronomy 5:7-21). This marked the signing and sealing of the Mt Sinai Covenant with "animal blood" (Exodus 24:6-8). Did Yisrayah adhere to YHWH's instruction to follow Him and never heed the "gods" or "lords" of the Gentiles? No! They didn't obey Him, and as a result, after many prompts, warnings, teachings, and redirections to keep the Covenant without success, they were scattered into the world until today.

The renewed Covenant YAHWEH made with Yisrayah was based on the fact that they would learn His ways and be OBEDIENT to His LAWS, COMMANDMENTS, AND STATUTES. The main clause of the Covenant says, *"Now therefore, if you will obey My voice indeed, and keep My covenant, then ye shall be a peculiar treasure unto Me above all people: for all the earth is Mine. And you shall be unto me a kingdom of priests and a set-apart nation"* (Exodus 19:5-6; 1 Peter 2:5, 9; Rev. 5:10). Unfortunately, the TORAH [LAW] & TEN COMMANDMENTS were abandoned for Gentile ways of life. The people of YHWH did not keep His Covenant, and as a result, they were scattered all over the world until today. Again, the Covenant required RENEWAL for the latter age. Once again, the goodness and mercy of YHWH were rekindled by the coming of the only SON – YAHSHUA HAMASHIACH – to fulfil the promise to Adam for a SEED that would deliver mankind from the power of sin and liberate them from the yoke of Satan and death. YHWH's promise of a New Covenant is here observed:

Jeremiah 31:**33**

For this is the covenant that I will make with the house of Yisrayah after those days, declares YHWH: I will put My Torah (Law) within them, and I will write it on their hearts. And I will be their FATHER, and they shall be My people. 34 And no longer shall each one teach his neighbour and each his brother, saying, 'Know YHWH,' for they shall all know Me, from the least of them to the greatest, declares YHWH. For I will forgive their iniquity, and I will remember their sin no more."

Indeed, the coming of YAHSHUA HAMASHIACH provides mankind with a new Covenant, a Covenant of hope, a Covenant of salvation, a Covenant of eternal inheritance on earth, and eternal life in YHWH (Heb. 8:6; Heb. 9:15).

SUMMARY

FIRST

YAHWEH made His first COVENANT with Adam and continued the renewal with Noah, Abraham, Yisrayah and their descendants. The first Covenant was enshrined in the TORAH (first five books: Genesis, Exodus, Leviticus, Numbers, and Deuteronomy). Leaders of Yisrayah entered into a covenant or agreement with YHWH that they and their children must obey and keep the WORDS OF TORAH (see Exodus 24:6-7). Are you keeping the Covenant or disobeying it?

If you're a Covenant-keeper, well done! Continue to fear HIM, keep the covenant, daily obey His commandments, and love Him with all your hearts and with all your souls. Also love the brethren and your neighbours; then wait for YAHSHUA HAMASHIACH's appearing. Below, we examine the Covenant renewed in the Person of YAHSHUA – who is today the Mediator of the Renewed Covenant.

PART 2
CHAPTER 8:
FIFTH COVENANT YAHSHUA
YAHSHUA

THE MEDIATOR OF THE RENEWED COVENANT

From Genesis Chapter 3 verse 15 to Matthew Chapter 26 verses 27-28, YAHSHUA was appointed by the FATHER to RENEW THE ENTIRE COVENANT with His people who will submit to HIM and the rest of mankind who also will believe in HIM and the FATHER and be grafted into the family of Yisrayah. YAHSHUA, the Promised Seed, is the Deliverer, Saviour, Mashiach, the High Priest, and the King of Yisrayah who will defeat the kings and globalists of this world and deliver the PROMISED LAND (Kingdom) of YISRAYAH to them forever. All those, whether they are born of the Abrahamic seed or Gentiles grafted into the family of Yisrayah by virtue of their obedience to YHWH's Covenant and faith in YAHSHUA HAMASHIACH, are today called true Yisrayah. Conversely, Yisrayah who reject YAHSHUA and the Covenant Way lose their crown and the Kingdom. The Scripture says, they are replaced by those grafted into the family of Yisrayah [read Hosea Chapters 1-14; Romans Chapter 11]. Some Yisrayah by birth will be replaced because they lived in unbelief by following the religions of this world; they served Baal – the god of the Gentiles – who thrives in religions.

Seed & Land: The PROMISE of "SEED" and "LAND" rests on YAHSHUA MASHIACH. YAHSHUA, as the promised Seed, was destined to save His people from their sins so that "they which are called might receive the promise of eternal inheritance." Also, He is not only "the Mediator of the BETTER COVENANT which was established upon better promises," but "the Mediator of the Renewed Covenant" (Hebrews 8:6; Heb. 9:15; Jer. 31:31-34). In YAHSHUA, those who will inherit the coming Kingdom must keep the Covenant Law and Commandments, which depict the LOVE of the Father and the Son (John 14:15; John 14:21, 23-24). "Hereby we do know that we know Him, if we keep His commandments" (1 John 2:3). "He that says, 'I know Him,' and keeps not His commandments, is a liar, and the truth is not in him." (v. 4). YAHSHUA said, "If you love Me, keep My commandments" (John 14:15). Do you keep His commandments?

Sacrifices

Sin has no option of being removed except through the BLOOD of YAHSHUA HAMASHIACH. Blood of animals sacrificed to atone for the sins of men was not cleansing nor removing the sins of men. It wasn't the COVENANT TORAH or LAW OF OBEDIENCE handed to Yisrayah as a permanent legacy. If they were to obey the commandments and keep His statutes, they were to live and possess the Land and live in it safely without anyone pursuing or driving them away; but anytime they violated HIS instructions, they were punished, chased away, and killed, even till today in the Gentile world where they dwell. However, in order to temporarily keep Yisrayah from being wiped out, animal sacrifices were permitted – although YHWH did not sanction them – He only prepared a BODY IN YAHSHUA as the LAMB OF SACRIFICE so that men's sins would be atoned for once and for all. YAHSHUA says, FATHER, "You have given Me a body to offer. You were not pleased with burnt offerings or other offerings for sin." (Heb. 10:5-6). The will of the FATHER was for the SON to die for sinful mankind, and that was fulfilled so that covenant-keepers would be saved (Heb. 10:7; Isaiah 53:1-12). The excerpts below from Hebrews Chapter 10 attest that YAHSHUA is the only SACRIFICE acceptable to the FATHER, made available to redeem mankind from their SINS even before the foundation of the world was laid. After YAHSHUA was offered as the living sacrifice, no more animal sacrifices were required for atonement.

YAHSHUA MASHIACH'S SACRIFICE ONCE FOR ALL

Hebrews Chapter 10 [NLT]

¹The old system under the law of Mosheh was only a shadow, a dim preview of the good things to come, not the good things themselves. The sacrifices under that system were repeated again and again, year after year, but they were never able to provide perfect cleansing for those who came to worship. [NKJV: "make those who approach perfect"] ² If they could have provided perfect cleansing, the sacrifices would have stopped, for the worshipers would have been purified once for all time, and their feelings of guilt would have disappeared.

³ But instead, those sacrifices actually reminded them of their sins year after year. ⁴ For it is not possible for the blood of bulls and goats to take away sins. ⁵ That is why, when MASHIACH came into the world, he said to YHWH,

"You did not want animal sacrifices or sin offerings. But You (YHWH) have given Me a body to offer.

⁶ You were not pleased with burnt offerings or other offerings for sin.

⁷ Then I said, 'Look, I have come to do your will, O YHWH — as is written about Me in the Scriptures.'"

⁸ First, Mashiach said, "You did not want animal sacrifices or sin offerings or burnt offerings or other offerings for sin, nor were you pleased with them" (though they are required by the law of Moshe). ⁹ Then

he said, "Look, I have come to do Your will." *He cancels the first covenant in order to put the second into effect.* [i.e., the animal blood sacrifices were cancelled so that the BLOOD of YAHSHUA will take effect]. ¹⁰ For YHWH's will was for us to be made holy by the sacrifice of the BODY OF YAHSHUA MASHIACH, once for all time.

¹¹ Under the old covenant, the priest stands and ministers before the altar day after day, offering the same sacrifices again and again, which can never take away sins. ¹² But our High Priest [YAHSHUA] offered Himself to YHWH as a single sacrifice for sins, good for all time. Then he sat down in the place of honour at YHWH's right hand. ¹³ There he waits until his enemies are humbled and made a footstool under His feet. ¹⁴ For by that one offering He forever made perfect those who are being made holy.

¹⁵ And the Holy Spirit also testifies that this is so. For he says,

¹⁶ "This is the RENEWED COVENANT I will make with my people on that day, says YHWH: I will put my laws in their hearts, and I will write them on their minds." [Jer. 31:31-34; Matt. 26:27-28].

¹⁷ Then he says, "I will never again remember their sins and lawless deeds."

¹⁸ And when sins have been forgiven, there is no need to offer any more sacrifices.

There was no time YHWH delighted in the killing of animals or the shedding of their blood for purposes of atoning for the sin of mankind. Rather, what He gave them was His Covenant, to follow it and be blameless. Keeping His covenant would have saved them from evil and wickedness, which lawbreakers fall into and are consumed by. However, animal sacrifice was permitted – not because it was capable of atoning for or saving souls from sin and death – but because it was allowed to keep the wrath of YHWH from wiping out the disobedient Yisrayah until YAHSHUA, whose body was prepared for the sacrifice and atonement of sin, came and fulfilled the onerous task. Indeed, He came, taught His people to repent and return to the FATHER; He then paid the ultimate price of our rebellion – He died for sinful mankind that they might repent and be reconciled to the FATHER for eternal salvation. To those who believe in Him and keep the Covenant Commandments of the FATHER, they shall be saved. Today, YAHSHUA is our New Mediator of the Covenant.

YAHSHUA–MEDIATOR OF THE RENEWED COVENANT

Hebrews 8 (NKJV)

"**6.** But now He (YAHSHUA) has obtained a more excellent ministry, inasmuch as He is also Mediator of a better covenant, which was established on better promises. **7.** For if that first covenant had been faultless, then no place would have been sought for a second. **8.** Because finding fault with them [first covenant of animal sacrifices], He says: "Behold, the days are coming, says YHWH, when I will make a new covenant with the house of Yisrayah and with the house of Yehudah — **9.** not according to the covenant that I made with their fathers in the day when I took them by the hand to lead them out of the land of Egypt; because they did not continue in My covenant, and I disregarded them, says YHWH. **10.** For this is the covenant that I will make with the house of Yisrayah after those days, says YHWH: I will put My laws in their mind and write them on their hearts; and I will be their FATHER, and they shall be My people. **11.** None of them shall teach his neighbour, and none his brother, saying, 'Know YHWH,' for all shall know Me, from the least of them to the greatest of them. **12.** For I will be merciful to their unrighteousness, and their sins and their lawless deeds I will remember no more." **13.** In that He says, "A renewed covenant", He has made the first obsolete (i.e., the covenant of animal sacrifices, not the LAW itself). Now what is becoming obsolete and growing old (i.e., animal blood sacrifice) is ready to vanish away."

CONSEQUENCES OF CONTINUOUS SIN

To YHWH be the glory, who through His unchangeable Word quickens us to awake to His Covenant Way, not religion, and not the commandments of men or traditions of the elders. The Book of the Covenant is clear that only the ultimate sacrifice of the BODY and BLOOD of YAHSHUA MASHIACH was provided by the FATHER to atone for our sins. Continuous sin, as in disobedience to YHWH's express Covenant Commandments or making animal sacrifices as a means of sin cleansing, makes such a person liable to damnation, because he or she has refused to abide in the instruction of the FATHER, who commands all men to be baptised into the Name of YAHSHUA and have faith in Him as our ONE and only SAVIOUR in these last days of human history. He accomplished His promise made in Genesis Chapter 3:15, Isaiah Chapter 53, Jeremiah 31:31-34, and Matthew Chapter 26:26-28, etc., by giving us His only SON YAHSHUA, that whosoever will believe in Him and keep the Covenant Commandments shall be saved. The blood of animals has never saved and will not save men from their sins. The sacrifice of animals and their blood for atonement is no longer required, as YAHSHUA is the LAMB of sacrifice that fulfilled YHWH's promise of the Seed for human salvation. Anybody sacrificing the blood of animals for atonement of sins is trampling upon the PRECIOUS BLOOD OF YAHSHUA MESSIYAH. Henceforth, the faithful and believers are saved by trusting and believing in YAHSHUA's finished sacrificial work. Below, the Covenant Book states the consequence for those who would sin wilfully after receiving the knowledge of the truth about animal sacrifices, which are no longer tolerated by the FATHER, YHWH, having accomplished the gift of His SON to die for and atone for our sins.

HEBREWS 10 [NKJV]

"**26.** For if we sin wilfully after we have received the knowledge of the truth, there no longer remains a sacrifice for sins, **27.** But a certain fearful expectation of judgement, and fiery indignation which will devour the adversaries (enemies, foes). **28.** Anyone who has rejected Mosheh's law dies without mercy on the testimony of two or three witnesses. **29.** Of how much worse punishment, do you suppose, will he be thought worthy who has trampled the Son of YHWH underfoot, counted the BLOOD OF THE COVENANT by which he was sanctified a common thing, and insulted the SPIRIT OF GRACE? **30.** For we know Him who said, "Vengeance is Mine, I will repay," says YHWH. And again, "YHWH will judge His people." **31.** It is a fearful thing to fall into the hands of the living YHWH."

SUMMARY

RENEWED COVENANT

Renewed Covenant and Religion: YAHSHUA MASHIACH is the Mediator of the Renewed Covenant. Only He, the FATHER chose to fulfil the promise of human deliverance. YAHWEH made His renewed COVENANT in YAHSHUA HAMASHIACH and commanded all mankind to follow HIM, for HE is the "Way, the TRUTH, and the LIFE; no man can come to the FATHER but through HIM" [Jn. 14:6]. The Renewed Covenant that holds YAHWEH's WORD is made flesh as contained in the Torah, the Prophets, and the Writings. YAHSHUA is the purpose and the goal of the Law. The three Tanach (Scriptures) mentioned above are enshrined in what is today called the SCRIPTURES upon which YAHSHUA taught (Luke 24:27, 44–46). These constitute the BREAD OF LIFE, which is also described as SPIRIT and LIFE, that every covenant-keeper must eat to have life, even eternal life (Jn. 6:53–56; Jn. 6:63, 68; 2 Cor. 3:6).

From the Tanach and the doctrine of YAHSHUA, the Disciples and the Apostles wrote the Gospels and Epistles that were heavily corrupted in today's New Testament Bibles. The corruption constitutes religion in Christianity. Anyone who follows man-made RELIGION other than the COVENANT Way commanded by YHWH is simply following and serving the prince of this world in his religion, which YHWH forbids [Ex. 23:13]. Such an individual is liable to hellfire. Faithful believers are commanded to follow the Covenant Way of YHWH through YAHSHUA HAMASHIACH [Ex. 20:1–17; Deut. 5:7–21; Jn. 14:6; Jn. 14:15; Jn. 15:10].

The prince of this world established religion through priests, pastors, imams, clergy, etc., to deceive those who would not submit to YHWH's Covenant Way. The false leaders mix the Scriptures with the commandments of men and traditions of elders, which is religion (see Matthew 15:1–9). YAH warns His people to flee from religions and every appearance of idolatry. No observance or teaching of religion will lead anyone to the everlasting Kingdom. Eternal life is in YHWH and YAHSHUA. Strive to enter the Kingdom; fear YHWH and have faith in YAHSHUA; and keep the everlasting Covenant Commandments of the FATHER. This is the whole duty of man! Those who abide by and perform YHWH's instructions shall be saved.

CHAPTER 9: COVENANT OF PEACE

COVENANT OF PEACE IS COMING

The Hebrew meaning of 'Covenant' is to create or cut in agreement between YHWH and His people. In English common law, a Covenant may refer to an Agreement, Pact, Treaty, Contract, Accord, Bond, Settlement, Deal, Unity, Consensus, Harmony, Consent, Commitment, Vow, or assurance between two or more parties who agree to perform a specific task. However, YHWH's Covenant is far more than a human Agreement between Him, the Creator of heavens and earth [hereinafter called FATHER], and His people Yisrayah. The FATHER began a Covenant with the first parent, Adam, Noah, Abraham, Yisrayah, and continues unto the SAVIOUR, YAHSHUA HAMASHIACH. Covenant is a continuum. Another "Covenant" is coming after the return of YAHSHUA MASHIACH. It's called the COVENANT OF PEACE! It will usher the whole of Yisrayah into everlasting PEACE, and consequently, the entire world will be at PEACE as in heaven. The prophets affirm that in the latter days, YHWH will establish a new Covenant through YAHSHUA HAMASHIACH that will free the world from war and destruction (Jer. 31:33-34; Isaiah 2:3-4).

Isaiah 54:9,10 For this is as the waters of Noah to me: for as I have sworn that the waters of Noah should no more go over the earth, so have I sworn that I would not be wroth with you nor rebuke you.

Ezekiel 34:25 And I will make with them a COVENANT OF PEACE and will cause the evil beasts to cease out of the land, and they shall dwell safely in the wilderness and sleep in the woods.

Ezekiel 37:26 Moreover, I will make a COVENANT OF PEACE with them; it shall be an everlasting covenant with them, and I will place them and multiply them and will set my sanctuary in the middle of them forevermore.

Jeremiah 1:31-34 "Behold, the days are coming," declares YHWH, "when I will make a new covenant with the house of Yisrayah and the house of Judah, not like the covenant that I made with their fathers on the day when I took them by the hand to bring them out of the land of Egypt, my covenant that they broke, though I was their husband," declares YHWH. For this is the covenant that I will make with the house of Yisrayah after those days, declares YHWH: I will put My Torah (Law) within them, and I will write it on their hearts. And I will be their FATHER, and they shall be My people. And no longer shall each one teach his neighbour and each his brother, saying, 'Know YHWH'. For they shall all know Me, from the least of them to the greatest, declares YHWH. For I will forgive their iniquity, and I will remember their sin no more."

Covenant Lessons

From Adam, Noah, Abraham, Yisrayah, and YAHSHUA HAMASHIACH, the masterplan of YHWH to redeem mankind from sin became apparent as He continued to call people to abide in His COVENANT Way. Each of the covenants He made with the fathers was based on obedience to His LAW. To rescue mankind, His WORD was made flesh (John 1:1-2, 14). The Word is YAHSHUA MASHIACH (Rev. 19:13). Through Him, the believing Yisrayahlites and the Gentiles shall be saved (Matt. 1:21; John 3:16). Through Him righteousness will be established in the earth. As He reigns in the earth at His return, the whole world will experience peace and blessings forever. He will stop wars and the production of weapons of destruction. YAHSHUA, the WORD of YHWH, has all the characteristics of the FATHER captured in the Set-apart Spirit (Galatians 5:22-23). His death and resurrection brought forgiveness to repented and believing people who were before cut off by sin. By His Spirit, He transforms believers from the kingdom of darkness into His marvellous light, thus making them inheritors of the everlasting kingdom. Through YAHSHUA, believers become the light of the world. Today, the SPIRIT of YAHSHUA empowers believers to live obedient lives, which mankind has been failing to achieve. Unfortunately, many today are still saying that the COVENANT LAW was cancelled and 'nailed to the stake'. This is Satan's deception, instituted from the time of Adam to cause mankind to perpetually rebel against their Creator, YHWH. If the angels in Heaven are governed by YHWH'S Laws, and the world leaders govern their people with human laws and decrees, why can't mankind obey the COVENANT LAW of YHWH given to them for their own good and eternal existence? The law of the Covenant says if you keep it, you'll live by it; if you break it, you die. The Covenant which commenced from Adam still exists today, and through the Word of the Covenant, mankind will be judged when YAHSHUA HAMASHIACH returns (John 12:48). The unbelieving mankind will be wiped out by fire for breaking His Covenant (Isaiah 24:5-6). Therefore, covenant breakers are called to REPENT from breaking His Covenant LAWS (e.g., Sabbath, His Name — YHWH, Feasts, Ten Commandments, etc.) and be SAVED! Notice that only one MESSIAH and SAVIOUR [not two] is given to mankind for their salvation, and that Saviour is YAHSHUA HAMASHIACH OF YISRAYAH (Acts 4:10, 12).

PART 3
CHAPTER 10:
YISRAYAH

In this part, we should seek to find out, who are the Yisrayahlites? Did Christianity replace the Yisrayahlites? Where are the Yisrayahlites today? Meanwhile, let's examine Yisrayah under the promises that established who they are as a people and nation. YHWH's promises to His people are many, but the fulfilment of Genesis Chapter 3:15 — the promise of the gift of the "Seed" — was renewed in the Seed that would come through the descendants of Abraham. The promised "Land" would be the headquarters of the chosen family from which the Seed would come. These two vital promises form the foundation upon which the call for obedience and righteousness was first announced to Abraham and later enshrined in the Covenant of Circumcision (Genesis 17:1-14). For Yisrayah to receive the promised Seed and the Land, they must live a life of obedience to YHWH's commandments; they must live a life of love for YHWH; they must live a life of love for their neighbours; they must keep the covenant and follow Yahshua HaMashiach all the days of their lives, even after the Seed is born in their midst and assumes the government or the Kingdom of the Land, which Yahweh promised to establish on the earth through them.

SEED & LAND PROMISED FROM THE BEGINNING

From Abraham to this date, the covenant relationship between YAHWEH and His people is based on four concepts:

    (1)   OBEDIENCE TO HIS WORD, and
    (2)   FAITH IN YHWH and YAHSHUA.
    (3)   LOVE FOR YAHWEH,
    (4)   LOVE FOR NEIGHBOUR,

The relationship between Yisrayah and their FATHER is based on these four as prescribed in the Ten Commandments and described as the Torah Obedient criteria in Figure 1. Yisrayah and the Gentile people who would believe in YHWH are called to internalise His Torah Laws. The Torah commandments are to be received with enduring love and faith that would bind them and the Creator together forever. Attributes of the Saviour are based on observing the covenant. Following its instructions leads to the restoration of righteousness and opens the way for the return of humanity to the FATHER and the regaining of the lost earth through the establishment of the Kingdom. In YAHWEH's infinite favour, two powerful PROMISES were made to Abraham and his descendants. The promises include SEED and LAND, amongst others, so that He can restart the earth anew through the SEED that would bear no sin.

The promise of the Seed began in Genesis Chapter 3 verse 15, where Adam and Eve were promised a Seed that would save mankind from the clutches of sin. The promise was renewed to Abraham through his descendants and was fulfilled through the loins of Yoseph and Miriam in the Land of Yisrayah about 2000 years ago. The Seed, who took the form of the WORD of YAHWEH, was made flesh in His likeness. He was born in Judea during the reign of the Roman Emperor Caesar (Octavian) Augustus. He was named YAHSHUA HAMASHIACH. The Book of the Covenant declared that He is the Seed promised to be born in the Land of Yisrayah to save His people from their sins and restore them to their Land in these latter days (Matthew 1:21; Luke 2:11, 21, 26–35; see Genesis 15:13–16, 18; Genesis 17:7–10; Isaiah 9:6–7). Having come to teach repentance from sin and salvation on earth, He would return to set up the FATHER's Government, where He would reign over Yisrayah and the entire human race.

However, the second promise, LAND, is awaiting fulfilment because the Yisrayahlites are still scattered all over the world, and they have not repented from their sins to be restored to the Promised Land. They're still under the law of sin; as a result, they're still scattered abroad serving their punishment. When the Yisrayahlites shall repent and confess their sins and come into obedience and favour with Yahweh, He will restore them back to their Land (Leviticus 26:40–45; Deuteronomy 4:27–31; 30:1–10). And this will be the second time they will be delivered from the annihilation of the Gentile nations. According to the Book of the Covenant, Yahweh knows where the Yisrayahlites are today. He keeps His eyes on them, and they cannot be destroyed as long as the Covenant of YAHWEH and His promises remain. Yisrayah remains YAHWEH'S firstborn son, the natural Olive Tree of YAHWEH, the chosen generation, a royal priesthood and a peculiar people; the only nation chosen by YAHWEH to be His people. As the scattered Yisrayahlites are beginning to call upon the Name of YAHWEH, they will soon be gathered and restored back to their Land as YAHWEH and YAHSHUA promised (Matthew 23:38–39; Matthew 24:31; Joel 2:32; Isaiah 11:10–16; Ezekiel 20:33–40; Ezekiel 34:11–16, etc.).

YAHSHUA the SEED was the expected Yahweh's Messiah whom Simon saw and declared: "Mine eyes have seen Thy SALVATION" (Luke 2:30). Oh yes! Yahshua is the salvation of anyone who receives Him and serves the Father. The Covenant and Promise of 'SEED' YAHWEH made with Abraham was about YAHSHUA ["Salvation"]. The Promise spoke about "Seed" and not "Seeds", and that referred to only One Man – YAHSHUA HAMASHIACH – THE SAVIOUR OF Yisrayah. Apostle Paul wrote:

"Now to Abraham and his Seed were the promises made. He does not say, "And to seeds," as of many, but as of one, "And to your Seed," who is Messiah (Galatians 3:16; NKJV).

YAHSHUA The Seed Is from Yisrayah

The Seed referred to one, not two, and the title of the Seed is "HaMashiach" [The Anointed One], known as the Saviour of Yisrayah. During the earthly ministry of YAHSHUA, He confirmed that He is the Saviour of Yisrayah and their King (John 5:24, 39; Luke 23:3; Mark 15:2). He also declared that "salvation is of the Yisrayah" (John 4:22), thus affirming that He is the fulfilment of the PROMISE of the Seed whose Name shall be called YAHSHUA that will save Yisrayah from their sins (Matt. 1:21; Luke 1:31-33; Luke 2:21). Thus, YAHSHUA is the Good News that affirms the fulfilment of YAHWEH'S PROMISE to Abraham that began with Adam (Gen. 3:15; see Gen. 17:7-11). Luke concords: "And now we proclaim to you the good news: what YAHWEH promised our fathers" (Acts 13:32). Yahshua HaMashiach is from the tribe of Judah, a nationality of Yisrayah, and a Hebrew in origin. No Gentile nation bears the Hebrew name, YAHSHUA, nor possesses the above attributes associated with Yisrayah's Mashiach and Saviour. Except for YAHSHUA of the Hebrew Yisrayah, no Gentile name fulfils the status of 'Messiah and Saviour' promised to humanity. The Gentile people were regarded by Yisrayahlites as the uncircumcised sinners. The BOC declared that the Gentile nations worship Baal, Elohim, i.e., "the Lord" or "God", as their Saviour. They do not serve or worship the Biblical YAHWEH of Yisrayah. When the Greek Empire defeated the tribe of Yehuda (Jews), the biblical history records that their leader Antiochus Epiphanes polluted the Temple of YAHWEH in Yerusalem with his image of abomination that desecrated YAHWEH's Temple.

YAHWEH did not only promise Seed and Land to Yisrayah, but He also promised to keep and secure Yisrayah, wherever they may dwell. Although they would sin and desert Him and be scattered abroad from their Land, He would preserve them and have them return to repossess the promised Land in the latter days of the human age. Unfortunately, having lost their land because of the unfaithfulness of some, most of Gentile Christianity thought that Yisrayah had been cast away completely, as they were unable to keep the Torah Law of YHWH, and they had assumed the replacement of these people of YHWH. The BOC stated otherwise and promised that YHWH, who chose them, will show favour again to them and restore them back to their own land (Romans 11; Jeremiah 30:1-24; 31:1-39; Ezekiel 20:33-45; Ezekiel 37:1-28).

CHRISTIAN REPLACEMENT OF YISRAYAH

COVENANT-YISRAYAH IS IRREPLACEABLE

Ever since the RCC and all the Protestants, or "daughters" of the RCC, had the notion that they replaced the Covenant-keeping Assembly of Yisrayah founded by YAHSHUA HaMashiach, the entire Christendom has farther separated themselves from the only ONE SAVIOUR, YAHSHUA HAMASHIACH, given to mankind for their salvation. Apostle Paul forewarned the Gentile Churches that Yisrayah and the head – YAHSHUA Mashiach – are the Olive Tree, which is irreplaceable and can never be destroyed nor cast away, just as the covenant commandments can never be done away with. Yisrayah is the original source of salvation after the days of Noah, and they remain so forever. Through the Yisrayahlites, the Torah (Law), Scriptures, or Bible was given for instruction and guidance. YAHSHUA Mashiach was sent to the house of Yisrayah, not to the Gentiles: "Go not into the way of the Gentiles, and into any city of the Samaritans enter ye not. But go rather to the lost sheep of the house of Yisrayah" (Matthew 10:5-6). YAHSHUA asserts, "I am not sent but unto the lost sheep of the house of Yisrayah" (Matthew 15:24). However, by YAHWEH's mercy, the Gentiles are to be grafted in if they receive Yahshua. Apostle Shaul knew that someday the Gentile

Christians would boast that they are the custodians of the Assemblies. He reminded them that Yisrayah is his kinsman. They still retain salvation status and covenant-keeping.

Apostle Shaul told the Gentile believers who the Yisrayahlites are: Who are the Yisrayahlites, to whom pertain the adoption, and the glory, and the covenants, and the giving of the Law, and the service of Yahweh, and the promises; whose are the fathers, and of whom, as concerning the flesh, Yahshua Mashiach came, who is over all, Yahweh blessed forever. (Romans 9:4-5). Apostle Shaul went further to inform the Gentile Churches that the Word of YAHWEH is not taken away from Yisrayah, but that some who are not Yisrayah are removed from the covenant. Not all in Yisrayah that profess to be the seed of Abraham are his children. The promised descendants, or seeds, are those born of Isaac, who must live in accordance with the covenant and follow Yahshua. For the seed to qualify for the Kingdom (i.e., the Land of Yisrayah), he or she must be rooted in the VINE or the OLIVE TREE and become a BRANCH. Following the 'breaking off' of some Yisrayahlites as a result of sin, an opportunity was granted to the Gentiles to be partakers in the Olive Tree (Israel). They also must be willing to keep YHWH's Shabbat and His Covenant Commandments to qualify as a Yisrayahlite (Isaiah 56:1-8). "The same law shall apply to both the native and the foreigner who resides among you." **"The same law applies both to the native born and to the foreigner residing among you." "This instruction applies to everyone, whether a native-born Yisrayahlite or a foreigner living among you." "There is to be one law and one ordinance for you and for the alien who sojourns with you."** (Exodus 12:49; Numbers 9:14; 15:14, 16; see Exodus 20:10; Leviticus 19:34; 24:22; Numbers 9:14; Deuteronomy 5:14).

Today's Christians think that the Law is replaced by faith and grace alone. They don't even read from the Bible that YHWH spoke of one law in Yisrayah for the native-born and for the foreigner. The Torah is one, the commandments are one, and the statutes are one for everybody. Apostle Shaul corrected the replacement theologians, stating that he was a Yisrayahlite who still upheld the one Law given to Yisrayahlites to keep. Yisrayah cannot exist without the Torah.

I ask, then, has YAHWEH rejected His own people, the nation of Yisrayah? Of course not! I myself am a Yisrayahlite, a descendant of Abraham and a member of the tribe of Benjamin. No, YAHWEH has not rejected His own people, whom He chose from the very beginning. Do you realise what the Scriptures say about this? **"YAHWEH, they have killed your prophets and torn down your altars. I am the only one left, and now they are trying to kill me, too."** And do you remember YAHWEH'S reply? He said, **"No, I have**

7,000 others (Israelites) who have never bowed down to Baal" (Romans 11:1-4; also see Revelation 7:3-8; 9:4; 14:1).

Christianity is a religion that thinks to replace Yahweh's Covenant-keeping Yisrayah. Apostle Shaul rejects replacement theology and warns the Gentile Christians that Yisrayah is irreplaceable because they are Yahweh's covenant people from the beginning: they are the firstborn son of Yahweh; they are the chosen nation; they are the peculiar people; they are the holy priesthood – these are not applicable to the Gentile Christians, Muslims, Buddhists, or Hindus, etc., except those grafted into the Olive Tree. Shaul, however, explains that some of the people of Yisrayah have remained faithful to YAHWEH. These remnants are the natural branches of the Olive Tree that obey the voice of Yahweh and keep His commandments. Shaul reiterated that not all Yisrayah found favour with Yahweh; as a result, they were broken off – scattered into the world. Those that found favour are YAHWEH's chosen people because of their faithfulness to His Covenant Commandments (Revelation 3:8, 10; 14:12; 17:14; 22:14). What is the problem with those unbelieving Yisrayahlites? They reject the covenant commandments; as a result, YAHWEH shuts their eyes and ears to His gospel of truth. This is exactly what is happening to Christianity today. They rejected His covenant commandments right from the time the RCC falsely assumed ownership of the Church. All those who reject the covenant way fall into the deception of the enemy.

Apostle Shaul wrote:

"YAHWEH has put them into a deep sleep. To this day He has shut their eyes so they do not see and closed their ears so they do not hear" (Romans 11:8).

The hearts of many are hardened against YAHWEH'S covenant way. YAHWEH does not want anyone to abhor His Covenant. Rejection of the Covenant way is rejection of Yahweh and His Son, and the Scripture says such people love death (Proverbs 8:30-36). YAHWEH has put both fallen Yisrayah and fallen Gentile Christians into a deep sleep and shut their eyes (see Acts 13:46-48; Acts 18:6; Isaiah 29:10-14).

David was furious about how these fallen people rejected YAHWEH's truth. He wrote:

"Let their bountiful table become a snare, a trap that makes them think all is well. Let their blessings cause them to stumble, and let them get what they deserve (punishment). Let their eyes go blind so they cannot see, and let their backs be bent forever" (Romans 11:9-10; Psalm 69:22-23; Isaiah 29:10).

Who do the Yisrayahlites of old and new worship? Baal – 'the Lord', and Elohim – 'God', of course! They turned to bowing their knees to Baal, to the idols of nations. They reject the covenant of YAHWEH and follow the worship of idols of stone and wood; they reject their Maker and follow Gentile gods that come newly (Deut. 32:16-17). This is what the prophets and the apostles called the "falling away" (2 Thessalonians 2:2-12). Worship of God is evil and an abomination that provokes YAHWEH's wrath and destruction (Deuteronomy 8:19; Jeremiah 11:1 23; 14:1-22; 15:21; Revelation 14:9-11; Luke 13:3, 5). However, YAHWEH says if they return to Him, He will deliver them out of the land of the wicked and will redeem them out of the hand of the terrible (Jeremiah 15:21). Shaul avers that YAHWEH's people did not stumble and fall beyond recovery. He predicts that Yisrayah, in these latter days, shall awake from their slumber and be saved.

SALVATION IS OF YISRAYAH, NOT OF GENTILES

Is salvation of the Yisrayah or the Gentile Christians? Many Gentile Christians quote Apostle Shaul as one who taught the cancellation of the Law, and most of them believe that salvation is of the Gentile Christians. This belief is unbiblical! Listen to Apostle Paul:

"Brethren, my heart's desire and prayer to YAHWEH for Yisrayah is that they might be saved. For I bear them record that they have a zeal for YAHWEH, but not according to knowledge. *For they, being ignorant of YAHWEH's righteousness and going about to establish their own righteousness, have not submitted themselves unto the righteousness of YAHWEH. For Messiah is the end [goal or purpose] of the LAW FOR RIGHTEOUSNESS to everyone that believeth"* (Romans 10:1-4).

What was missing amongst most Yisrayahlites was a lack of faith in YAHSHUA HaMashiach (the Righteousness they were seeking), Who Himself was the Law the Yisrayahlites were seeking, even the end of the Law. He is today the Covenant bearer of Yisrayah, even the Mediator of the New Covenant. Yahshua called them, but they rejected His invitation, seeking their own righteousness and "another messiah". Yahshua said of Yisrayah:

"And ye will not come to Me that ye might have life. I receive no honour from men. But I know you, that ye have not the love of YAHWEH in you. I am come in my FATHER's NAME, and ye receive Me not; if another shall come in his own name, him ye will receive" (John 5:40-43).

Yahshua invited Yisrayah to come to Him as their Mashiach and Saviour, but they rejected Him, hoping to receive "another messiah" that will come in his own name and honour of men. This expectation was fulfilled in part in A.D. 325 by Constantine and the Bishops of

Rome when the name "Jesus" was created to receive honour from men. Today, most Jews and Yisrayahlites alike worship the Gentile Christian Jesus. However, in the latter days, "the false messiah" will manifest either in the same name of "Jesus" or in another false messianic name to receive honour from men. This does not apply to YAHSHUA, who remains unchangeable and will return afterwards to defeat His enemies and rule this Earth forever (John 5:41; Revelation 19:11-16; Daniel 7:26-27; Isaiah 9:6-7).

Who Are the Yisrayahlites?

Perhaps it can be worthwhile to reiterate here that Yisrayah were the called or chosen of YHWH the FATHER. They were called to hearken to His Word, obey His commandments, and keep His covenant and live. They are promised that their lives would be prolonged, saved from their enemies, and blessed if they do the will of the FATHER. Disobedience to His commandments would lead to curses, afflictions, sicknesses, and eventually, to eternal death. Yisrayah was given the oracle, the law, the covenant, the promise, and the service of YAHWEH. "Who are Israelites; to whom pertaineth the adoption, and the glory, and the covenants, and the giving of the law, and the service of YAHWEH, and the promises. Whose are the fathers, and of whom, as concerning the flesh, Messiah came, who is over all, YAH blessed forever. Amein" (Romans 9:4-5).

Here, Apostle Shaul (Paul) told us that Yisrayahlites are called to know YAHWEH, serve Him, worship Him, and attend to His service beginning from the priests (pastors, apostles, teachers, and evangelists, etc.) to all the members of the Yisrayahlite families, including the Gentiles who acknowledge and receive the Law of YHWH. Yisrayah is a people of YHWH set apart for Him. The Gentiles and their religious bodies, including Christians, are not called or chosen by YHWH unless they confess their sins and receive Him as their Saviour (John 1:12). The Gentiles are different because they do not keep His laws and do not exclusively worship Him. They worship the gods of this world. These gods are found amongst various world religions. They are not equal to nor associated with YHWH (Exodus 23:13; Hosea 13:4; Isaiah 42:8; Isaiah 48:11, etc.).

Shaul further defines a Yisrayahlite in line with YAHSHUA's description: "A Yisrayahlite is a believer in YAHSHUA MASHIACH who keeps the Covenant of the Father." According to the Torah, a Yisrayahlite possesses the following traits:

    (1)   Adoption
    (2)   Glory
    (3)   Covenants
    (4)   Giving of the Law
    (5)   Service of YAHWEH
    (6)   Receiving of the promises (Seed, i.e. Yahshua, and Land i.e. Israel)

Yisrayah of Today: regardless of physical ancestral heritage, today those who obey YHWH and hold to YAHSHUA's TESTIMONY are defined as true Yisrayahlites or children of the Promise (read Romans 2:29; Galatians 3:7). Shaul unequivocally asserts that Yisrayah are Yahweh's people, the very branch and lump from the Vine (YAHSHUA) who is given the Land of Yisrayah for inheritance. Promises of the Covenant, Law, etc., are given to Yisrayah, not to Christianity, who serve the deities of this world. Until Gentile Christians repent and are grafted into the Olive Tree (Yisrayah), they have no inheritance of salvation in Yahshua HaMashiach. He says, "If you love Me, keep My commandments" (Jn. 14:15). Christianity teaches that the Law of commandments is nailed to the 'cross'. They believe that by 'faith' and 'grace' without obedience to the commandments, they would obtain righteousness and salvation. Faith and grace without commandments contradict the Tanach (Scriptures) and the Renewed Covenant Law of Yahshua.

Yisrayah Are Not Cast Away: Apostle Shaul, quoting the Prophets, argues that Yisrayah, called the 'branch' and the set-apart 'lump', was not cast away; but because of sin (breaking of the covenant commandments), some of them were "broken off, and thou (i.e., Gentile Christians), being a wild olive tree, were grafted in among them (Yisrayahlites), and with them partakers of the Olive Tree"; therefore, "Boast not against the branches (Israelites), but if thou boast, thou bearest not the root, but the root thee" (Romans 11:16-18). It's unfortunate that Christianity thought that Yisrayah had been broken off completely; as a result, they boast that they have been chosen to replace Yisrayah. This is deception of Satan. The Bible says no! Yisrayah is still the chosen covenant people of YAHWEH. Although some of them were broken off because of unbelief, soon they will be restored. In these latter days, YAHWEH will call them back to Himself, and by this time, the number of Gentiles grafted in would be completed (v. 25).

The foregoing clarifies that SALVATION is of Yisrayah and not of the Gentile nations or Christian Churches (except those that repent). Obedient Yisrayahlites are the Covenant-keepers; they hold the Covenant relationship with YAHWEH to obey His voice and keep His Commandments. This is what makes them peculiar people: chosen priests and a set-apart nation (Exodus 19:5-6; 24:7; 1 Peter 2:9). Anyone grafted into Yisrayah must queue into the set-apart Covenant way of Yahweh (read Isaiah 56). They will honour His Shabbat day and set it apart. YAH will reveal His Name to them, and they will know Him. No one who obeys Him refuses His Law. Such people are not exempt from covenant commandments; else they will be cast away. There is only ONE LAW or COMMANDMENT that governs YAHWEH's people. On the return of YAHSHUA, He'll govern the earth with that ONE COVENANT LAW from Jerusalem (Isaiah 2:2-3). YAHWEH's coming Kingdom is based on obedience to His Word and having faith in YAHSHUA MESSIAH; otherwise, the nation of Yisrayah will cease to exist. Jeremiah wrote:

Behold, the days come, saith YAHWEH, that I will make a NEW COVENANT with the House of Yisrayah and with the House of Judah... But this shall be the COVENANT that I will make with the House of Yisrayah: After those days (these days), saith YAHWEH, I will put My LAW in their inward parts and write it in their hearts and will be their YHWH, and they shall be My people... 'IF THOSE ORDINANCES (LAWS) DEPART FROM BEFORE ME, SAITH YAHWEH, THEN THE SEED OF YISRAYAH ALSO SHALL CEASE FROM BEING A NATION BEFORE ME FOREVER' (Jeremiah 31:31, 33, 36; Jeremiah 32:40-41; Isaiah 54:9-10).

If Yisrayah or anyone grafted into it shall stop obeying YAHWEH's Covenant, he or she will be cut off; and if the whole Yisrayah reject YAHWEH and His Covenant, there will be no more Yisrayah. Every believing Yisrayahlite understands this. Keeping the Covenant Commandments and following Yahshua is living a life of righteousness, and it's compulsory. Covenant-keeping and following Yahshua is the gateway to righteousness. The Covenant Way of YAHWEH is also a set-apart way of living a sanctified life; this is the reason Yisrayah is called a peculiar treasure, a set-apart nation, and a kingdom of priests (Exodus 19:5-6; see also Matthew 19:17-22). Yisrayahlites are the firstfruits, not the Gentile Christians; Yisrayahlites are called the sons and daughters of Yahweh; Yisrayahlites are the apple of YAHWEH'S eye; and Yisrayahlites are given the Covenant, the law, the commandments, and the statutes, and all grafted Gentile people must follow suit.

Gentiles Are Invited: Any Gentile that receives YAHSHUA and keeps the Covenant Commandments is an Yisrayahlite. In other words, anyone that obeys the FATHER'S voice and follows YAHSHUA becomes part and parcel of Yisrayah, and he or she is called "blessed" (Revelation 22:14; Isaiah 56:2-8). Why did some unbelieving Yisrayah and Gentile Christians fall away? They reject the LAW, the COMMANDMENTs and YAHSHUA MESSIAH. Fallen Yisrayahlites pursued the doctrine of sacrificial and ceremonial laws (instead of moral and spiritual laws); they are self-righteous seekers and at the same time rejected YAHSHUA MESSIAH, whereas the Gentile Christians pursue righteousness of grace without obedience (good works) and choose the Gentile 'Jesus' as their messiah instead of the FATHER's sent MESSIAH, YAHSHUA. The

Gentile Christians hold the doctrine of grace alone that is destructive to faith, and this has caused many of them to fall away from the Covenant of the FATHER. Favour never replaced the moral law of Yahweh; rather, unmerited favour is empowerment to obey the law. Without favour (e.g., love, peace, joy, long-suffering, kindness, goodness, faith, self-control, etc.; see Gal. 5:22-23), the law would be difficult to obey. Favour is given for obedience, not disobedience. Christians lean on the 'under grace' dictum to excuse themselves from obedience to the Law. What is under grace and under the law? They invert the response to this question each time they care to explain it. But Torah declares that to live 'under grace' is to live a life of obedience to the commandments of YHWH that leads to righteousness, favour, blessings and prolonged life, whereas to 'live under the law' is to live a life of disobedience that leads to curse and damnation. Discover the truth and be set free!

TIME OF GENTILES IS RUNNING OUT

The time given to the Gentile Christians to repent and be grafted into the Olive Tree is running out. The Gentile Christians and other religious bodies are encouraged to repent from breaking YAHWEH'S Law so that they can be grafted into the Olive Tree (Yisrayah) before the "fullness of the Gentiles comes in" (Romans 11:25; Luke 21:24). The New Living Translation Bible explains it this way:

"I want you to understand this mystery, dear brothers and sisters (i.e., Gentile Christians), so that you will not feel proud about yourselves. Some of the people of Israel have hard hearts, but this will last only until the full number of Gentiles comes to Messiah." (v. 25).

"For if YAHWEH spared not the natural branches (some broken off Yisrayahlites), take heed lest He also spare not you. Behold therefore the goodness and severity of YAHWEH: on them which fell (sinned), severity; but toward thee, goodness, if thou continue in His goodness: otherwise thou also shall be cut off" (Romans 11:21-22).

Be sober; don't boast any longer! Stop rejecting and breaking the Covenant Commandments, and receive YAHSHUA MESSIAH before the time given to the Gentiles runs out. Yisrayahlites are the chosen people, not the Gentiles! Gentile Christians and others may be grafted into the Olive Tree of Yisrayah – if they repent and accept YAHSHUA and the Covenant Law of YAHWEH (read Isaiah 56:1 8; Rom. 11:11-26, etc.).

This book proves that only ONE OLIVE TREE of YISRAYAH, called the TRUE VINE – YAHSHUA MASHIACH – is given to mankind as their Messiah and Saviour, and in Him all covenant-keeping mankind shall be saved (Joel 2:32; Acts 4:10, 12). Yisrayah as the Assembly of YAHWEH remains, and it is never replaced by Gentile Christianity. YAHSHUA MESSIAH will return to believing Yisrayah at His appearance to establish righteousness on Earth via His exemplary leadership that the world has never known. Since YAHSHUA MESSIAH is the only Saviour, who then is 'Jesus'? He is the Baal Gad ['Lord God'] created by the Greco-Roman Empire through the act of Constantine and the Bishops of Rome. Biblical history clearly proves that the Gentile Christian messiah is different from the Yisrayahlite Messiah and Saviour. History traced the name of 'Jesus' from ancient Babylonian BAAL ["the Lord"], through Medes and Persia, down to the Greco-Roman Catholic Church, where Constantine and the Bishops of Rome selected names of deities and merged them together to form the name 'Jesus Christ', whom Gentile Christians honour today (Professor J.C.J. Melford, Dictionary of Christian Lore and Legend, 1983, p. 126).

CHAPTER 11: WHAT DID BOC PROMISE YISRAYAH? RAPTURE OR SECOND EXODUS?

RAPTURE OR EARTHLY INHERITANCE?

Heaven is not the promised reward of the saved people. YAH's Kingdom on earth is. YAHWEH is letting His Kingdom dwell on Earth as promised to Adam and other patriarchs. One day, the kingdom of men here on Earth will be the kingdom of YAHWEH. In the end, there will be a New Heaven and a New Earth! The Kingdom of Yahweh, or the Kingdom of Heaven, is being prepared for the righteous. All those seeking YHWH's righteousness and salvation today will inherit the

Kingdom of Yahweh here on earth, while the wicked or evildoers shall be destroyed. Evildoers are those who refuse to listen and hear YHWH's instructions. They refuse to serve Him according to His WORD of TRUTH. They refuse to worship YHWH based on His Covenant with them. They avoid His Covenant Commandments by giving excuses based on human theology and the commandments of men. David wrote: "

For evildoers [the wicked] shall be cut off; but those who wait on YHWH, they shall inherit the earth… the meek shall inherit the earth, and shall delight themselves in the abundance of peace." (Psalm 37:9, 11).

RAPTURE: The rapture message is deceptive! YHWH didn't promise Heaven to His people but the Earth. From Adam, Noah, Abraham, Yisrayah, and YAHSHUA HAMASHIACH, YAHWEH never promised mankind that He will 'rapture' them into heaven. Instead, YAHSHUA promised to return to the Earth to commence the Kingdom of the FATHER. This is in fulfilment of the FATHER's covenant with Adam (Gen. 3:15) and Abraham (see Gen. 17; 12:1-5; 15:18-19; 26:4), and other descendants of Yisrayah. YAHSHUA is the Seed, or a descendant of Abraham, chosen by YAHWEH the FATHER to fulfil this Promise at the time He will be returning to save Yisrayah and all obedient people that have kept the FATHER's Commandments (Jn. 14:15; 15:10). The Promised Land stretched from the River Nile to the River Euphrates. Those that will inherit the earth are today being taught the righteousness of YHWH, and YAHSHUA MESSIAH will return to renew the earth, and the righteous shall reign with Him (Rev. 1:6; Rev. 5:10; Rev. 20:6).

SPIRITUAL OR PHYSICAL KINGDOM: Some religious folks teach that the Kingdom is a spiritual one, not a physical world. But Daniel and many other prophets disagree with them (read below: Dan. 2:44; Dan. 7:27).

Daniel 2:44 "And in the days of these kings, **YAHWEH** of heaven will set up a kingdom which shall never be destroyed; and the kingdom shall not be left to other people; it shall break in pieces and consume all these kingdoms [i.e., kingdoms of men here on earth], and it shall stand forever."

Daniel 7:27 "Then the kingdom and dominion, and the greatness of the kingdoms under the whole heaven, shall be given to the people, the saints of the Most High. His kingdom is an everlasting kingdom, and all dominions shall serve and obey Him."

Luke 1:31-33 "You [Mary] will conceive and give birth to a Son, and you are to call Him YAHSHUA (not Jesus). He will be great and will be called the Son of the Most High. YAHWEH ALMIGHTY will give Him the throne of His father David, and He will reign over Jacob's descendants forever; His kingdom will never end."

The above passages refer to the Kingdom of YHWH here on Earth, not in Heaven. They refer to a physical kingdom here on Earth, not a spiritual kingdom. We are not going to inherit the imaginary world that most religious people have been conditioned and programmed to believe in — the one where they believe their dead loved ones currently inhabit. They were lied to that when they die, they go straight to heaven. Others believe that their dead brethren are already in heaven. Yet others believe that they would be raptured into heaven before the Great

Tribulation begins. All these are the lies of the devil. The Scriptures never teach rapture! "No one has ascended into heaven but the One who came down from heaven, and that is the Son of Man (Yahshua) who is in heaven." (John 3:13; see Jn. 1:18; 5:37). YAHSHUA, the Son of YAH, was prophesied tobe born great and succeed the throne of David. According to Luke 1:33, at His return, He will "reign over Jacob's descendants forever; His kingdom will never end." His seat of government shall be in Jerusalem. Daniel, Isaiah, and many other prophets declared this good news vividly. Daniel wrote:

Daniel 2:34-35, 44 (NKJV): "You watched while a stone was cut out without hands, which struck the image on its feet of iron and clay and broke them in pieces. Then the iron, the clay, the bronze, the silver, and the gold were crushed together and became like chaff from the summer threshing floors; the wind carried them away so that no trace of them was found. And the stone that struck the image became a great mountain and filled THE WHOLE EARTH. And in the days of these kings the Elah of heaven will set up a kingdom which shall never be destroyed; and the kingdom shall not be left to other people; it shall break in pieces and consume all these kingdoms, and it shall stand forever."

ISAIAH 9:6-7 REVEALS:

6 "For to us a child is born, to us a Son is given; and the Government shall be upon His shoulder, and His name shall be called Wonderful Counsellor, Mighty YAHWEH, Everlasting Father, Prince of Peace. 7 Of the increase of his government and of peace, there will be no end, on the throne of David and over his kingdom, to establish it and to uphold it with justice and with righteousness from this time forth and forevermore. The zeal of the Lord of hosts will do this."

Revelation 5:9-10 (ESV): And they sang a new song, saying, "Worthy are you to take the scroll and to open its seals, for you were slain, and by your blood you ransomed people for YAHWEH from every tribe and language and people and nation, and you have made them a kingdom and priests to our YAHWEH, and they shall reign ON THE EARTH."

None of these prophets mentioned that mankind shall be raptured into heaven. Where then did men pick up the teaching of rapture? The theory of "rapture" was propounded within the Western world about the 16th century and sold to the Gentile Christian world from France to the United Kingdom and then publicised as religious theology in America about the 18th and 19th centuries to date. It's all Satan's distraction and confusion so that mankind would continue to believe a LIE! Beloved, let's continue to believe Abba YAHWEH and our SAVIOUR YAHSHUA MASHIACH, whose Promise can never fail. Let's continue to keep His Covenant Commandments as we follow YAHSHUA to walk on the "narrow way" which leads to eternal life. Watch and pray always so that you will not miss the Kingdom YAHSHUA is returning to establish here on earth.

YISRAYAH'S RESTORATION DRAWS NEAR

What Is the Second Exodus and When Does It Occur?

A Look at End-Time Bible Prophecies Relating to the Second Exodus

The Issue in People's Hearts

The Bible clearly teaches that the ten tribes of the ancient northern kingdom of Yisrayah (known biblically by various names such as the House of Yisrayah, *Samaria* or *Ephraim*) were exiled among the nations of the world because of:

Sin of Worship of Gods – Idols:

The Scriptures kept warning the fathers that because of their prostitution with the gods of nations, they would be scattered into the Gentile world – and they would humiliate, enslave, and degrade them until they destroy them. In YHWH's favour, He raised judges, seers, prophets, priests, and later Yahshua to restore them back to the Father, but to no avail. They were told that if scattered into the Gentile world, they would lose their identity (name and who they are), but they didn't pay attention. They were told that they would cease to serve and worship their Maker and the Father YHWH that chose them – still all these warnings fall on deaf ears. However, in the latter days when their host nations would have suffered and humbled them to destruction, they would cry to YHWH, and He would have mercy on them and hear their prayers and return to restore them back to their land. Here are but a few of many instances in which Yisrayah abandoned YHWH and served gods, which led to many years of warnings to desist from gods' worship, but to no avail.

Deuteronomy 32:15-17 *Then he (Yisrayah) abandoned YHWH, who made him, and rejected the Rock of his salvation. They moved him to jealousy with strange Gods [El, Elohim, mighty ones]. They provoked Him to anger with abominations. They sacrificed to demons, not YAH, to gods [El, Elohim, mighty ones] that they didn't know, to new gods [El,*

Elohim, mighty ones] that came up recently [newly], which your fathers didn't dread.

1 Kings 18:21 *"Elijah went before the people and said, 'How long will you waver between two opinions? If YHWH is the Almighty Father, follow Him; but if Baal (the Lord) is the Almighty Father, follow him.' But the people said nothing."*

Jeremiah 11:13 *"Your gods are as many as your cities, Judah, and the altars you have set up to burn incense to that shameful god, Baal, are as numerous as the streets of Jerusalem."*

Hosea 4:12 *"My people consult a wooden idol and are answered by a stick of wood. A spirit of prostitution leads them astray; they are unfaithful to their YHWH."*

2 Kings 17:16 *"They forsook all the commands of YHWH their Father and made for themselves two idols cast in the shape of calves and an Asherah pole. They bowed down to all the starry hosts, and they worshipped Baal."*

Ezekiel 8:16 *"He then brought me into the inner court of YHWH's temple, and at the entrance to the temple, between the temple and the altar, were about twenty-five men. Their backs were toward the temple of YHWH, and they were facing east; they were bowing down to the sun (God) in the east."*

In all these abominable behaviours, YHWH begged them to return to Him, yet they did not give ear to His appeal.

Joel 2:13 *"Rend your heart and not your garments. Return to YHWH your Father, for He is gracious and compassionate, slow to anger and abounding in love, and He relents from sending calamity."*

Acts 3:19 "Repent, then, and turn to YHWH, so that your sins may be wiped out, that times of refreshing may come from YHWH."

Having seen that their hearts were hardened in worshipping of the Gentile Gods, YHWH explicitly told them that He will scatter them into nations where they would worship "wood and stone", and not YHWH that called them. However, in the latter days, YHWH will show them favour; if they repent and diligently seek Him, He will restore them to Himself.

Deuteronomy 4:27-30 *"YHWH will scatter you among the peoples, and you will be left few in number among the nations where YHWH will lead you away. There you will serve gods, the work of men's hands, wood and stone, which neither see, nor hear, nor eat, nor smell. But from there you shall seek YHWH your YAH, and you will find him when you search after him with all your heart and with all your soul. When you are in oppression, and all these things have come on you, in* the latter days you shall return to YHWH your Father and listen to his voice. For YHWH your Father is a merciful YAH. He will not fail you nor destroy you, nor forget the covenant of your fathers which he swore to them."

In Deuteronomy 28:64, *Moshe warns the Yisrayahlites, "Then YHWH will scatter you among all nations, from one end of the earth to the other." This dispersion was both a punishment for idolatry and a means to preserve a remnant that would eventually return to the land."*

The prophets further stated:

Jeremiah 9:16 "I will scatter them among the nations, whom neither they nor their fathers have known; and I will send the sword after them until I have annihilated them." 1 Kings 14:15 "For YHWH will strike Yisrayah, as a reed is shaken in the water; and He will uproot Yisrayah from this good land which He gave to their fathers, and will scatter them beyond the Euphrates River, because they have made their Asherim, provoking YHWH to anger."

1 Kings 14:15 *"For YHWH will strike Yisrayah, as a reed is shaken in the water; and He will uproot Yisrayah from this good land which He gave to their fathers, and will scatter them beyond the Euphrates River, because they have made their Asherim, provoking YHWH to anger."*

Lamentations 4:16 *"The presence of YHWH has scattered them, He will not continue to regard them; they did not honour the priests. They did not favour the elders."*

Ezekiel 11:16 *"Therefore say, 'Thus says YAH Almighty, "Though I had removed them far away among the nations and though I had scattered them among the countries, yet I was a sanctuary for them a little while in the countries where they had gone."'*

Thus, Yisrayah were scattered all over the world because of their love for the worship of gods of nations and other numerous abominations they were into that broke the everlasting covenant He made with them.

News of the Return of the Ten Tribes

At the same time, the biblical prophets and Jewish sages over the past 2000 years have predicted that in the end times (at the coming of the Messiah), through a series of supernatural events, the nine and a half tribes of the Northern tribe of Yisrayah will be regathered and return to the land of Yisrayah to be reunited with their brethren, the two and a half tribes of Judah, who are descended from the southern kingdom of Judah. Furthermore, there is clear biblical and historical evidence that the ten northern tribes of Yisrayah, who were scattered about 721 B.C.E. and collectively known as Ephraim, are largely to be found among the Christian peoples scattered across the earth. Scholars have attempted to prove this point from biblical, linguistic, archaeological, historical and rabbinic Jewish sources and many works that are today in the public domain.

In these last days before Mashiach's Second Coming, more and more redeemed believers in Yahshua are discovering a newfound love for the name of Yisrayah and the land of Yisrayah itself. At the same time, they are awakening to the need to return to the Hebrew roots of Covenant faith by adhering to a more Torah centred lifestyle and spiritual walk. It then follows that some are coming to the fundamental truth taught in numerous places in the Testimony of Yahshua (the more biblically accurate name for the Saviour), who is to restore His people and those Gentiles being born again to be redeemed into the family of Yisrayah. In these last days, those that are literal biological children of Yisrayah or the "grafted in" descendants of Abraham outside the Covenant, or the grafted Gentile believers, all would be brought into the two sticks of Ephraim and Judah under one stick of Yisrayah as a nation (see Ezekiel 37). As such, many are beginning to see that the numerous promises YHWH made to Abraham and his descendants apply to them — especially the promises that the land of Yisrayah is an important aspect of their promised future inheritance. With these revelations often comes a newfound zeal and enthusiasm about returning to the land of Yisrayah. For many, it is a question of not if, but "when do we return?" Oh! One can begin to see the beauty of YHWH's love and His favour towards His chosen people. For He said, "Though I had removed them far away among the nations, and though I had scattered them among the countries, yet I was a sanctuary for them a little while in the countries where they had gone" (Ezekiel 11:16). Despite all the provocation Yisrayahlites caused Him, He did not forsake them nor allow the enemies to eat them up completely. In these latter days, He is set to recall them back to Himself and restore them to their native land forever.

But when is their return?

This question has been the real matter this work has been trying to grapple with, to respond to the question which brings joy and delight to all Yisrayah. The subsequent chapters will attempt to showcase more biblical proofs to the covenant-keepers, which will bring more heartwarming bliss and hope to the people of the Most High YAH. In attempting to determine the timing of the return of Ephraim to the land of Yisrayah, often referred to as the Second or Greater Exodus, the words of the Father, the prophets, and Yahshua would be deeply sought for guidance and proof of the planned journey back home. This is a difficult and complex subject, and many factors need to be considered. No one has all the answers, and neither does this book promise to pinpoint the time and season when it would happen, but hopefully, the presentation you are about to read will provoke thought and discourse that will move believers toward a greater understanding of this subject – the Second Exodus of Yisrayah.

In this work, effort will be made to cover much ground in a panoramic manner without delving into the fine details of any one biblical passage (a variety of the Word would be consulted). Following biblical evidence that would be presented, and hopefully, the overall analysis would be correct, then the findings will set up an agenda for other biblical researchers to make their own input with the evidence adduced here, and synergistically, researchers can collectively fine-tune the details and elucidate this subject. Already, the roadmap of what led to the fall and being scattered has been clearly established above. An outright walk away from the Covenant led to where Yisrayah found themselves today – in the land of suffering and affliction.

Since there is no direct place in the Scriptures that tells us the exact year or date when Ephraim will be regathered and return to the land of Yisrayah (although many believe that the process will begin on a Jubilee year, plus within any of the Feast periods), we must examine many prophecies and prophetic scenarios in order to extrapolate from them the answer to our question. Before we take the plunge, let's review some fundamental biblical truths.

Ephraim's Return to the Land of Yisrayah Is a Fundamental Truth of the Torah

As the very words of YHWH dictated to and written down by Moshe, the Torah (i.e., Genesis through Deuteronomy) is the bedrock of biblical truth upon which the rest of biblical revelation is founded — whether the Prophets or Bible Writers. This is the place to begin when discussing the timing of Ephraim's return.

In Jewish thought, Deuteronomy 30:1–10 is the embryo from which all the other Scriptures discussing Ephraim's return are birthed. Here YHWH promises to gather Yisrayah from all the nations where He has scattered them (because of spiritual apostasy), and He promises to return them to the land of Yisrayah after they repent and return to Him (see Lev. 26:40-45; Deut. 4:27-30). This prophecy has not yet been fulfilled, nor is it referring to the tribe of Judah held captive in Babylon who returned from their 70 years of exile. There are specific terms used, e.g., "Ephraim" and "all nations" — these were not applied to Judah but to the return of Ephraim from all nations. The ancient empire of Babylon is not "all nations", and the people of "Ephraim" did not go to Babylon but to all nations!

Here is the prophecy in its entirety:

Deut. 30:1-10 "And it shall come to pass, when all these things are come upon you, the blessing and the curse, which I have set before you, and you shall call them to mind among all the nations whither YHWH your Father has driven you, and shall return unto YHWH your Father, and shall obey His voice according to all that I command you this day, you and your children, with all your heart, and with all your soul; that then YHWH your Father will bring you back from captivity, and have compassion upon you, and will return and gather you from all the nations wherever YHWH your Father has scattered you. If any of you be driven out unto the outermost parts of heaven, from thence will YHWH your Father gather you, and from thence will He fetch you; and YHWH your Father will bring you into the land which your fathers possessed, and you shall possess it; and He will do you good, and multiply you above your fathers. And YHWH your Father will circumcise your heart and the heart of your seed to love YHWH your Father with all your heart and with all your soul, that you may live. And YHWH your Father will put all these curses upon your enemies and on them that hate you, which persecuted you. And you shall return and obey the voice of YHWH and do all His commandments which I command you this day. And YHWH your Father will make you plenteous in every work of your hand, in the fruit of your body, and in the fruit of your cattle, and in the fruit of your land, for good: for YHWH will again rejoice over you for good, as He rejoiced over your fathers, if you shall hearken unto the voice of YHWH your Father, to keep His commandments and His statutes which are written in this Book of the Law, and if you turn unto YHWH your Father with all your heart and with all your soul."

The Jewish Sages Affirm That Ephraim Will Return

The biblical prophets predicted that all the tribes of Yisrayah (including the ten tribes of the Northern Kingdom, or Ephraim) would be scattered to other lands outside of Yisrayah, and that YHWH would regather them in the last days and return them to the land of Yisrayah. This has also been the dominant belief of the Jewish sages as recorded in their writings and in their oral traditions, including the Talmud. For example, the Scriptures tell us about the scattering of the twelve tribes.

"And YHWH rooted them out of their land in anger, and in wrath, and in great indignation, and cast them into another land [eretz acheret], as it is this day." (Deut. 29:28) The Babylonian Talmud, in Yevamot 17a (written ca. A.D. 500, The Soncino Talmud), confirms this when it states,

"They had declared them [i.e., the ten tribes of Yisrayah] to be perfect heathens [or Gentiles]; as it is said in the Scriptures, 'They have dealt treacherously against YHWH, for they have begotten strange children.'" A rabbinic footnote on this passage states, "The ten tribes; Hosea. 5:7."

The ArtScroll Tanach Series Bereishis/Genesis (an Orthodox Jewish commentary on Genesis) states, regarding Genesis 48:19, quoting the Orthodox Jewish sage of the Middle Ages, Ibn Ezra:

Many nations will descend from him [Ephraim]. That is, the word "fullness" (melo) connotes "abundance", the phrase meaning "and his seed will become the abundance of the nations" (Neter; Karnei Or, p. 2121). According to Radak's (R. Dovid Kimchi, a Torah scholar in the Middle Ages) commentary on the same verse, This refers to the Exile, when the lands of others will be filled with his scattered descendants. See also Hoshea 7:8: "Ephraim shall be mingled among the nations" (Ibid.).

Pertaining to the end-time regathering of the twelve tribes, the late well-known Orthodox Jewish leader, Menachem Schneerson, stated that the future King Messiah (Messiah Ben [Son of] David) will not only redeem the Jews from exile but will restore the observance of the Torah commandments to its complete state, which will only be possible when the Yisrayahlites are living in the land of Yisrayah. At this same time, Schneerson, who is quoting the notable rabbinic sage of the Middle Ages, Moshe Maimonides, also known as the Rambam, says, **"There will be an ingathering of the dispersed remnant of Israel. This will make it possible for the Davidic dynasty to be reinstated and for the observance of the Torah and**

its mitsvot to be restored in its totality." According to Jacob Immanuel Schochet, the ten tribes of the northern kingdom of Yisrayah [Ephraim] will also return (as substantiation for his claim, he cites b. Talmud, Sanhedrin 110b) to serve YHWH (he also cites Ezek. 20:32–37, 40–42).

According to Jacob Immanuel Schochet, the ten tribes of the northern kingdom of Yisrayah [Ephraim] will also return (as substantiation for his claim, he cites b. Talmud, Sanhedrin 110b) to serve YHWH (he also cites Ezek. 20:32–37, 40–42).

Furthermore, The ArtScroll Bereishis, vol. 1(b), states in its commentary on Genesis 48:19 regarding Ephraim, R. Munk explains:

"While it is true that the dispersion [of the descendants of Ephraim and Manasseh] was caused by the unfaithfulness and sinfulness of Ephraim's descendants (Hos. 7:8ff), Jacob's blessing was not in vain, for 'they will return to [YAH]' and will have their share in the world to come ([Talmud] Sanhedrin 110b)." And R. Eliezer adds, "Even the darkness in which the Ten Tribes were lost will one day become as radiant as the day" (according to the version of Avos d'Rabbi Nosson 36). "And in the perspective of history, did not these exiled children of the Patriarchs enlighten the nations among whom they were scattered? They did so by teaching their conquerors the fundamental ideas of the

knowledge and love of [YAH], ideals they had never forsaken. Hence, they too have a messianic vocation, and their Messiah, the Mashiach ben Yosef, Messiah son of Joseph (Succah 52a), also called Messiah son of Ephraim (Targum Yonasan on Exodus 40:11), will play an essential role in humanity's redemption, for he will be the precursor of the Mashiach ben David, Messiah son of David. It is therefore not surprising to find that the prophet Jeremiah (3:12) speaks affectionately of Ephraim. In this light, Jacob's words, 'His offspring will fill the nations,' assume the significance of blessing."

The ArtScroll Stone Edition Chumash goes on to say, quoting Samson Raphael Hirsch, in regard to Deuteronomy 32:26, which says, "I said, I would scatter them into the corners ..." (KJV),

This refers to the exile of the Ten Tribes, who were scattered to an unknown place where they have never been heard of again.

On the phrase of the same verse, *"I would make the remembrance of them to cease from among men ...,"* the same Chumash states.

This is a reference to the exiles of Judah and Benjamin, the Davidic kingdom from which today's known Jews are descended.

It goes on to say that though the nations would seek to destroy Yisrayah entirely [during the government of the beast], YHWH would never allow Yisrayah to become extinct or disappear. Yisrayah's perpetual existence is a constant reminder of YHWH's plan, and eventually, Yisrayah will thrive and fulfil YHWH's intention for it.

The nineteenth-century Orthodox Jewish sage S. R. Hirsch, in his commentary on the Pentateuch on the same verse, translates the phrase *"I would scatter them into the corners ..."* as *"I would relegate them into a corner ..."* and then says that the Hebrew here refers to the "extreme end of a surface, the side or corner ..." He, too, relates this fate to the ten tribes who would be scattered "to some distant corner of the world, where, left entirely to themselves, they could mature towards serious reflection and ultimate return to Me ..."

What's more, Abraham Cohen, in his classic book, Everyman's Talmud — The Major Teachings of the Rabbinic Sages, states with regard to the Messianic Era (Millennial period).

"Another confirmed belief was that the Messiah would effect the reunion of the tribes of Yisrayah [Ephraim and Judah]. While we find the teaching, 'The ten tribes will have no share in the World to Come' (Tosefta Sanh. 13.12), the Talmud usually takes the opposite view. By appealing to such texts as Isaiah 27:13 and Jeremiah 3:12, the [Jewish sages] enunciated the doctrine of the

return of the lost ten tribes (Sanh. 110b). 'Great will be the day when the exiles of Yisrayah will be reassembled as the day when heaven and earth were created' (Pes. 88a). A law of nature will even be miraculously suspended to assist this great reunion. ' In the present world, when the wind blows in the north, it does not blow in the south, and vice versa; but in the Hereafter, with reference to the gathering together of the exiles of Yisrayah, the Set-apart One, blessed be He, said, "I will bring a northwest wind into the world which will affect both directions; as it is written, 'I will say to the north, Give up; and to the south, Keep not back; bring My sons from afar, and My daughters from the end of the earth' (Isa. 43:6)." (Midrash to Esther 1:8). The regathering of the tribes will be preceded by another wondrous event, viz., the restoration of the Set-apart City. If a man tells you that the scattered exiles of Yisrayah have been gathered together without Yerusalem having been rebuilt, do not believe him, for thus it is written, 'YHWH doth build up Yerusalem' (Ps. 147:2), and then, 'He gathereth together the outcasts of Yisrayah.'"

The Babylonian Talmud, Megilah 17b (Soncino Press), states,

"What was their reason for mentioning the gathering of the exiles after the blessing of the years? — Because it is written, 'But you, O mountains of Yisrayah, you shall shoot forth your branches and yield your fruit to your people Yisrayah, for they are at hand to come.' [Ezek.

34:8] And when the exiles are assembled, judgement will be visited on the wicked, as it says, 'And I will turn my hand upon you and purge away your dross as with lye,' and it is written further, 'And I will restore your judges as at the first.' And when judgement is visited on the wicked, transgressors cease, and presumptuous sinners are included with them, as it is written, 'But the destruction of the transgressors and of the sinners shall be together, and they that forsake YHWH shall be consumed.' And when the transgressors have disappeared, the horn of the righteous is exalted, as it is written, 'All the horns of the wicked also will I cut off, but the horns of the righteous shall be lifted up.' And 'proselytes of righteousness' are included with the righteous, as it says, 'You shall rise up before the hoary head and honour the face of the old man,' and the text goes on, 'And if a stranger sojourns with you.' And where is the horn of the righteous exalted? In Jerusalem, as it says, 'Pray for the peace of Jerusalem; may they prosper that love you.' And when Jerusalem is built, David will come, as it says."

Before going into the evidence of the Second Exodus, have a snippet of what led to YAHSHUA's revelation about the suffering of Yisrayah that would quicken them to repent and seek the return of Yahshua to save them.

CHAPTER 12: PRELUDE TO SECOND EXODUS

REJECTION OF YAHSHUA LEFT YISRAYAH DESOLATE: THEY NEED SAVIOUR BEFORE REGATHERING AND RETURN OF YAHSHUA HAMASHIACH

Before the decree is passed, prior to the escalation of trouble on earth, Yisrayah are expected to repent and seek the face of YHWH. To wait till the trouble begins will be a monumental disaster. The decree that would commence YHWH's judgement against rebellious mankind will hit unrepentant Yisrayah so much. This is biblically known as the time of Jacob's trouble, i.e., the time of great tribulation, and eventually the wrath of YHWH. They must repent and seek YHWH with all their hearts; then they would receive His favour and be hidden for protection [from 'trial', great tribulation, and the wrath of YHWH] before their regathering back [the second time] into the Promised Land of Yisrayah (Rev. 3:8, 10; see Zeph. 2:1-3; Lev. 26:40; 2 Chron. 15:4; Deut. 4:29; Is. 26:20-21; Is. 11:10-16; Ex. 12:22 23; Ezek. 20:20:33-44; Hos. 2:16-17). At the point of their repentance, they would call upon the Name of YHWH through Yahshua for deliverance. In Jerusalem, Yahshua told the leaders that it shall come to pass; Yisrayah shall pray, "Blessed is YAHSHUA who comes in the Name of YHWH" (Matt. 23:39; Matt. 21:9; Mk. 11:9 11; Lk. 19:39-44).

Must Yisrayah Seek the Saviour They Rejected? Yes, Yahshua said so! Why they must pray to seek Yahshua, whom they rejected, is because they were enticed and ensnared by the adversary – "the God of this world" – that deceived them to reject and forsake their Saviour YAHSHUA when He came to them the first time to teach them YAH's righteousness and to prepare them for the Kingdom of the Father here on earth, but they refused and denied Him (Jn. 8:44; 2 Cor. 4:4; Rev. 12:9). They disowned Him, betrayed and murdered Him – He was not the Saviour they were waiting for. Earlier they uttered comments that showed Yahshua wasn't the Messiah they were waiting to receive. They said, "We know where this Man is from, but when the Messiah comes, no one knows where He is from" (John 7:29). This statement revealed their rejection of Him. They called Him a Samaritan devil: "The Jews answered Him, "Aren't we right in saying that you are a Samaritan and demon-possessed?" [John 8:48]. They considered Yahshua a human being like them and thought He was not qualified as 'Man' to deliver them because their mind was on the coming of a heavenly Being that would suddenly emerge and announce His powers and superiority over creatures and take the government from the Roman Empire and rule them. They were looking for a powerful being to liberate them from the Roman powers and governance. Again, theirs was ignorance about the teachings of the prophets and John the Immerser on His coming (Isaiah 9:6-7; Dan. 2:44; 7:27; 9:20-26; Matt. 1:21; Luke 1:26-38; 2:22-40; etc.). The same lack of knowledge exists today – people do not understand the Torah – the instruction of YHWH's Covenant and the Second Exodus of Yisrayah back to their Land in these latter days.

Yahshua Reveals Yisrayah's Trouble Prior to Second Exodus! The climax of their rejection was exemplified during His triumphant entry into Jerusalem, where the Temple leaders told Him to stop His followers from rejoicing and praising the Name of YHWH. At that time Yahshua was entering Yerusalem as the King of Yisrayah. Those leaders would not have Him as their King. Luke reported that the Sanhedrin leaders rejected Him, but the crowd loved Him and sang, *"Blessed is the King who comes in the Name of YHWH! Peace in heaven and glory in the highest!"* (Luke 19:38). This praise infuriated the Sanhedrin Temple leaders. They would not tolerate praises of Him offered to YHWH. They demanded that Yahshua should stop His followers from the praises. The crowd sang more! Matthew wrote: *"The crowds that went ahead of Him and those that followed shouted, "Hosanna to the Son of David! Blessed is He who comes in the Name of YHWH! Hosanna in the highest heaven!"* (Matthew 21:9; Luke 19:38; Psalm 148:1; Psalm 118:25, etc.). In Matthew 23,

YHWH reminded them that in the latter days, when they would be oppressed, afflicted, persecuted and destroyed by the Gentile nations, they would be in need of a Saviour to save them; then they would realise that He is the One the Father sent as their King and Saviour for their salvation. In this passage, Yahshua bemoans their ignorance and their rejection of Him and reiterates the trouble they would encounter in the latter days, except they return and cry out to YHWH for deliverance.

"Jerusalem, Jerusalem, who kills the prophets and stones those who are sent to her! How often I would have gathered your children together, even as a hen gathers her chicks under her wings, and you would not! Behold, your house is left to you desolate. For I tell you, you will not see Me from now on until you say, 'Blessed is He who comes in the Name of YHWH!'" (Matthew 23:37-39).

Unbelieving Yisrayah Shall Undergo Trial. Indeed, after the ascension of Yahshua, Yisrayah have been desolate, scattered all over the world because they rejected YHWH and worshipped gods of the Gentiles, and when their Saviour and Messiah came, they disowned Him and killed Him. However, they were reminded that in the latter days, they would face persecution and troubles from the beast and false prophet that would deceive them and overturn the covenant he would make with them; the beast would appear as Yisrayah's saviour whom they would receive

(John 5:43). Unfortunately, they would be disappointed, punished, and dehumanised. The trouble they would encounter will cause them to begin to seek Yahshua as their true Saviour. They would do so through earnest repentance and prayer to the Father for Yahshua to return and save them. When they truly repent, Abba YHWH will show them favour, and this will be during "the hour of trial [great tribulation and wrath of YAH], which shall come upon all the world, to try those who dwell upon the earth" (Rev. 3:8, 10; see Ps. 145:20). This is the dreaded time in human history when the beast would persecute Yisrayahlites (the saints) and all those who refuse to worship him. At this time, YHWH will remove, preserve, and shelter those who love Him and keep His commandments (Rev. 12:6, 14; see Exod. 20:6; Rev. 14:12). But the disobedient Yisrayah, the hardened of heart, shall undergo the trial that will come upon the earth, whereby many will perish because of their rebellion against YHWH and His Covenant Way. They refused to follow YAHSHUA – the Way, the Truth, and the Life – that leads repented souls back to the Father (John 14:6).

Disobedient Will Perish. After hiding His people away from the troubles of the beast (Is. 26:20-21), He will allow the destruction of the disobedient who hate him and refuse to obey His everlasting Covenant (Exod. 20:1-5; Prov. 8:36; Ps. 145:20; Rev. 11:18; Is. 24:5,6). In those days, YHWH will destroy those who destroy the earth (Rev. 11:18). YAHSHUA would supervise the protection and regathering of the remnant obedient Yisrayah. All these would happen before YAHSHUA's feet touch Mount Olive in Jerusalem. YAHSHUA will return to save the elect and reign over His obedient servants who fear YHWH and keep His commandments (Eccl. 12:13; Rev. 1:6; Rev. 5:10; Rev. 20:6; Rev. 3:8, 10). He will reign over Yisrayah and the entire world forever!

"Yahweh preserves all them that love Him:

But all the wicked will He destroy.

(Ps. 145:20; see Rev. 3:8, 10).

"He (YHWH) who scattered Yisrayah will gather him, and keep him as a shepherd does his flock."

(Jeremiah 31:10).

CHAPTER 13: EVIDENCE ON THE SECOND EXODUS

In this part, we shall search the Book of the Covenant[12] for proper guidance with a view to obtain evidence, indications or signs foretold by the Prophets

The place where it was said unto them, "You are not my people," there it shall be said unto them, "You are the sons of the living YAH." Then shall the children of Judah and the children of Yisrayah [ten tribes] be gathered together and appoint [or make, set, ordain, establish] themselves one head, and they shall come up out of the land, for great shall be the day of Jezreel.

At some time in the future, Judah (i.e., the two and a half tribes – Judah, Benjamin and part of Levi) and the children of Yisrayah (i.e., Ephraim) will be gathered together and appoint for themselves one head (Heb. rosh), and they shall be regathered from the earth where they have been scattered in the great day of Jezreel (another name for the great and terrible day of YHWH's wrath). This event has not happened yet anytime in Yisrayah's long history. This one passage gives us

---

[12] The Book of the Covenant (BOC) is Sacred Name Bible that restores the sanctified Name of the Creator, Yahweh, and reveals the Savicur, Yahshua HaMashiach. The Second Exodus of Yisrayah evolved out of the BOC.

some powerful evidence as to the timing of Ephraim's return. It is after the proverbial "battle of Armageddon" (Rev 16:16 cp. 19:11–21), which occurs in the Jezreel Valley, where the armies of the east (Rev 16:12) and the kings of the earth (verse 14) gather together to battle against YAH Almighty "on that great day" (verse 14) during the period known as "the wrath of YHWH" (verses 1 and 19). This event occurs at the return of YAHSHUA when, at his second coming, He will destroy Babylon the Great[13] ('the New World Order Anti-Mashiach system', see Rev 16:18–21; Chapters 17 and 18; 19:11–21), at which time both houses of Yisrayah (Jews and Christians) will (begin to?) accept him as their Messiah or head (Heb. rosh). Again, these events haven't happened yet. The acceptance of Jews and Christians is explicitly mentioned in Revelation 2:9 and implied in and Yahshua that would herald the return of the children of Yisrayah. Just as in the days of ancient Yisrayah in Egypt who out of their troubles, YHWH heard them and called Moshe to go and deliver them. Our information about the Second Exodus would be ascertained from the records of the Torah, the Prophets, and Yahshua's instructions. Let's examine the evidence.

---

[13] Babylon is fallen. *Many scholars opine that 'Babylon the Great' points to America, who was the sole slave trader of Yisrayah. YHWH foretold that nations that afflicted, persecuted, and destroyed, and killed Yisrayah shall be visited in YAH's wrath and destruction – see Rev. 18; Isaiah 47; Jeremiah 50; Jeremiah 51, etc.

First Evidence:

The Timing of Ephraim's Return to the Land of Yisrayah

Now that we know that the Torah and the Prophets aver that Ephraim will return in the end time, let's now begin examining the pieces of the puzzle in the Scriptures pertaining to the timing of Ephraim's return. As we do so, these pieces will begin to come together in your understanding, and a picture will emerge allowing us to pinpoint likely the signs that would place every covenant-keeper on the part of readiness, which would mark a time frame for Ephraim's return to the land of Yisrayah.

1st Evidence: Hosea 1:10–11

Yet the number of the children of Israel shall be as the sand of the sea, which cannot be measured nor numbered; and it shall come to pass, that in the place where it was said unto them, "You are not my people," there it shall be said unto them, "You are the sons of the living YAH." Then shall the children of Judah and the children of Yisrayah [ten tribe] be gathered together, and appoint [or make, set, ordain, establish] themselves one head, and they shall come up out of the land: for great shall be the day of Jezreel.

At some time in the future, Judah (i.e., the two and half tribes – Judah, Benjamin and part of Levi) and the children of Yisrayah (i.e., Ephraim) will be gathered together and appoint for themselves one head (Heb. rosh), and they shall be regathered from the earth where they have been scattered in the great day of Jezreel (another name for the great and terrible day of YHWH's wrath). This event has not happened yet anytime in Yisrayah's long history. This one passage gives us some powerful evidence as to the timing of Ephraim's return. It is after the proverbial "battle of Armageddon" (Rev 16:16 cp. 19:11–21), which occurs in the Jezreel Valley, where the armies of the east (Rev 16:12) and the kings of the earth (verse 14) gather together to battle against YAH Almighty "on that great day" (verse 14) during the period known as "the wrath of YHWH" (verses 1 and 19). This event occurs at the return of YAHSHUA when, at his second coming, He will destroy Babylon the Great13 ('the New World Order Anti-Mashiach system, see Rev 16:18–21; Chapters 17 and 18; 19:11–21), at which time both houses of Yisrayah (Jews and Christians) will (begin to?) accept him as their Messiah or head (Heb. rosh). Again, these events haven't happened yet. The acceptance of Jews and Christians are explicitly mentioned in Revelation 2:9, and implied in Revelation 3:9 – which appear to suggest that, although they may be into worship of 'another', they would repent and seek YAH their Creator, and would worship under the feet of Yisrayah that have already found YHWH and keep His commandments and His Name (Revelation 3:8,10). Meanwhile, these strayed Yisrayahlites are presently in the sanctuary of 'Synagogue of Satan.'

Two Sticks of Judah & Ephraim

A corollary passage to Hosea 1:10–11 is the famous two-stick prophecy of Ezekiel 37:15–27. Here, YHWH tells the prophet to take two sticks or trees for the two houses of Yisrayah and bring them together in his hand so that they become one stick with one king over them (a resurrected David) and united in a covenant between them and YHWH. At that time, YHWH will make His sanctuary or tabernacle among them, and together this united Yisrayah kingdom will worship YHWH. Clearly, Hosea's and Ezekiel's prophecies speak of the same event, which has yet to happen. Both prophecies are speaking of events surrounding the second coming of the Messiah, the resurrection of the dead, and the establishment of the Messiah's millennial kingdom on earth.

Second Evidence:

The Repeating Paradigm of Yisrayah's Redemption

Biblically, the concept of the return of exiled and scattered Yisrayah (including Ephraim) to the land of Yisrayah is tied to the idea of redemption. Biblically, the concept of redemption involves a stronger person (the Redeemer) intervening on behalf of the weaker person (the enslaved, i.e., the one needing redemption), defeating the captor of the slave, thus allowing the enslaved to go free. Captors include all those nations and their leaders that enslaved Yisrayah in the trans-Atlantic slave trade that lasted about 400 years (1619–2019).

Egypt & First Exodus Experience

The first biblical example of this process occurred when YHWH redeemed Yisrayah out of Egypt. The biblical prophets compared this First Exodus to a Greater, or Second, Exodus that is yet to occur as humanity heads into the future. In Jewish thought, the Exodus out of Egypt is called the First Redemption, yet the biblical prophets also speak of Yisrayah going into captivity again — this time not to Egypt, but into the exile of the nations. (They are in exile now in nations because of disobedience – see the above biblical warnings of Yahweh.) From this place of exile and spiritual enslavement, affliction, persecution, destruction of their identity, and forgetfulness of their Father, YHWH, YAH Almighty promises to redeem Yisrayah from slavery again, but this time in the last days. The Jewish sages refer to this momentous event as the Final Redemption.

When are the last days?

Check out YAHSHUA's description of those days in Luke 13, 17, 21, and Matthew 24. The world would be in tension, seeking for a Saviour; there would be serious wars, food shortages, high cost of living, economic downturns, natural disasters, earthquakes, floods, ocean falls, and tsunamis, and economic, political, and religious tensions would be the order of the day, etc. These were described as signs. Then the emergence of false pastors, teachers, and apostles would be everywhere. Finally, the emergence of the beast — the man of sin, the son of perdition, and the false prophets — would calm the world that is experiencing troubles, and subtly they would assume power and deceive many. Thus, the government would last for seven years, divided into two. In the first three and a half years, the beast would hide his evil identity, and in the second half of the seven years, he would sever accord with Yisrayah (possibly those claiming they are Jews); he would betray the agreement of "peace" signed with Yisrayah and other religious folks and command them and all the rest of humankind to worship him. This pronouncement will stir trouble all over the world. People would be commanded to worship the beast by the image they set up for him. Those who rebel against taking his "mark" shall be killed; the rest of the people shall gladly worship the beast. According to the prophets and the Book of Revelation, the people of the covenant shall be hidden away by YHWH in the wilderness where they would tarry until the trouble has overpassed, and they would be caused to return home (see Isaiah 26; Ezekiel 20:33–40; Revelation 12, etc.).

In the prophecies of the Bible and in Jewish thought, the concept of the Final Redemption is synonymous with the idea of a Second or Greater Exodus of Yisrayah from its exile in the nations of the world. According to the Jewish sages, and based on their understanding of the biblical prophecies, this redemption of the tribes of Yisrayah (including the ten northern tribes) will occur at the end of 6000 years, which they refer to as the Age of Messiah. This is to occur just prior to a time period they refer to as the Messianic Age, which the Book of Revelation says will last 1000 years, and which believers in Yahshua refer to as the Millennium.

Again, the concept of the Final Redemption has its origin in the promises of Deuteronomy 30:1–10, where we read (in summary):

"YHWH your Father [will] ... gather you from all the nations whither YHWH your FATHER has scattered you. If any of you be driven out unto the outmost parts of heaven, from thence will YHWH your Father gather you, and from thence will he fetch you, and YHWH your Father will bring you into the land which your fathers possessed, and you shall possess it..."

The Jewish sages teach, again based on their understanding of the Hebrew Scriptures, that the following notable events will occur in conjunction with the Final Redemption:

- There will be an ingathering of the dispersed remnant of Yisrayahlite exiles to the land of Yisrayah, including both the exiles of the ten tribes of the northern kingdom and those of the southern kingdom of Yisrayah (comprised of the tribes of Judah, Benjamin, and part of Levi, collectively known as the Jews) from the lands where they have been scattered. According to Isaiah 11:10–16, Yisrayahlites will be moved from various parts of the world — YHWH would achieve this secret plan by His Mighty Arm — carrying His people on His two eagles' wings.

- Messiah, the King of kings, and the High Priest will assume rulership over the earth, and the Messianic Age will be established upon this earth for 1000 years. The Torah will be imposed as the law of the earth.
- King David will rule over a reunited Yisrayah (i.e., the tabernacle of David). This means the dead would rise, and the living would return to the land.

- The resurrection of the dead will occur at the coming of the Messiah, whereby Yahshua will establish His Kingship Headquarters in Yerusalem, where He will govern the entire earth.

The biblical prophets and Jewish sages view Yisrayah's redemption from Egypt as a precursor, antitype, or prophetic model of Yisrayah's final redemption in the end times and as one of the events accompanying the coming of the Messiah, the Word of the Living YHWH, the King of kings, and the High Priest. In Christianity, this is known as the second coming of "Jesus", and many of them believe He would "rapture" them and take them back to heaven, where they would stay until the wicked are all destroyed by the beast; then they would return with their "Jesus" to commence government on earth. The Bible did not teach rapture, nor did Yahshua give any hint about this false doctrinal theology.

How Long a Time?

As an aspect of the Final Redemption, an obvious question must be asked: how long will the regathering of scattered Israel back to their land take? Is the "day of YHWH's wrath" a literal day or a time period, since the Hebrew word for day (yom) can mean both? The prophet Isaiah may give us a clue. In several places, he mentions "the day of YHWH's vengeance". This is the time period when YHWH will judge the nations, including Babylon the Great, which occurs at YESHUA'S second coming (see Rev. 18 and 19). In three places, Isaiah indicates that the day of YHWH will last for one year (Isa. 34:8; 61:2; and 63:4). Interestingly, in Isaiah 63:4, the prophet couples the idea of the day of YHWH's vengeance being a year long with the Jubilee Year — "the year of my redeemed has come." This occurs as HaMashiach (the subject of Isa. 63:1–6) judges the enemies of Yisrayah (notably Edom, spreading to Amon and Moab) as He is at the same time about to redeem (i.e., regather and return) the scattered Yisrayah to its Promised Land inheritance. It appears that while Yahshua is judging Yisrayah's enemies, such as Edom (Isaiah 34:5), at His second coming, He will at the same time be regathering the lost and scattered twelve tribes of Yisrayah — a process that will take no longer than a year.

Nations Shall Receive YHWH's Punishment

Following the example of the first redemption, where Yisrayah was delivered by the strong arm of YHWH the Redeemer (the Egypt experience), the biblical prophets and Jewish sages do not explain exactly how Yisrayah will be redeemed the second time, but simply that she will be redeemed by the strong arm of YHWH when He defeats her enemies, sets her free and allows her to make her way to the Promised Land, as occurred in the first redemption of ancient Yisrayah – i.e., the First Exodus. Her being set free will involve mighty and divine judgements against disobedient Yisrayah and those who held Yisrayah captive [Isaiah 34:1-17]. As Yisrayah was not set free from Egypt through her own efforts, except by having faith in YHWH and leaving Egypt when he opened the door, there is every indication in the biblical prophecies that the same will occur in the final redemption, i.e., the Second Exodus of Yisrayah. He will judge the nations that caused so much punishment, affliction, persecution, wounds and murder against His people, Yisrayah. With iron hands, just as He judged Egypt and Pharaoh, YHWH will trash those nations that hate the true covenant, Yisrayah, and afflict them with so much slavery, torture, pain, and disgrace. As we shall discuss below, the people of Yisrayah will first need to recognise that they are Yisrayah by YAH's choice and calling. Reference Genesis Chapters 12 and 22; Exodus Chapters 19, 20, and 24; Amos 3:1-3; and Hosea 11:1-2. Yisrayah should be sober and sincerely accept that they have sinned and turned away from YHWH and His Torah and that they need to repent of their sins and return to YHWH and the Torah (Lev. 26:40; Deut. 4:27-29; Deut. 30).

While the Jewish sages view the final redemption as a precursory event to the coming of HaMashiach at the end of the age, Yahshua and the apostolic writers teach us that this process of the redemption of mankind actually began with the first coming of Yahshua and will continue until His second coming — a process that has been ongoing for 2000 years! This process can be summarised as follows

The Redemption Process Had Already Commenced!

The final redemption of Ephraim began 2000 years ago when ten men of nations took hold of the fringes of a

Jew (Zech 8:23). As we have already noted, 'Ephraim' is a biblical colloquialism for the Ten Tribes of the Northern Kingdom of Yisrayah, whose biological and/or grafted-in descendants largely comprise the Christian and Moslem peoples of the earth today. This is the reason you hear about the three-tier Abraham's family. This is often referred to in religious circles as the Abrahamic Accord [Judaism, Christianity, and Islam]. These Yisrayahlites are lost in the religions of this world, having separated themselves from YAH that called them. They offered themselves to the worship of Gentile 'new' gods, which they were forewarned would happen to them (Deuteronomy 32:15-17). The Ten Tribes, or Ten Men of the nations, is a prophetic reference to the lost sheep of the house of Yisrayah (i.e., the ten tribes of the Northern Kingdom of Yisrayah) whom YAH sent into captivity and who were scattered among the Gentile nations. This Yehudah, to which Zechariah makes reference, was Yahshua, HaMashiach, who declared that He and His disciples were sent to regather the lost sheep of the house of Yisrayah (Matt 10:6; 15:24), and whose gospel message has been going out to the nations of the world for 2000 years now. So, the final redemption started with the ministry of Yahshua. Redemption has been ongoing for two millennia. The First Exodus of Yisrayah back to Egypt was the first phase. The Second Exodus and the last of it will happen in this latter age. It's the second phase, and after it, Yisrayah will never go into captivity again forever.

The Torah Will Be Taught Before the Second Exodus

Since Yahweh has been trying to cleanse Yisrayah and place them in their own Land, His strategy to achieve their righteousness, which they need before the Kingdom (Land) inheritance, is to teach them. He began to teach them His way of righteousness and set-apartness (holiness), living in Egypt for 30 years before He got them out. Having noticed they were still not educated enough in His Torah instructions, He took them through the wilderness for 40 years so that they would be isolated from cultures and 'doings' of nations that may entice, ensnare and corrupt them, just as they were corrupted with the idols and worship of the gods of Egypt. YHWH cannot keep Yisrayah in His Land (Land of Israel) except and unless they thoroughly learn His good ways captured in the Torah and the Ten Commandments, and as were taught by the Prophets and Torah Scribes. They must be taught by YAHWEH, not by themselves. This is what many do not know. For this reason, YAH revealed how His people will be taught through His Shepherd (pastors and teachers) He will appoint them. When YHWH was rebuking Yehudah, He revealed how His backsliding people would be taught and restored:

Jeremiah 3:11 Yahweh said to me, "Backsliding Yisrayah has shown herself more righteous than treacherous Judah. 12 Go, and proclaim these words toward the north, and say, 'Return, you backsliding Yisrayah,' says Yahweh; 'I will not look in anger on you, for I am merciful,' says Yahweh. 'I will not keep anger forever. 13 Only acknowledge your iniquity, that you have transgressed against Yahweh your Father, and have scattered your ways to the strangers under every green tree, and you have not obeyed my voice,'" says Yahweh. 14 "Return, backsliding children," says Yahweh, "for I am a husband [i.e. Father] to you. I will take one of you from a city and two from a family, and I will bring you to Zion. 15 **I will give you shepherds according to my heart, who will feed you with knowledge and understanding.**

Fantastic! Although YAH had been angry against His people, He would no longer be angry with them; He will show them favour and mercy. But they must acknowledge their sins – that they have broken His laws – that led to their being scattered to the nations. He promised to visit them in the nations where they are scattered and teach them His Law they rejected. He will send His teachers, pastors, and those whom He trained in things of His knowledge according to His Own heart to feed (train) them with His knowledge and understanding. This is another glorious promise many have overlooked.

YOU MUST BE TRAINED BY YHWH

"And they will all be taught by YHWH" [Jn.6:45]

Do Not Teach Others Except You Have Been Taught!

You must not teach the Word of YAH unless you have been trained by YHWH's appointed servant (Jer. 3:15). YHWH trains His shepherds through His Spirit in Yahshua, Who is the Word made flesh and the Word of YHWH (Jn. 1:1–3, **14; Rev. 19:13**). The reason why you must be trained is to remove Satan's infiltration in the Word so that the servant of YAH would not teach errors. About 2000 years ago, Yahshua came, training, teaching, **and** preaching the Word of Yahweh so that His people would mend their wicked ways and return to the Father. After Yahshua completed His work, He appointed **shepherds** that learnt from Him to continue the work of training and teaching the people of Yisrayah. He instructed that His training and teaching **of** the Covenant Way must continue from generation to generation until He returns. Yahshua gave a strong warning that the **disciples** must never commence teaching or preaching the Word until they are properly equipped with the Set-apart Spirit (Holy Spirit). After 40 days of Yahshua's ascension, the Set-apart Spirit was given to them on the day of Shavuot [Pentecost].

The Spirit is what everyone needs to receive knowledge expressly from Yahshua before the disciple can teach or preach the Word to others. If YHWH taught them for 30 years in Egypt plus 40 years in the wilderness, why would you risk teaching YAH's Truth without the required training yourself? When YHWH said, "My people perish for lack of knowledge" (Hos. 4:6), that's exactly what He meant. It's lack of knowledge that causes people to teach the Sunday lies instead of the Shabbat day of rest. It's unforgivable ignorance that makes people teach and lead astray many souls to believe that 'God' is YHWH, and people end up praying to God. Those who teach wrong doctrines shall perish (Deut. 8:19–20). Lack of knowledge is a baggage of confusion, and it kills. It's wrong to teach others without knowledge and understanding of the truth. Knowledge about the Kingdom comes from the FATHER through YAHSHUA, not the other way around. The BOC impresses it on disciples to learn first before rushing to teach others. Who sent you to teach without being appointed? Who asked you to train others when you are not called, ordained, or trained by the Spirit of YAH? If YAHSHUA spent three-and-a-half years training and teaching His disciples and even asked them to wait for the coming of the Set-apart Spirit, why would you disobey YHWH's instruction by rushing to establish an assembly without being trained? Do you want to ruin the souls YAH is trying to save?

We are commanded to follow the example of our Leader, King, and High Priest, YAHSHUA HAMASHIACH. YHWH tells us that any attempt to deviate from His Word would be met with death. You must not do what you are not commanded to do, or else you will end up offering a strange fire like the two children of Aaron, whom YHWH killed for their disobedience. Again, in this age, you must be taught by YAHSHUA's servant whom He appointed for the Father's work. Notice YAH's instruction that all His people must be taught by Him through Yahshua, the Set- apart Spirit, and His pastors:

Jeremiah 3:15 "I will give you shepherds (pastors) according to My heart, who will feed you with knowledge and understanding."

John 6:45 "It is written in the Prophets: 'And they will all be taught by YHWH.' Everyone who has heard the Father and learnt from Him comes to Me."

Isaiah 54:13 "All your children will be taught by Yahweh, and your children's peace will be great."

John 14:26 "But the Advocate, the Set-apart Spirit, whom the Father will send in My Name, will teach you all things and will remind you of everything I have told you."

Today, whosoever YAH appoints to lead His people benefits from the teaching of the Spirit. There are steps to follow for one to benefit from the teaching of the Spirit and to receive the fruit of the Spirit that enables the individual to obey the Word of YAH that is taught. Being taught is a vital aspect of Covenant-keepers' walk. We need guidance to grow in our faith and to understand our Father's will for our lives. As obedient children, it is essential for us to seek wisdom and knowledge that come directly from YHWH, allowing ourselves to be instructed by the Word of YAH and by those He places in our lives. We are encouraged to embrace learning, as it helps us mature spiritually and develop a deeper relationship with our Creator. YHWH calls us to teach and to be taught, creating a beautiful cycle of learning within our communities. The Bible is our primary source of instruction, guiding us through the challenges of life with divine wisdom.

The redemption process requires one to have Torah knowledge and understanding about spiritual matters. Most people think they know when they are already lost. To achieve salvation and truly return to the FATHER, learning is expedient. Learning helps the individual to appreciate the 'eternal way' of YAH. His way is not man's way. There are hidden truths we do not know, which only the Spirit reveals to the leaders elected to teach others. The Word of YAH must be learnt as humanity enters the days of trouble. Without knowledge of the WAY of YAHWEH, many will be lost and cut off because of ignorance. In the restoration of all things and the turning of the hearts of the children back to the fathers of their faith (Mal. 4:1–6), just before the day of YHWH's wrath, it started in the 20th century and is picking up pace as more and more Covenant-keepers are returning to the Hebraic roots of their faith. The idea of the final redemption is tied to the Book of the Covenant (Bible) concept of Yisrayah's First Exodus from Egypt and her future Second Exodus from the nations of the world. Let's now examine the prophecies that pertain to this Second Exodus.

Third Evidence

Understanding the Second Exodus

The concept of the Messianic Age in Hebraic thought involves an understanding of the first and final redemptions, which are two separate events. The First Redemption, or First Exodus, occurred when the Yisrayahlites obeyed the Word of YHWH and placed the blood of the lamb on the doorposts of their homes, resulting in YHWH delivering them out of Egypt. It is understood by redeemed believers that Yisrayah's Exodus from Egypt was prototypical of the ones placing their faith in Yahshua (the Lamb of YAH) who redeems them from sin's death grip through his shed blood at the tree and then leads them out of their spiritual Egypt of sin and worldliness toward the promised land of a new spiritual life in Mashiach Yahshua.

By contrast, the Final Redemption, or Second Exodus, is a series of events that will occur at the end of the age prior to the return of Mashiach Yahshua at the beginning of the Messianic Age (or Millennium). The signs that characterised the regathering of Yisrayah are already seen everywhere and all the time. The people of YAH need to wake up and listen to the call to come out of the Gentile Gods' worship, which destroyed the faith of the fathers of old.

For those who have placed saving faith in Yahshua HaMashiach, at the final redemption, the redeemed believers will receive their spiritual or glorified bodies at the resurrection of the dead, which occurs at the second coming of Yahshua. After that, they will rule and reign with Yahshua for a thousand years during the Messianic Age.

Now let's explore some of the biblical prophecies that pertain to the Second Exodus and how the 'trouble' that will unfold would herald unity between Yisrayah and Judah. This will yield us more evidence as to the timing of the return of Ephraim to the land of Yisrayah.

JUDAH & EPHRAIM AND THEIR HERITAGE

"Now a new moon [month] shall devour them and their heritage" (Hosea 5:6-7). This seems to mean that in the future 'trouble', great tribulation, unbelieving – Judah and Yisrayah (who are in today's religions) – will fall within one month. Refer to Revelation chapters 2 and 3. But covenant- keeping Assembly shall be delivered (Isaiah 11:10-16; Revelation 3:8-10; Revelation 12:6,14).

Unity of Yisrayah and Judah

The outcome of the trouble Yisrayah and Judah will experience will galvanise them into a common goal – to unite under Torah and obedience to Yahshua, as their King and Saviour. At this time, Yahshua's Word would be fulfilled: "*For I tell you, you will not see Me again until you say, 'Blessed is He who comes in the Name of YHWH'*" (Matthew 23:39).

Let's examine some prophecies about the unity of Yisrayah and Judah.

Isaiah 11:10-12:6 (NKJV)

[11] It shall come to pass in that day
That Yahweh shall set His hand again the Second time
To recover the remnant of His people who are left,
From Assyria and Egypt,
From Pathros and Cush,
From Elam and Shinar,

From Hamath and the islands of the sea.
¹²He will set up a banner for the nations,
And will assemble the outcasts of Yisrayah,
And gather together the dispersed of Judah
From the four corners of the earth...

Although consisting of two chapters, this passage of the Scriptures is part of the same prophecy and speaks about the coming of Yahshua Messiah and the regathering of the outcasts of Yisrayah from the nations to which they have been scattered. Below is a list of the salient points that pertain to the Second Exodus along with commentary.

➢ **11:10**, The "root" of Jesse (the Messiah) will be an ensign or banner to the Gentiles of the nations. We know that Yahshua was that root of Jesse who commanded his followers to preach the gospel to the Gentile world. The gospel went to the entire Gentile world only in the 20th century via the means of modern travel and mass communications.

➢ **11:11**, In this verse, the prophet seems to be talking about another group of people — a remnant of his people (the outcasts of Yisrayah, verse 12) as opposed to the larger group of Gentile believers from among the nations (who have heard the gospel message) referred to in verse 10. These "outcasts" are people of YAH [those exiled who today live without YAH's Law]. YHWH will recover these scattered people of His — who are the remnant of Yisrayah — the second time (i.e., in the coming Second Exodus) from all lands, including the islands of the sea (North and South America, England, Australia, Japan, etc.).

➢ **11:12,** YHWH will set up an ensign or banner for the nations and shall assemble the outcasts of Yisrayah and the dispersed of Judah. Yahshua is that banner. Even though Yahshua is the ensign for the Gentiles of the nations and for the remnant outcasts of Yisrayah who are scattered among the nations, only the outcasts of Yisrayah will be regathered along with the dispersed of Judah [plus foreigners that joined the house of Yisrayah].

➢ **11:13**, It is among this remnant group of scattered redeemed Yisrayahlites and dispersed Judah that peace between the two groups will occur. As awareness of YHWH increases among Yisrayah and Judah, they would begin to unite based on their common historical experiences of sufferings, afflictions, persecutions, troubles, etc., which both have suffered from the nations. How, may we ask, are you saying these two previously antagonistic brethren would be brought together? Exactly, that's what YAH said. However, their unity will occur as they examine who they are, what's written about them (see Lev. 26; Deut. 28, etc.), and the kinds of suffering experiences they have encountered; majorly, they would come together based on a common adherence to the Torah Covenant and a belief in Yahshua HaMashiach – as their Saviour. The Spirit of YAH will unite them in One New Man – Yahshua, as the Gentile Christians who also receive Him call on His Name and accept His Shabbat, feasts, etc. (Isaiah 56:1-8; Eph 2:11–19). At the same time, the adversaries of Judah and Ephraim (the Edomites, Moab, Amon, Moslems and their Islamo-fascist terrorist allies [more on this later]) will be cut off.

➢ **11:14–15**: Together, Judah and Ephraim will defeat Edom, the Philistines of the West Bank, Moab, Amon, Iran, Iraq, etc. (Note that all these enemies of Yisrayah are predominantly Moslem nations! Compare this with the prophecies of Obad 18 and Zech 9:13.) Perhaps there are two groups of Judahites and Ephraimites: the remnant and the greater group. It appears that greater or national (secular) Judah and national (secular) Ephraim will defeat Edom, as it seems less likely that a remnant of Yahshua-followers (the end times Torah-observant saints) will be the ones to do this. However, the Scriptures declare that the Yisrayah that will unite as one stick, who will obey YAH's Torah and commandments, will defeat their enemies like when the fathers were returning from Egypt in the days of Moshe.

➢ **11:16**, The scene switches back to the remnant again, where a highway will be formed for YHWH's people to return to Yisrayah from Assyria (the nation of their captivity). This Second Exodus will be similar to Yisrayah's leaving Egypt the first time. As YHWH led ancient Yisrayah through the wilderness en route to the Promised Land, He will do the same in the last days when Yisrayah will return to the Land of Yisrayah from the nations of her exile – from all paths of the world.

➢ **12:1–12**, This chapter seems to describe a millennial setting. For example, verse three is understood in Hebraic thought to be a reference to Hoshana Rabbah, the last great day of the fall biblical Feast of Tabernacles (or Sukkot), which is a prophetic picture of the Millennium when the Spirit of YHWH will be poured out upon the earth.

Ezekiel 37:15-23

The Reunification of Yisrayah

The word of YAHWEH came to me: *"Son of man, take a single stick and write on it: Belonging to Judah and the Yisrayahlites associated with him. Then take another stick and write on it: Belonging to Joseph — the stick of Ephraim — and all the house of Yisrayah associated with him. Then join them together into a single stick so that they become one in your hand. When your people ask you, 'Won't you explain to us what you mean by these things?' — Tell them: This is what YAH Almighty says: I am going to take the stick of Joseph, which is in the hand of Ephraim, and the tribes of Yisrayah associated with him, and put them together with the stick of Judah. I will make them into a single stick so that they become one in my hand. "When the sticks you have written on are in your hand and in full view of the people, tell them: 'This is what YAH Almighty says: I am going to take the Yisrayahlites out of the nations where they have gone. I will gather them all around and bring them into their own land. I will make them one nation in the land, on the mountains of Yisrayah, and one king will rule over all of them. They will no longer be two nations and will no longer be divided into two kingdoms. They will not defile themselves anymore with their idols, their detestable things, and all their transgressions. I will save them from all their apostasies by which they sinned, and I will cleanse them. Then they will be My people, and I will be their Father."*

Discuss!

Now let's note Isaiah 11:10–12:6 in the broader context of the chapters following this passage. Perhaps there is some additional understanding to be found as to the timing of Ephraim's return by examining the event foretold therein.

Isaiah Chapter 13:6, 9, and 13 speak of the day of YHWH's wrath, which occurs at the end of the age when YHWH will judge the nations as described in the seven bowl judgements of Revelation 15 and 16. The wrath in Isaiah 13 is directed at Babylon, and in Revelation 15 and 16 YHWH's wrath is toward the nations of the world as represented by Babylon the Great, which is a greater, world-ruling version of the original Babylon. Because of the proximity of Isaiah describing the Second Exodus with Chapter 13 prophesying the fall of Babylon, it would appear that these two events are related.

After this, Isaiah Chapter 14 goes on to talk about the fall of the king of Babylon with verses 13 through 20 and then curiously links this to Lucifer's (Satan's) rebellion against YHWH and his fall from glory and his being cast into a pit (verse 15). The Book of Revelation also speaks of similar events—Satan's fall from heaven (Rev 12:7–9), Babylon the Great's destruction (Rev 18) and Satan being cast into the bottomless pit (Rev 20:1–3). Are Isaiah's and John's prophecies speaking about the same events that are to occur at the end of the age and about YHWH's end-times judgement of Babylon the Great with Satan the devil as its head (see Rev 13, 18, 19 and 20)? This could be the case.

In chapter 14, Isaiah then goes on to prophesy another judgement against the king of Babylon, then a judgement against the Assyrians, Philistines (Isa 14), Moab (Isa 16), Syria (Isa 17), and America — a land beyond and due west of Ethiopia that is accessible only by ocean ships (Isa 18) — and, finally, judgement upon Egypt (Isa 19–20). These are nations that afflicted and troubled Yisrayah. They will all come under YAH's judgement.

Then Chapter 21 readdresses the fall of Babylon, wherein verse nine the phrase "Babylon is fallen, is fallen" is repeated as if to say that Babylon fell once, but that it will fall again in the end times. Most people are familiar with this phrase from John's Book of Revelation (Rev 18:2) but are unaware that John is actually quoting Isaiah. It's as if John is calling our attention to Isaiah's prophecy as a corollary antecedent statement that relates to his own prophecy.

Isaiah then goes on to pronounce judgement against Edom and Arabia (Isa 21), against Phoenicia (Isa 23) and then against the whole earth (Isa 24). Could these prophecies of Isaiah be what John is seeing in Revelation when he describes YHWH's bowl judgements against the whole earth just prior to the return of Yahshua (Rev 15 and 16), which John refers to as the wrath of YHWH (Rev 14:19; 15:1,7; 16:2,19)? In the chronology of the Book of Revelation, the fall of Babylon the Great occurs after the bowl judgements of the wrath of YHWH are poured out upon the whole earth. After this, Yahshua returns to this earth with his heavenly army to bring final judgement upon the armies that have gathered at Armageddon (Rev 19 and Jude 14–15). At this time, Satan and his Antimessiah confederacy, who dared to exalt themselves against YHWH and his Anointed One, will be dashed to pieces and destroyed for good (Rev 19:11–21; 20:1–3)!

So we see from this series of passages additional evidence as to the timing of the Second Exodus and the return of Ephraim to the land of Yisrayah. As the first exodus of Yisrayah from Egypt occurred in conjunction with Egypt's judgement and demise, so it appears that similar events will surround the second exodus. YHWH will judge all the nations which are part of end times Babylon the Great, and the devil, who is the instigator of man's rebellion against YHWH Yahshua, and then the dispersed captives of Yisrayah will be set free to return to her promised inheritance. By the three-and-a-half-year rule of the beast, the Torah Covenant Yisrayah shall be led away from the government of the beast and taken to the wilderness, where they would await the intervention of Yahshua, who at the sound of the last trumpet (seventh trumpet), will be returning and will arrest the beast and false prophet. Satan the devil will be caught and thrown into a bottomless pit until after about 1000 years of the reign of Yahshua on earth.

Perhaps this whirlwind tour of all these prophecies is overwhelming, and my analysis may seem to be too broad and speculative. But before jumping to any conclusions one way or the other, let's continue to examine other biblical prophecies on this subject to determine if a pattern of events will begin to take shape that will shed light on the timing of Ephraim's return. After you begin to see how the pieces of the puzzle fit together to form the whole picture, you will be in a better position to determine if there is enough evidence from the whole counsel of the Scriptures to support what has been proposed. As the Scriptures say, "Despise not prophesyings. Prove all things; hold fast that which is good" (1 Thess 5:20–21).

Jeremiah 16:14–15

Another solid Second Exodus reference is found in Jeremiah 16:14–15. Here we read,

"Therefore, behold, the days come," says YHWH, "that it shall no more be said, 'YHWH liveth, that brought up the children of Yisrayah out of the land of Egypt'; but 'YHWH liveth, that brought up the children of Yisrayah from the land of the north, and from all the lands whither he had driven them: and I will bring them again into their land that I gave unto their fathers.'"

What stands out about this passage is that the Second Exodus will be much greater in scope than the First Exodus and will involve scattered Yisrayahlites being regathered from the countries north of Yisrayah, across Africa, America, Europe, Asia, and Australia, and from wherever else they have been scattered. It must be remembered that the lands of Babylon and Assyria into which ancient Yisrayah were exiled were primarily east and northeast of Yisrayah and not due north of Yisrayah, as this prophecy indicates. So, this prophecy has yet a future fulfilment.

Yisrayah's Punishment

What's more! In the future when these prophecies are fulfilled, YHWH promises to punish Yisrayah for its iniquity (or Torahlessness, verses 17–18). This will happen when the Yisrayahlites who have been scattered among the Gentiles begin to wake up and realise that much of what they have been taught for religious truth is nothing more than worthless, anti-Torah lies (verse 19)! At the same time, they will come to know the name of YHWH (verse 21) — a possible reference to the restoration of the Hebrew-biblical names of deity, which is happening in our day among many Christian faiths who are rediscovering the Hebrew roots and returning to them. Those in Judaism, Christianity, Islam, Hinduism, and Buddhism being told to return to YHWH's covenant way would regret their disobedience; however, they will attribute their rebellion to their fathers who told them lies: "Our fathers inherited nothing but lies, worthless idols of no benefit at all." Jer. 16:19. Those who pick up this book will do himself or herself a world of good. It will enable the individual to hear the truth revealed here and come out of idol worship, which is inherent in the religions of this world that lead people away from YHWH. Moshe sums up YAH's revelation as secret things that belong to YAH, but things revealed are for the people of YAH that they may obey His Law.

"The secret things belong to Yahweh our Father, but the things that are revealed belong to us and to our children forever, that we may do all the words of this law" (Deuteronomy 29:29).

Jeremiah 23:7-8

This Second Exodus prophecy is almost a direct quote from Jeremiah's earlier 16:14–15 prophecy, just discussed above.

It is interesting to note the timing of this prophecy's fulfilment. This Second Exodus regathering corresponds with Yahshua's reigning over this earth and executing judgement (verses 2–5) — something that will not happen until Yahshua's second coming when He will defeat his enemies and establish his millennial kingdom on earth. So, we see from this passage that the Second Exodus, when scattered Yisrayah (including Ephraim) is regathered and returns to dwell safely in the land of Yisrayah (verse 6), coincides with the second coming of Yahshua and the beginning of the millennium.

The First Exodus Compared to the Second Exodus

Let's now examine the First Exodus and compare it to the Second Exodus that many end-time believers and Jewish sages believe will happen at the end of the age, prior to the coming of the Messiah and arrival of the Messianic Age or Millennium. Perhaps, this will give us some more clues as to the timing of Ephraim's return to Yisrayah.

First, what are the similarities between the first and second exodus?

✓ The children of Yisrayah could not leave Egypt as long as they were bound as slaves to that land. When YHWH brought judgement against Egypt and crushed that nation, Egypt no longer had the power to keep Yisrayah enslaved, who was free to leave at this point. This was Yisrayah's First Redemption, or First Exodus.

✓ According to Isaiah 11:16, the First and Second Exodus will be somewhat similar. If the Second Exodus will follow the pattern of the First Exodus, then in the end times, the worldwide system known as Babylon the Great, which enslaves men, including scattered Yisrayahlites (Rev 18, especially note verse 13), economically, politically and religiously (Rev 13), will have to be judged first and destroyed before her captives are set free. Biblical scholars and most schools of thought believe that America is today's capital city of the Great Babylon; hence, it assumes the status of the most powerful nation in the world today. Many writers are of the opinion that Revelation 18 describes America precisely as the transformed Babylon of old. Only after Babylon has fallen, when Yahshua destroys it at his second coming, will Yisrayah be free to return to the land of Yisrayah en masse. This is when the Jubilee trumpet of freedom will sound to proclaim liberty throughout the earth. In ancient Yisrayah, the Jubilee trumpet sounded every 50 years on the biblical set-apart day of Yom Kippur. Because of this and other reasons, we believe that Yahshua will return to this earth on Yom Kippur.

✓ Exodus 13:20, the first place the Yisrayahlites came to after leaving Egypt was Sukkot. Is this a prophetic indicator that Yisrayah will largely return to the land of Yisrayah on or during the fall biblical festival event known as the Feast of Tabernacles (or Sukkot)? The Yisrayahlites weren't able to leave Egypt until that nation was judged and destroyed. Similarly, it would seem that only after Yahshua judges and destroys Babylon the Great during the seven bowl judgements and at the battle of Armageddon will Ephraim be able to leave their captive nations for the Land of Yisrayah. However, when we put side by side the prophecies of Ezekiel 20:33-40, Isaiah 26:20 and Revelation 12:6,14, which reveal that Yisrayah was helped to escape into the wilderness until the trouble was over, it may suggest that at the escalation of the beastly power (last three and a half years) to annihilate the people of the Covenant who would not submit to the beast's image worship, the beast plotted to destroy the people of YAH; hence, the people were temporarily helped to escape into the wilderness until YHWH's wrath overthrew the beastly government, as was the case of Pharoah's government in Egypt.

One should remember that Yisrayah lived in the land of Goshen, away from the dominant population of the Egyptians. Yisrayah received YAH's protection in the land of Goshen until the plagues were over, and they were moved out of Egypt after the 10th plague. Given the technological sophistication of the modern world to track people, YAH may decide to take His people away from the eyes of the beast until the trouble is over, then He would move them to the Land of Yisrayah. Whichever scenario, Yisrayah in some way shall remain on the planet Earth when the beast will be unleashing mayhem. They are not going to be raptured into heaven, as false teachers and pastors have already deceived billions of people.

The prophecies of moving Yisrayah into the wilderness until the trouble is over have merit. Ezekiel and Hosea aver that Yisrayah shall receive Torah training in the wilderness, and YAH will "purge the rebels from among you, and those who transgress against Me; I will bring them out of the country where they dwell, but they shall not enter the land of Yisrayah" (Ezek. 20:38). Verse 39 reveals that YHWH refers to those who would still be worshipping the Gentile Gods – who do not want to cast away idol names in their mouths but continue to call YHWH those abominable names of idols, which defile and blaspheme His Set-apart Name. It was using those idol names to continually profane His set-apart Name that made YAH scatter the fathers of old into nations. "So, I scattered them among the nations, and they were dispersed throughout the countries; I judged them according to their ways and their deeds. When they came to the nations, wherever they went, they profaned My set-apart name... But I had concern for My set-apart Name, which the house of Yisrayah had profaned among the nations wherever they went." (Ezek. 36:19, 20-21; see Deut. 28:36, 64; Jer. 16:13; Rom. 2:6). Those people shall be cut off in the wilderness and shall not enter the Land of Yisrayah, as it happened during the First Exodus (Ezek. 20:38-39; 34:17; Jer. 44:14; Hos. 2:16-17).

➢ Next, in the First Exodus, the children of Yisrayah had to wander in the wilderness for a while, where YHWH refined out of them the spiritual corruption of Egypt. It was in the wilderness that he gave them his Torah, trained them to follow the Torah, and formed them into a righteous nation that was ready to enter the Promised Land. Similarly, biblical prophecies speak of the end times saints/righteous people going through a wilderness enroute to the Promised Land. Those who survive the beast's power and escape from him would be taught the Law of Yahweh in the wilderness. There they will be spiritually refined. He will prepare them as a righteous nation that would possess the Land. Those who refuse to follow YHWH's Torah will be excluded, while those who do will be permitted to return to the land of Yisrayah (Ezek 20:34–38). Additionally, other prophecies speak of a highway being made through the wilderness for scattered Yisrayah to return to the Promised Land. For certain, the saints of end times Yisrayah will come into her promised inheritance by way of the wilderness (Isa 11:16; 40:3–4 cp. 35:8; 43:19), as did the children of Yisrayah during the First Exodus.

➢ In the first exodus, Joshua (Heb. Yehoshua) led the Yisrayahlites into the Promised Land. In the Second Exodus at his second coming, Yahshua (short for Yehoshua – Joshua) will lead the saints of redeemed Yisrayah into the Promised Land in the end days according to Hebrews 4. This will commence a thousand-year-long millennial Sabbath rest for the Yisrayahlite saints of YHWH (again, see Heb 4).

➢ Judah was the tribe to lead the way into the Promised Land in the First Exodus (Num 10:13–14). The Jews of the tribe of Judah have been the first to return to the land of Yisrayah in our time. If the prophecies of the BOC (Bible) are true, and I believe they are, then the rest of the tribes will follow after Judah. If they don't, then the Bible lies when it speaks of all the tribes returning to the land of Yisrayah in the last days.

➢ YHWH promised to go before Yisrayah as a consuming fire to destroy her enemies who were illegally inhabiting the land YHWH had promised to Yisrayah and who were hindering Yisrayah's entrance into the land (Deut 9:3). In the end times at the Second Exodus, Yahshua will destroy with consuming fire all of redeemed Yisrayah's enemies who will be hindering her return to her promised inheritance (1 Thess 1:8–9; 2 Thess 2:8; Heb 10:27; Rev 18:8–10; 19:20; 20:10).

➢ Yisrayah had to drive out the inhabitants of Canaan — at least those who were antagonistic against them (the Gibeonites were an exception) — under Joshua the warrior's leadership. This feat Yisrayah was able to do only with YHWH's miraculous help (Deut. 9:3; 11:23). In the end times, Yisrayah (YHWH's warrior bride), under the leadership of Yahshua, the warrior-king, will drive out and defeat her enemies (Edom and Babylon the Great), who will be preventing her from entering the Promised Land.

➢ As ancient Yisrayah had to come into Torah obedience in preparation for entering the Promised Land (Deut. 11:8), so in the last days, a return to Torah will be a precursor requirement for redeemed Yisrayah to enter her promised inheritance in the land. Many biblical prophecies attest to this fact. The rebels and Torahless [lawless or lawbreakers] will not enter the land of Yisrayah (Ezek 20:37–38).

Finally, what are the dissimilarities between the First and Second Exodus?

The children of Yisrayah went out of Egypt as a unified group in the first exodus, since they all lived in the land of Goshen in Egypt. However, in the Second Exodus of the last days, scattered Yisrayah, by virtue of the fact that they have been scattered around the world, will not return to Yisrayah as a single unified group. They will likely return in waves at various times from various places. Isaiah 11:11 16 agrees that they would be returning from different places of the nations. Some from the tribe of Judah have already returned to the land of Yisrayah. The first wave of Ephraimites will likely include those resurrected saints who will enter the Promised Land at His second coming. Thereafter, and on into the Millennium, little by little, more lost and found Yisrayahlites (those of both Judah and Ephraim) will begin to make their way back to the land of Yisrayah from the spiritual wilderness to where they have been scattered for so long. This will occur as little by little they realise that they're Yisrayahlites (biologically or grafted in), repent of their sins, and return to YHWH, the Elohim of Yisrayah, and accept the Messiah and His Torah.

Remember, the first exodus involved the ancient Israelites coming out of Egypt. The Bible prophesies that the Second Exodus will involve the last days' descendants of those ancient Yisrayahlites who have been scattered to the four corners of the globe returning to the Land of Yisrayah. As noted above, the biblical prophets predicted this would occur, and this has been the consensus of many Hebraic scholars, including the Jewish Talmud, for nearly 2000 years. All things being equal, and assuming these analyses stick to the biblical narratives between the First and Second Exoduses are correct, Ephraim will return to the land of Yisrayah at or just after the second coming of Yahshua and after He has destroyed Babylon the Great, and not before. One must admit that this aspect of the Second Exodus is not easy to nail on the head. However, scholars are still studying this part of the movement. Furthermore, when examining the context of the Isaiah-Ezekiel-Hosea scenario discussed above and Revelation Chapter 12, YHWH's intervention to lead the "woman" (true Assembly – Yisrayah) out of the presence of the beast on two eagles' wings into the wilderness, one may conclude that the Covenant-keepers will be in the wilderness (to be taught YHWH's Torah) at Yahshua's second coming. From there, they would return to the Land of Yisrayah to participate in the Marriage Supper of the Lamb. Since the outcast Yisrayah will be redeemed to be part of the wedding with Yahshua HaMashiach in Yerusalem, it would be biblically correct to conclude that these saints from the wilderness will be guided home into the Land of Yisrayah at the return of their Saviour. Therefore, "Let us be glad and rejoice and give Him glory, for the marriage of the Lamb has come, and His wife has made herself ready. And to her it was granted to be arrayed in fine linen, clean and bright, for the fine linen is the righteous acts of the saints." Write: "Blessed are those who are called to the marriage supper of the Lamb!... These are the true sayings of YHWH." (Rev. 19:7-9; Matt. 22:2; 25:10). All those saved and invited by YHWH into His eternal glory will participate in this glorious marriage banquet of the Lamb that will mark the beginning of a new dawn, freedom from the world, sin, and the enemies.

Fourth Evidence:
Ezekiel's Wilderness of the Peoples Prophecy

Further evidence as to the timing of Judah and Ephraim's return ("house of Yisrayah") to the land of Yisrayah is found in Ezekiel 20:31, 33–44. At this time, I recommend that you read this entire passage in your BOC (Bible). Below, I will present a verse-by-verse commentary on what you have just read. In this evidence, we shall learn that worship of the Gods of the Gentiles, which the fathers loved and which caused YHWH to scatter them, continued with the children to the point they intended to maintain the status quo – serving Gentile Gods and YHWH at the same time. But YHWH hated it and would someday bring them out and lead them through the wilderness and bring the remnant home to the Land of Yisrayah.

- **Verses 31–32:** In this verse, YHWH revealed that the whole "house of Yisrayah" held to perpetually serve the Gentile idols – "wood and stone" – and still wanted to call His sanctified Name, and YHWH told them: "What you have in your mind shall never be, when you say, 'We will be like the Gentiles, like the families in other countries, serving wood and stone.'" YHWH forbids when His people serve idols and at the same time call on His Name. YHWH promised them that their desire to continually worship the gods of nations must someday stop, and He will "surely with a mighty hand, with an outstretched arm, and with fury poured out, bring them out and rule them."

- **Verses 33–34:** As YHWH supernaturally and with His outstretched arm of judgement brought the Yisrayahlites out from Egypt, so in the end times, in these last days, He will bring the "house of Yisrayah" out of the captive nations where they have been scattered. He will lead them out through the wilderness of the people (nations), and from there, He will take them home to the Land of Yisrayah.

- **Verses 35–36:** YHWH will bring the house of Yisrayah into "a wilderness of the people." Is this a literal wilderness similar to what the children of Yisrayah went through, or a spiritual wilderness where a remnant of faithful Yisrayahlites will exist, isolated and rejected in the midst of the heathen peoples of the nations? I don't think it is a place of abandonment. Remember that the ancient fathers were led out from the wilderness of the peoples to the land of Yisrayah. This same thing will happen during the Second Exodus. This is not a spiritual journey or travel. No! Not at all! However, many modern-day redeemed Yisrayahlites are 'sensing' that they are currently in a spiritual wilderness where they feel alienated from the pagans around them and, at the same time, have been rejected by their Jewish and Christian brothers. Whatever covenant Yisrayah is going through now is physical, and their journey back home will be physical too. YHWH has a physical wilderness experience in store for His people, as was the case in the days of the fathers. YHWH gave out this revelation for His people to begin the preparation. All they need is to "watch and pray", as requested by the Saviour Mashiach (Luke 21:36). In this wilderness of the peoples, YHWH will plead with Yisrayah face-to face like He did in the wilderness of Sinai. Here is yet another reference to a future Second Exodus.

- **Verses 37–38:** In that wilderness, YHWH will separate or purge out from His people the rebels from the righteous and the Torahless or lawless from the Torah obedient, as He did with ancient Yisrayah for 40 years. Those who refused to obey Him died in the wilderness. Only those who were obedient to Him were permitted to enter the Promised Land. In the wilderness, the fathers made a calf and worshipped it; similarly, during the Second Exodus, most religious Yisrayah in Christianity, Islam, etc., will go along with their gods that are in their mouths. YHWH would try to purge those from them, but many will choose to die rather than do away with worship of "Master" or "the Lord" (see Hosea 2:16–17).

- **Verses 38–39:** During this time of testing and purging, the house of Israel will not be returning to the land of Yisrayah until they have put away their spiritual idols (or false doctrines and unbiblical belief systems and vain traditions). This is the hardest part amongst the children of Yisrayah in terms of finding faith in YHWH. Many think they have escaped idol worship[14] – no! It's worse today than in the days of the ancient fathers.

- **Verses 40–41:** After this process of spiritual purification and refinement occurs, "all the house of Yisrayah" (both Judah and Ephraim) will be acceptable to YHWH and will serve Him on His Set-apart Mountain (in Jerusalem). This prophecy obviously has yet to be fulfilled. It's on this mountain that the Marriage Supper of the Lamb will take place. This is a strong confirmation that Yisrayah will get home from the wilderness to the Land of Yerusalem after receiving the required training in the wilderness.

---

[14] "In the Book of Covenant Yahweh Is Not God" is a groundbreaking book you must never miss. Get a copy to flush out spiritual idols plaguing the minds of covenant-keeper.

- **Verses 42–44**, "All the house of Yisrayah" (i.e., Judah and Ephraim) will not return to the land of Yisrayah until they loath their spiritual pollutedness (state of Torahlessness or lawlessness). This prophecy has not yet been fulfilled either. The same Law they run away from and says it's nailed to the 'cross' will be the same Law YAHSHUA will train them to know YHWH and learn His righteous way (Isaiah 2:2-3).

Possibly correlating with Ezekiel's wilderness of the people's prophecy is a verse in Revelation 12. There we find a prophecy about an end-times remnant of Torah obedient followers of Yahshua (verse 17) who, due to persecution, are forced to flee into the wilderness for three-and-a-half years (verses 6 and 14). YHWH helps them to escape into the wilderness of the people until the troubles of the enemy are over. While in the wilderness, they will receive training that will enable them to return to YAHWEH's righteousness. The knowledge of Torah is very important to those who must enter the Land of Yisrayah. This is an acid test to covenant keepers!.

Another corollary passage to Ezekiel's wilderness of the peoples prophecy is Hosea 2:14–23. Here YHWH speaks of alluring Ephraim (Yisrayah) into a wilderness where he will speak kindly to her. After that, YHWH will give her vineyards and the valley of Achor (meaning "trouble") for a door of hope. Yisrayah will go through a time of trouble (a likely reference to "Jacob's trouble", discussed below) before entering the Promised Land. It's the disobedient people that will partake in trouble or "trial" (Rev. 3:8). What is the significance of Achor? You will recall that it was there that Achan and his family were stoned to death because they brought sin into the camp of Yisrayah (Josh 7:1–26). Yisrayah could not go forward in its conquest of the Promised Land until the sin was put out of their camp.

Remember: secret things belong to YHWH, but the things that are revealed belong to the children. Only the wise would hear this and learn and live!

In Ezekiel's wilderness of the people, YHWH will deal with sin in the camp by passing His people under the rod of His judgement as a shepherd separates out his sheep. There He will purge out the rebels from Yisrayah and those who are the transgressors or who walk in Torahlessness (LAWLESSNESS) (Ezek 20:37–38) even as YHWH purged Yisrayah of the sin of Achan before they were allowed to enter the Promised Land.

In his prophecy, Hosea likens this "Second Exodus" to the First Exodus when Yisrayah came out of Egypt with joy. The Second Exodus will be a time when Yisrayah will become endeared to YHWH as a wife to her husband, and He will take the names of foreign gods from out of her mouth. He will then make a covenant with Yisrayah and will betroth himself to Yisrayah forever. This is an event that the Book of the Covenant clearly associates with the second coming of YAHSHUA.

Fifth Evidence:
Understanding Jacob's Trouble & Time of Return

What is the time of Jacob's trouble? The phrase "Jacob's trouble" is found in Jeremiah 30:7. There has been much speculation among Bible commentators as to the meaning of this phrase prophetically. Classical commentators see 'Jacob's trouble' as relating to the Babylonian exile of the Yehudis and their redemption from captivity. The error with this interpretation is that Jeremiah speaks of not only the Yehudis (the house of Judah, i.e., the southern kingdom), but also of the "*people of Israel*" (or the house of Israel, i.e., the northern kingdom; see verse 3.) Furthermore, this prophecy (see verse 9) speaks of a resurrected David ruling over a redeemed Judah and Yisrayah. Clearly, this hasn't happened yet, as it refers to the two houses of Jacob.

On the other hand, many modern Bible commentators view Jacob's trouble as a future end-time event related to the Jewish people, Daniel's seventieth week, the Great Tribulation, the man of sin, and the Antichrist. The problem with this interpretation is that, although it takes the Yehudis (the house of Judah) into account, it also fails to consider the house of Yisrayah and a resurrected David ruling over both houses of Yisrayah. For context, I will cite verses two through nine. This is an end-times prophecy about both houses – Ephraim and Judah.

² Thus speaks YHWH of Yisrayah, saying, 'Write you all the words that I have spoken unto you in a book. ³ For, lo, the days come,' says YHWH, 'that I will bring again the captivity of my people Yisrayah and Judah,' says YHWH, 'and I will cause them to return to the land that I gave to their fathers, and they shall possess it.' ⁴ And these are the words that YHWH spoke concerning Yisrayah and concerning Judah. ⁵ For thus says YHWH, 'We have heard a voice of trembling, of fear, and not of peace. ⁶ Ask you now, and see whether a man does travail with child? Wherefore do I see every man with his hands on his loins, as a woman in travail, and all faces are turned into paleness? ⁷ Alas! For that day is great, so that none is like it; it is even the time of Jacob's trouble, but he shall be saved out of it. ⁸ For it shall come to pass in that day,' says YHWH of Hosts, 'that I will break his yoke from off your neck and will burst your bonds, and strangers shall no more serve themselves of him. ⁹ But they shall serve YHWH their Father, and David their king, whom I will raise up unto them.'"

Perhaps when Jeremiah spoke of Jacob's trouble, he had in mind an antecedent event that occurred in the patriarch's life that could be prophetic of something that would recur in a broader scope to his future descendants — the twelve tribes of Yisrayah. In other words, perhaps an understanding of Yisrayah's history will yield clues as to her future! The cyclical nature of biblical history — that is, the repetition of biblical events — is the paradigmatic view through which Jewish sages interpret many Old Covenant events. For example, I have already discussed the cycles of redemption that have occurred in Israel's history and that will happen in her future. Because Yisrayah is under the hand of divine guidance, the prophets and Jewish sages realise that this unseen heavenly hand deals with different generations of Yisrayahlites in similar fashions. This appears to be the case when it comes to understanding the meaning behind Jacob's trouble.

With this in mind, what event in Jacob's life was his darkest day and would merit the rubric of "Jacob's trouble"? Doubtless, it would have been when he was returning to his home in Canaan after 20 years of exile in Haran under the servitude of Laban. After labouring hard and starting with nothing, he had gained two wives, many children, and much wealth. Now Esau, his hate-filled brother, was seeking his life, and he was about to lose everything.

While I am not aware that the Jewish sages have connected this event in Jacob's life with Jeremiah's usage of the phrase "Jacob's trouble", they do have the sense that Jacob's perilous encounter with his brother Esau (or Edom) foreshadows future experiences Yisrayah would have with Esau's descendants. They see Edom as an allusion to the nations in whose lands the people of Yisrayah are currently exiled and from which, I might add, captive Yisrayah would be set free, enabling them to return to the land of Promise, Yisrayah, even as Jacob did when leaving Laban.

Now let's analyse Jeremiah 30 verse-by-verse to find more clues to help us ascertain the timing of Ephraim's return to the Land of Yisrayah as it relates to Jacob's trouble.

❖ **Verse 3:** this is a future prophecy concerning Yisrayah and Judah involving their returning to the land YHWH gave their fathers. ❖ Verse 5, this period is a time of trembling and fear and of dread and terror (or terrorism?) and not of peace (Heb. shalom). ❖ Verse 6, It is likened to a woman's birth pains (see Rev. 12:2).

❖ **Verse 7**: It is a time of Jacob's trouble (the Hebrew word for "trouble" means "straits, distress, tribulation, affliction, adversity"); YHWH promises to save Jacob "out of it".

❖ **Verse 8**: YHWH of Hosts promises to break the yoke from Yisrayah's neck.

❖ **Verse 9**: YHWH will "raise up" [or resurrect] David, and he will be king over a united kingdom. This sets the time period to that of the Ezekiel 37 valley of dry bones and the two sticks prophecies pertaining to Ephraim's and Judah's "resurrection" and reunification at the coming of the Messiah, when David will rule over the united kingdom of Yisrayah.

❖ **Verses 10–11, 17**: YHWH will bring the seed of Jacob (or the outcasts, verse 17) back from afar from the land of their captivity and will judge the nations where he had scattered them. YHWH will destroy the nations in which he scattered Yisrayah, but he will preserve Yisrayah out of them, although YHWH will punish the unrepentant Yisrayah as well. This is an aspect of Jacob's trouble – where the rebellious Yisrayah would face "trial" and great tribulation but the obedient will be delivered (verse 7; see Rev. 3:8,10; Dan. 12:1; Matt. 24:21, 29; Mk. 13:19; Rev. 7:14). Even as Jacob was wounded in his struggle with the Angel or Messenger of YHWH (Gen 32:22–32), so the scattered Yisrayah will be wounded or punished because of the multitude of their iniquities and sins (i.e., Torahlessness, verses 14–15).

Let's now look at Jacob's trouble in Genesis 32 to see if it will yield some evidence pertaining to the timing of and the events surrounding the return of Ephraim's end days.

Jacob's Trouble and Return of Yisrayah

A Brief Commentary on Genesis 32 & 49; Isaiah 11: What will happen to Yisrayah in the latter days?

Genesis 32 is the story of Jacob's return to Canaan after having been exiled from his homeland for 20 years. His exile occurred after he obtained his birthright from Esau through nefarious means, resulting in his having to leave Canaan for fear of his life due to Esau's desire for vengeance. Jacob found refuge in the realm of Babylonia at his uncle Laban's home, where he married Laban's two daughters, Leah and Rachel. Genesis 32 recounts Jacob's encounter with Esau, who, along with his small army, physically stood in Jacob's way of entering his promised homeland. This, I believe, is the "Jacob's trouble" to which Jeremiah is referring.

The events of Genesis 32 appear to be a prophetic prototype of what will happen to Jacob's descendants when they return to the land of Israel in the end times, after being exiled among the nations of spiritual Babylon. Why do I say this? It is because the biblical prophets predict events that will happen to Jacob's descendants that fit the scenario we see in Genesis 32.

For example, Jacob divided his family into two camps (Gen 32:7) in preparation for meeting Esau. In the end times, the descendants of Jacob will be divided into two camps (Judah and Ephraim) as they prepare to enter the Promised Land. But blocking them will be the descendants of Esau, or Edom, many of whose descendants comprise the modern Palestinian-Arab Muslims. Both camps are returning out of spiritual Babylon (as Rev 18:4 prophesies), where they have been in servitude to the Babylonish world system, even as Jacob was a servant to Laban (who lived in the area of ancient Babylon). They will not defeat Esau through appeasement (Gen 32:20), as Jacob tried to do with Esau. Appeasement got Jacob nowhere except monetarily poorer, and the modern "State of Israel" (Jews) and the Western Christian nations led by America and Great Britain (America and Ephraim, loosely speaking) are dealing with the Palestinians as Jacob did with Esau by giving in to their demands in exchange for a peaceful existence in the land. Appeasement didn't work for Jacob, and it's not working for his descendants today.

As our father Jacob did, so the end-time Yisrayahlites will have to "wrestle" with man (Edom and his allies) and YHWH (Gen 32:28) in the wilderness of the peoples (Ezekiel 20:33–41) to come into the Promised Land. End-time Yisrayah (both Ephraim and Judah) will have to prevail with YHWH and demonstrate to Him that they are serious about **"hearing His voice and keeping His covenant"** (Exod. 19:5) and also that they are serious about wanting to possess their promised inheritance and, at the same time, overcome themselves (the carnal, rebellious, anti-Torah man within) — their pride and self-reliance and the notion that they will return to the Land of Yisrayah by their own strength and prowess apart from YHWH's divine direction and empowerment. Only after Jacob was brought low, after wrestling all night in the dirt with the Messenger of YHWH (the preincarnate Yahshua), did he wake up to his own spiritual inadequacy. It was when he was humbled and lay wounded in the flesh that he saw YHWH face-to-face, and he became a new man spiritually with a new name and a new identity – Yisrayah.

Similarly, when YHWH's end-time people repent of their pride and die to "self" as a people-group (both Judah and Ephraim), this will please the FATHER, and He will give His people victory over their enemies. Each will have to wrestle with Yahshua, the Messenger of YHWH. The Judeans, wherever they are scattered, will have to accept Yahshua, the Living Torah made flesh, as their HaMashiach, while the Ephraim (i.e., scattered Yisrayah) and Yahweh-believing 'Gentile Christians' and other believers will have to accept the Written Torah – YHWH's Name, Shabbat, Feasts, and the Word of YAH, which was the Word that became flesh. They'll all have faith in Him. Yahshua has been a stone of stumbling to both houses of Yisrayah, and only when they stumble and fall and are broken by Him (Isaiah 8:14–15; 56:1–8) will they be ready to enter the Promised Land.

The good news is that Jacob will be transformed into Yisrayah. He will prevail with YHWH, who will give him victory over his enemies who are attempting to prevent him from entering the land of his inheritance.

How can I be so sure of this? You can be sure of this promise because it is written in YHWH's Book of the Covenant!

There appear to be some additional parallels between the steps Jacob or Yisrayah took en route back to Bethel and the end-time return of Yisray'lites to the land of Yisrayah. Please consider the following. After his showdown with and triumph over Esau (or Edom), which, as we will see more clearly below, is prophesied to occur in the end times between greater Yisrayah and greater Edom, Yisrayah journeyed to Succoth (or Sukkot, Gen 33:17). From there he went to Shechem, where the son of the king of that city raped and kidnapped Dinah, the daughter of Yisrayah. Simeon and Levi avenged their sister's rape by killing all the men of Shechem, spoiling the city, and taking the rest of the people captive (Gen 34). From there, Yisrayah and his children went to Bethel, where they made an altar to YHWH and made their residence. In ancient Yisrayah, there were two towns by the name of Bethel: one was located 10–15 miles north of Jerusalem, and the other (also possibly known as Bethuel) was situated some distance southwest of Jerusalem, en route to Beersheba, where Abraham and Isaac dwelt. But the

Bethel where Yisrayah chose to abide was neither of these, but rather one that was near Bethlehem, which is only several miles from the current Old City of Jerusalem and the Temple Mount (Gen 35:16; 48:7).

What is the prophetic significance of this in helping us to determine the timing of Ephraim's return to the Land of Yisrayah in the last days?

As we shall see below, the Scriptures seem to indicate that end-times Ephraim will return to the Land of Yisrayah after he has been tested in a wilderness experience (Hosea 2:1-17; Ezekiel 20:33-40) and has overcome hateful and jealous Edom (with YHWH's help), who is militarily blocking Yisrayah's entrance into the Promised Land. The Scriptures further seem to indicate that these events roughly coincide with the great and terrible day of YHWH's wrath against the rebel nations of the world and the second coming of Yahshua, which immediately precedes the fall biblical Feast of Tabernacles, or Succoth (also *Sukkot*), which is a prophetic picture of Yahshua's millennial rule on this earth.

However, after defeating Edom, Jacob still had to face Shechem, another aggressor, who this time sought to defeat Yisrayah politically through intermarriage and assimilation, as opposed to Edom's tactic of frontal military assault. Is it possible that the prophet Zechariah had this in view when he wrote concerning the day of

YHWH that the nations of the world will come against Jerusalem and will take the city and rape the women (Zech 14:1–2)? Is Dinah's rape and capture a prophetic picture of this? I think Dina's story wasn't an ordinary flash in a frying pan! Let's pin Zechariah's ideas together.

Zechariah then goes on to tell us that YHWH (Yahshua at his second coming) will destroy those nations, and His feet shall stand on the Mount of Olives. This is a clear prophecy pointing to Yahshua's second coming. Of this event, the prophet Malachi says that YHWH's Messenger (Yahshua) will suddenly come to his Temple (Bethel or the House of YHWH, another name for the Temple of Solomon). [Nevertheless, this is a reflective emergence of Yahshua in the Second Temple when He was on earth during His first coming]. After Simeon and Levi defeated Dinah's rapist and captors, Jacob led his family to Bethel, where he chose to dwell with his family — the 12 tribes of Yisrayah (Gen 35:1).

End-time Yisrayah is following in their father Jacob's footsteps, leaving their exile and captivity in Babylon (false religious systems — both Christians and Jewish, which contain a mixture of both good and evil; see Revelation 18:4), returning westward across the Jordan River into the land of promise, to their spiritual inheritance, which is defined in terms of YHWH's covenants with Yisrayah (Ephesians 2:12–14).

Isaiah 11:11-16: Isaiah revealed that both houses shall embark on a Second Exodus, just as they did during the First Exodus, when they left Egypt.

"It shall come to pass in that day that YHWH shall set His hand again the second time to recover the remnant of His people who are left, from Assyria and Egypt, from Pathros and Cush, from Elam and Shinar, from Hamath and the Islands of the sea... But they shall fly down upon the shoulder of the Philistines toward the West; together they shall plunder the people of the East; they shall lay their hand on Edom and Moab; and the people of Ammon shall obey them. YHWH will utterly destroy the tongue of the Sea of Egypt; with His mighty wind, He will shake His fist over the River, and strike it in the seven streams, and make men cross over dry-shod (Isaiah 11:11,13-15).

According to Isaiah, the two houses shall return through two Seas: "the Sea of Egypt" and "the Rivers", i.e., the River Euphrates. The Sea of Egypt may be referring to the Red Sea [vv. 11,15]. The ten tribes of Yisrayah and their companions will be returning from the southern hemisphere, e.g., Egypt, Ethiopia, Sudan, and those from the East, West, North and South regions of Africa. The Spirit of YHWH will be upon them as they will be empowered to destroy enemies [e.g. Edom, Moab, Amon, etc] that may want to stand in their way. Another batch described as "the dispersed of Judah" shall be returning with those from the Islands of the sea (often associated with the British Isles); they will return through "the River" [River Euphrates] from the western hemisphere (e.g. South and North America, Europe, Asia) [vv. 11,15]. Similarly, they will be empowered by the Spirit of YHWH to destroy their enemies, as YAH will strike the River in the seven streams for the people to cross over the dry-shod (verse 15). Why seven ways? It's because a multitude would be crossing the Western Hemisphere. The prophets Isaiah, Jeremiah, Ezekiel, and Hosea, among others, are sure that both houses of Yisrayah shall return through the two different sea routes, as identified above. Isaiah added that, "There will be a highway for the remnant of His people who will be left from Assyria, as it was for Yisrayah in the day that he came up from the land of Egypt" (Isaiah 11:16). YHWH is calling out a growing remnant of redeemed covenant-keepers to return to repent and return to Him so that He can restore them to their Land. We are instructed to study Jacob's life [as revealed above], which is a prophetic roadmap of what each believer must go through to obtain their spiritual inheritance, as well as what all Yisrayah collectively or nationally must go through to enter the Promised Land in these last days.

Sixth Evidence:
Ephraim Refined Through Judgment Before Returning

We have just seen how YHWH called Jacob and his sons out of exile in Babylon and required them to go through a time of trouble (i.e., Jacob's trouble) or spiritual refinement and cleansing at the hands of Laban and Edom to prepare Jacob's family to enter the land of Yisrayah. Similarly, the biblical prophets tell us that history will repeat itself in the end days for the descendants of Jacob — Judah and Ephraim. For the Jews (Judah), the humbling process started in the Nazi Holocaust. After that, they began returning to the land of Yisrayah en masse. Ephraim will undergo a similar humbling process before YHWH allows them to return to the Land of Yisrayah.

As happened with Jacob, YHWH will drive the nations and people of Ephraim to a place where, in their state of spiritual apostasy, they will be forced to bend their knees before the Almighty YHWH. Most have forgotten who they are as YHWH's people; they have forsaken their YHWH that chose them and their spiritual heritage, and believe instead that their power, wealth, and world prestige have been gained through their own efforts. Out of the depths of spiritual, economic, political, and military despair, these descendants of the patriarchs will be forced to look up to YHWH, the God of their forefathers, and acknowledge that their blessings have only been a result of His favour and His promises to their forefathers. Getting Ephraim and Judah to acknowledge this will not be an easy task. They will both have to go through incredible hardships, and doubtless many will endure near annihilation before they acknowledge their sin of apostasy and repent and turn back to YHWH. Thus, Yahshua's prophecy would be fulfilled (Matthew 23:39).

Before the people of Ephraim return to the land of Yisrayah, they must first be judged for their apostate ways. The Christian nations and the Christian church have turned away from YHWH and His Torah, and YHWH chastens whom He loves (Heb 12:6). Of the lukewarm church, YHWH says He will spit them out of His mouth unless they are refined in the fires of adversity to bring them to repentance and back to Him. In these fires, their spiritual eyes, ears, and hearts will be opened, and their spiritual nakedness will be covered with robes of righteousness (Revelation 3:15–19; 7:14).

Judgement of the Lawless: The purpose of YHWH's judgements on Yisrayah is not to destroy His people, but to bring them back to Himself spiritually. As a loving FATHER (Hebrews 12:5–11), YHWH wants to have a spiritual relationship with Yisrayah. This cannot happen as long as His people are walking in sinful rebellion (Torahlessness or Lawlessness) against Him. Like a loving parent who has to spank His wayward child to bring him back to the right path, our Heavenly FATHER will be true to His promises and redeem Yisrayah and bring His people back into a covenantal relationship with Him. Together, Yisrayah and Mashiach Yahshua will rule over YHWH's Kingdom in the millennial or messianic age to come.

Freedom to the Obedient: The process of redeeming apostate and scattered Yisrayah is not an easy one. But the prophecies of the Scriptures are clear. Yisrayah will be redeemed and released from spiritual, economic, and political captivity, after which they will be free to return to the land of Yisrayah in fulfilment of numerous biblical prophecies. Again, this will happen, for it is written in the Word of YHWH! It will require the infinite wisdom and sovereign power of YAH Almighty to accomplish this seemingly impossible feat, but YHWH, through His prophets, has declared it so. After being brought low and humbled, the people of Yisrayah will repent of their sins and return to YHWH, their Father. All the obedient who kept YHWH's Word and never denied His Name shall escape without judgment. Those who ignored His Word and rejected His Name shall be tried and painfully punished, and many will be destroyed. There and then, the remnants will be protected and will return to the Promised Land and live in peace forever.

In Ezekiel 35:10–11, we read that YHWH will make Himself known among Judah and Ephraim because of

His jealousy over them and through His judgment against Edom.

Because you have said, 'These two nations and these two countries shall be mine, and we will possess them,' although YHWH was there, therefore, as I live," says YAH ALMIGHTY, "I will do according to your anger and according to the envy which you showed in your hatred against them, and I will make Myself known among them when I judge you. Good

Good things will happen to Ephraim (Yisrayah) and Judah as a result of being brought to their knees nationally. Not only will YHWH glorify His sanctified Name in their midst because they have returned to Him, and not only will YHWH give Yisrayah victory over their enemies, but YHWH will re gather Yisrayah from the lands where He has scattered them and bring them back to the Promised Land — the Land of Yisrayah.

Hosea 11:1–11: YHWH's love for Ephraim is indescribable. Even though he chose to worship "the Baals" (the Lord), YAH promised to keep him and promised that "Yisrayah shall not return to the land of Egypt" (vv. 1–2, 5), but before long, following their unrepentant heart, the Assyrians whisked them away to their land. Even in the foreign land, they "are bent on backsliding from Me. Though they call to the Most High YAH, [but] none at all exalt Him" (v. 7) (i.e., they kept worshipping the Gods of the Gentiles). At one point, YHWH thought of destroying them like Sodom, Gomorrah, Admah, and Zeboim. However, YHWH says of them, "My heart churns within Me; My sympathy is stirred. I will not execute the fierceness of My anger; I will not again destroy Ephraim. For I am YHWH, and not man, the Set-apart One in your midst" (vv. 8–9). YAH took a decision not to destroy them with terror (or terrorism). For their deliverance and their return, YHWH promised that they shall return to serve Him when He will "roar like a lion." Thereafter, Yisrayah shall be returning with trembling from the captivity of the Western world and from the captivity of Egypt (Africa) and from the rest of the Assyrian world of captivity (i.e., Babylon) (v. 11). All these happened to Yisrayah because they completely left Him to surround themselves with lies, deceit, and worship of the Gentile Lord God. (Notice, this prophecy has not been fulfilled yet, for in times past, Ephraim never did return to YHWH, but they will in these latter days and will never turn their back on Him again.) This prophecy reveals that the children of Ephraim shall tremble (be afraid or discomfited, or come trembling, according to the NAS) from the West, including Western nations, Asia, and Africa (e.g., Isaiah 11:11–16). What countries border Yisrayah's West? These include the dominant Islamic/Arab nations, e.g., Lebanon, Syria, and Jordan. The Southern Yisrayah includes Africa, Egypt, and Assyrian nations, which may consist of Iraq, Syria, Iran,

Turkey, and some Eurasian nations, as well as the east coast of America. Thus, they will come out of (spiritual) Egypt and Assyria and of all the countries where they have been scattered.

They shall walk after YHWH. He will roar like a lion. When He roars, then His sons shall come trembling from the west; they shall come trembling like a bird from Egypt, like a dove from the land of Assyria. And I will let them dwell in their houses, says YHWH (vv. 10–11).

Zechariah 10 elaborates further on what will happen to Ephraim and Judah after they have destroyed their enemies. In verse five, we see that YHWH will join with Judah and Ephraim to tread down their common enemies. "They shall be like mighty men, who tread down their enemies in the mire of the streets in the battle. They shall fight because YHWH is with them, and the riders on horses shall be put to shame." (Zech 10:5) Then in verse six, we see that YHWH will strengthen the house of Judah and the house of Joseph and have mercy upon them, and they shall be as if He had not cast them off (i.e., He will restore them spiritually).

I will strengthen the house of Judah, and I will save the house of Joseph [or Ephraim]. I will bring them back because I have mercy on them. They shall be as though I had not cast them aside, for I am YHWH, their Father, and I will hear them. (Zech 10:6)

As a result of YHWH's mercy upon Judah and Ephraim, they will rejoice in YHWH (v. 7), and He will whistle for them and gather them, for He has redeemed (ransomed, rescued, delivered) them.

I will whistle for them and gather them, for I will redeem them; and they shall increase as they once increased. (Zech 10:8)

YHWH will remember his people from all the far countries to which they have been scattered.

I will sow them among the peoples, and they shall remember Me in far countries; they shall live, together with their children, and they shall return. (Zech 10:9)

YHWH will bring Yisrayah back out of (spiritual) Egypt and (spiritual) Assyria (the places of their enslavement and captivity) to the land of Yisrayah. There will be so many returning that there will not be room for them in the land of Yisrayah.

I will also bring them back from the land of Egypt and gather them from Assyria. I will bring them into the land of Gilead and Lebanon until no more room is found for them. (Zech 10:10)

They shall cross seas and rivers to get there. Just as the children of Yisrayah passed through the Red Sea and the Jordan River on their way to the Promised Land, so when the Greater or Second Exodus occurs, YHWH will bring his people back to the land of Yisrayah supernaturally through oceans and rivers. Through YAH's education, they would learn how they commence their journey. The Spirit of YAH will work with them; Yahshua will be in action with His ministering angels. Yahshua will lead the leaders of Yisrayah, and they will lead the people. But will the people listen? This is the reason one must begin to learn the Covenant Way of YHWH. Always watch and pray to escape (Luke 21:36).

He shall pass through the sea with affliction and strike the waves of the sea: all the depths of the river shall dry up. Then the pride of Assyria shall be brought down, and the sceptre of Egypt shall depart. (Zech 10:11)

Before Ephraim and Judah return, Assyria and Egypt must be brought down. By the time Zechariah had written his prophecy, Egypt and Assyria had already fallen and were no longer empires. Likely, Zechariah's prophecy referred to end-time nations that would be like Egypt and Assyria, holding Yisrayah spiritually captive. This could be a reference to the end times coalition of nations the Book of Revelation refers to as Babylon the Great. Zechariah goes on to predict that the defeat of "Egypt" and "Assyria" will occur after Judah has trodden down her enemies (verse 5) with Ephraim's help (Zech 9:13). Through Yahshua, all Yisrayah held in prison, hostages of the enemies shall be released. As Yahshua returns as the King of Yisrayah, He will fight the enemies of His people and bring them down; He will rule over them and reign throughout the entire world.

I will cut off the chariot from Ephraim and the horse from Jerusalem. The battle bow will be cut off, and he will speak peace to the nations. His dominion will be from sea to sea, and from the River to the ends of the earth (Zechariah 9:10).

Unfortunately, to the Palestinians and all their alliances, including Egypt, Babylon and Assyria of these last days, though they may trample the people of YHWH as they like, YHWH will punish them severely for the evil they committed against His people. He will empower His people to be strong and do exploits. YHWH will bless Yisrayah with an abundance of wealth.

YHWH will be seen over them. His arrow will flash like lightning. YHWH will blow the trumpet, and will go with whirlwinds of the south. 15 YHWH of Armies will defend them. They (Yisrayah) will destroy and overcome with sling stones. They will drink, and roar as through wine. They will be filled like bowls, like the corners of the altar. 16 YHWH, their Father, will save them in that day as the flock of his people; for they are like the jewels of a crown, lifted on high over his land. 17 For how great is his goodness, and how great is his beauty! Grain will make the young men flourish, and new wine the virgins. (Zechariah 9:14-17)

The prophet Jeremiah describes these happy events in the following prophecy:

⁴ "In those days, and in that time," says YHWH, "the children of Yisrayah shall come, they and the children of Judah together, going and weeping: they shall go and seek YHWH their Father. ⁵ They shall ask the way to Zion with their faces towards it, saying, 'Come, and let us join ourselves to YHWH in a perpetual covenant that shall not be forgotten.' ⁶ My people have been lost sheep: their shepherds have caused them to go astray; they have turned them away on the mountains; they have gone from mountain to hill; they have forgotten their resting place. ⁷ All that found them have devoured them, and their adversaries said, 'We offend not, because they have sinned against YHWH, the habitation of justice, even YHWH, the hope of their fathers.' ⁸ Remove out of the midst of Babylon, and go forth out of the land of the Chaldeans, and be as the he-goats before the flocks." (Jer 50:4–8)

Historically, these prophecies have not been fulfilled. They are future in nature and will occur just before the day of YHWH's wrath upon the nations (Zech 14:1–3) and the return of Yahshua (Zech 12:10; 13:1; 14:4). In that day, many wicked will be killed, many of Judah and Ephraim will be saved, and many Yisray'lites will return to the land of Yisrayah. The return of Yisrayah out of the nations of the world to their Promised Land is, as already noted, often referred to as the Greater or Second Exodus (Jer 16:14; 23:7–8; Isa 11:11, 16; 27:13).

Seventh Evidence:
Yisrayah Must Begin To Repent From Their Sins And Return To Torah First

The biblical prophecies speak in unmitigated terms that a precondition for Ephraim's return to the land of Yisrayah will be its repenting of its sin (i.e., Torahlessness), which begins the process of Yisrayah returning to the Torah. Let's now document the scriptural evidence that confirms this truth.

Jeremiah 3:11–14

The prophet declares that "backsliding Yisrayah" (i.e., Ephraim, as opposed to "treacherous Judah", verse 11) will acknowledge its iniquity (i.e., Torahlessness, lawlessness) against YHWH (verse 13) before she can return to Zion (verse 13). It might be said that Judah returned to Torah when the Babylonian exiles returned to the land in the sixth century B.C., but in reality, only a small remnant of Jews returned. However, to be sure, this prophecy has yet to be fulfilled with regard to the northern ten tribes of Yisrayah (or Ephraim). Besides, after Yahshua came, and they rejected Him, He warned them that the Temple would be destroyed, and Yerusalem would be defeated and occupied by their captors. They will occupy the land till their time is over (Luke 21:24). The Temple and Yerusalem having fallen, the people were scattered all over the world. The Land is still being occupied by its conquerors. The Biblical Judah is still scattered and would return with Ephraim as one nation of Yisrayah (see Ezek. 34).

Ezekiel 36:1–38

Ezekiel 36 is a prophecy to "the people of Yisrayah" (verse 8) and to "all the house of Yisrayah" (verse 10), which includes both Ephraim and Judah. Because of their spiritual declension, YHWH punished them by scattering them among the heathen and dispersing them throughout the countries of the world (verses 19–23). However, he promises to gather his people and bring them to their own land (verse 24), where he will spiritually regenerate them, resulting in their return to Torah obedience (verses 25–38). Again, these prophecies have not been fulfilled heretofore in their fullest sense, since Ephraim has neither been regathered from its exile nor has it yet repented of its Torahlessness in any significant way, much less returned to the land of Yisrayah. This is yet to come.

Hosea 5:11–6:3

This prophecy is short but packed with prophetic significance. The key players are Ephraim and Judah (5:3, 5, 9–14; 6:4, 10, 11), who became sick spiritually (or Torahless, 5:13), resulting in the kingdom of Yisrayah being torn apart (when the kingdom was divided under Rehoboam, verse 14).

YHWH [Yahshua] then indicates that, in a sense, he will abandon them and return to his place (in heaven) until they acknowledge their offence (verse 15). Who but Yahshua left his people, Yisrayah, on earth and returned to his place in heaven after his resurrection?

In Heaven, Yahshua will stay until Ephraim and Judah acknowledge their sins [offences] (Ephraim, i.e., Yisrayah, has rejected the Law of Moses, or the written Torah-Word of YHWH, while Judah has rejected Yahshua, the Living Torah-Word of YHWH).

Today, both houses of:

- **Ephraim (Yisrayah)** rejected the Law of Moses, or the written Torah – i.e., the Word of YHWH, from which Yahshua taught (Luke 24:27,44).

- **Judah (Yehuda)** rejected YAHSHUA – the Living Torah-Word of YHWH – the Word made flesh.

In the meantime, both houses of Yisrayah will go through affliction, resulting in their seeking YHWH eagerly (verse 15). Jointly, they will acknowledge their offence and recognise that they are brother nations that YHWH had previously torn apart. Their epiphany or spiritual awakening will result in their seeking YHWH to heal the breach [hostility, animosity, enmity] between them (6:1). Hosea then goes on to prophesy that after two days (or prophetically, 2000 years from the time that Yahshua left earth to return to His place, 5:15), YHWH will revive Ephraim and Judah spiritually. Then on the third day (or the third millennium after Yahshua's first coming), he will raise them up (or resurrect them physically and spiritually), and together the two houses of Yisrayah will live in Messiah's sight, presumably during the Millennium through to the New Heaven and New Earth.

Again, this unique prophecy is yet to be fulfilled, and the timeframe for its fulfilment appears to be the end times and pre-millennial. Reader, take note!

In Hosea's prophecy, we see the same old story repeating itself: the people of Ephraim turn away from the Torah-based covenants of YHWH (Hosea 8:1, 12). To be true to his Word, YHWH is then forced to discipline his people by scattering them throughout the nations of the world (Hosea 8:8). However, in his mercy, YHWH will regather them after they demonstrate a sorrowful heart (Hosea 8:10).

For nearly 2000 years, the Torah (Instruction, i.e., the first five books of the Bible, or the "law of Moses") has been a strange or foreign thing to Christianity (Ephraim), which makes use of the BOC (Bible). It has developed theological philosophies to alienate its adherents from serious Torah obedience, claiming that the "Law has been done away with," is nailed to the "cross," and is against us, and that since we are not "under" the law, we are therefore free to break it. Never before has Ephraim acknowledged its Torahless state, but the day is coming when more and more Israelite-Christians [fallen Ephraim and Judah] will acknowledge their Torahlessness [lawlessness, see Matt. 7:21-23] and repent, returning to YHWH as prophesied by Hosea. This process is already beginning to happen as thousands of Christians worldwide are returning to the Hebrew-Torah roots of their faith. The number is increasing by the day.

Amos 9:8–15

Amos reiterates what the other prophets have said vis-à-vis Ephraim. Because of sin (breaking the Law), YHWH promises to punish the house of Jacob (verse 8) by sifting them through the nations of the world (verse 9). Those of the house of Jacob (both Jews and Christians) who refuse to repent of their sin (transgression of the Law, lawlessness or Torahlessness) shall die by the sword (verse 10; see Deut. 8:19-20).

After YHWH purges his people, he promises to raise the tabernacle of David, which, as discussed above, relates to the regathering and reuniting of the two houses of Yisrayah under a resurrected King David at the second coming of Yahshua (verses 11–15).

Eighth Evidence:
Israel's Captor Nations Must Be Judged First

YHWH brought judgment against Egypt, and the captive Israelites were set free. A thousand years later, YHWH brought judgment against Babylon by the Persians, after which the Jewish exiles were liberated and allowed to return to the land of Yisrayah. In our time, YHWH brought judgment against Nazi Germany. The Ashkenaz Jews and other foreigners (see Rev. 2:9; Rev. 3:9) subsequently obtained an independent "State of Israel" created by the United Nations (power of Babylon the Great???). Thus, the land space today called Israel was born in 1948 by decree of the UN. If they are biblical Judah and have returned, the prophecies of Yahshua in Luke 21:24, which state that foreigners will occupy the land until their time is over (i.e., the time Yahshua would return), will be a nullity. But we know that His Word remains alive and accomplishes its purpose. Therefore, the true Judah is still scattered in the Gentile world. As the time of the Gentiles in the Land of Yisrayah is being completed, Yahshua, prior to and at his second coming, will bring judgment against those that occupy His Land; He will bring judgement against Babylon the Great, Assyria, Egypt, and all the nations where the whole house of Yisrayah are held captive; and the captives of Ephraim will be set free to return to their promised inheritance in the land of Yisrayah, as well as the captives of Judah, who will return to their promised inheritance in the land of Yisrayah. Both houses of Yisrayah shall unite and fight their way back home with the backing of Yahshua and His host of angels to defeat the enemies of Yisrayah.

ISLAM & JIHADISM

Judgment on Ephraim's and Judah's enemies is a precondition for Yisrayah's return to the land of Yisrayah. The Nazis may have been judged in World War II, but the world is still full of anti-Semitism and anti-Christian (i.e., Torahless Yisrayah) hatred. The Palestinians and many of their Muslim brothers still hate Jews and Christians and are currently engaged in Koran-inspired jihad against the people of Yisrayah. Their aim is to destroy both America and Israel and to take over Christian nations and impose Islamic law on earth. The enemies of Yisrayah are alive and well and gaining strength! The children of Edom, Moab, Amon, and many others within the Arab and Islamic world who hate the people of YHWH are plotting to overrun and Islamise the covenant-keeping people of Yisrayah. The stage is being set for an end-times showdown between these two groups as predicted by the biblical prophets thousands of years ago. But in the end, the enemies of Yisrayah will be defeated. Finally, Yisrayah would conquer their archrival enemy and return to their land, dwelling safely as they would be led by their everlasting king, high priest, and Saviour of the whole world, Yahshua HaMashiach.

The prophet Ezekiel describes these happy events in the following prophecy:

⁴ "In those days, and in that time," says YHWH, "the children of Yisrayah shall come, they and the children of Judah together, going and weeping: they shall go and seek YHWH their Father. ⁵ They shall ask the way to Zion with their faces towards it, saying, 'Come, and let us join ourselves to YHWH in a perpetual covenant that shall not be forgotten.' ⁶ My people have been lost sheep: their shepherds have caused them to go astray; they have turned them away on the mountains; they have gone from mountain to hill; they have forgotten their resting place. ⁷ All that found them have devoured them, and their adversaries said, 'We offend not, because they have sinned against YHWH, the habitation of justice, even YHWH, the hope of their fathers.' ⁸ Remove out of the midst of Babylon, and go forth out of the land of the Chaldeans, and be as the he-goats before the flocks." (Ezek 50:4–8)

But before the captives of Israel are set free, Babylon will be destroyed (Ezekiel 50:1–3, 9–16, 21–32, 35–46; 51:1–49). Before this, YHWH will warn his people to flee Babylon and YHWH's vengeance or judgements against her (51:6 cp. Rev 18:4).

This prophecy was partially fulfilled by the Persians, as recorded in the Book of Daniel, but not entirely. In Daniel's day, only the house of Judah was liberated from Babylon. This particular prophecy, however, speaks of both the children of Yisrayah (the house of Yisrayah or Ephraim) and the children of Judah (the house of Judah), who both and together are repenting and seeking YHWH, their Father (verse 4). This has not happened yet. We therefore await a future and greater fulfilment of this prophecy in the end times.

WHEN WILL THE SECOND EXODUS OCCUR?

Numerous other biblical prophets speak of YHWH's judgment falling on Israel's captors, resulting in the outcasts of Yisrayah being liberated and allowed to return to the land of Yisrayah. **Yisrayah's First Exodus came after Egypt was judged. The Second Exodus will occur after the nations of the world are judged.**

Historically, the end-time judgment of the nations that numerous biblical prophecies speak about has not yet occurred. They are future in nature and will occur just before the day of YHWH's wrath upon the nations (Zech

14:1–3) and the return of Yahshua (Zech 12:10; 13:1; 14:4). In that day, many wicked people will be killed, while many people of Judah and Ephraim will be saved, and many Yisrayahlites will return to the land of Yisrayah. This is not to say that Yisrayah, who rebels against YAH, shall be saved. A lot of them will perish because they never recognised YHWH's Torah and Yahshua; they didn't keep His Word and His Name (see Rev. 3:8, 10). As noted above, the return of Yisrayah out of the nations of the world to their promised land is often referred to as the Second Exodus. As ancient Yisrayah was held captive as slaves in ancient Egypt, so in the end times, the people of YHWH are being held captive by the nations where they live. They are political, economic and spiritual captives to a worldwide New World Order, Babylon the Great, and the Anti-HaMashiach system that enslaves its inhabitants. Most of their laws will work against people of YHWH. They would intend to force them to obey those evil laws. The beast will enact a law similar to the one imposed by Nebuchadnezzar of ancient Babylon and Antiochus Epiphanes, requiring people to bow and worship the image of his god. The Torah keeping Yisrayah would reject it (those who did not escape, see Rev. 12:15-17), and many of them will be killed. However, YHWH will protect His true Assembly and take them into the wilderness, where He will look after them for three and a half years, until the power of the beast and the false prophets is destroyed. The government of Satan and his beast will come to an end as Yahshua will return to cut them off and assume the worldwide government of YHWH on earth. Meanwhile, biblical Yisray'lites are not free to return to the Land of Israel yet. If you think you are, just move to Israel and see how far you get if you can't prove that you're Ashkenazi Jewish!

There are still more prophecies that speak of YHWH's judgment against the nations that are Yisrayah's enemies.

Isaiah 24

Isaiah chapter 24 speaks of YHWH's judgment against the whole earth. Since Noah's flood, when has this ever happened? The earth will be turned upside down (verse 1). All people will be affected (verse 2). The earth will mourn and fade away (verse 4). Because man broke the Torah-Laws of YHWH (verse 5), the earth will be cursed, its inhabitants made desolate, and most will be killed, and few men will be left (verse 6). Even Yisray'lites who have been scattered to the isles of the sea will be punished (verse 15). The foundations of the earth will be shaken (verse 18), and the earth will be broken down, dissolved and moved exceedingly (verse 19). It will reel to and fro like a drunkard (verse 20). On that day of judgment, YHWH will punish the leaders of the earth (verse 21), after which YHWH of Hosts will rule in Zion and Yerusalem (verse 23). Does anyone reading this doubt whether this prophecy is yet to be fulfilled?

In chapter 25

Isaiah breaks into praising YHWH, who has brought low the haughty nations and given strength to the poor (verses 2–4), and who has swallowed up death in victory and wiped away the tears and shame of his people (verse 8), who are now rejoicing in his salvation (verse 9) from their enemies (verse 10).

Chapter 26

continues the song of praise and refers to YHWH's judgments upon the earth's inhabitants (verse 9) for oppressing YHWH's people (verse 11). Only those who acknowledge the Name of YHWH and reject other names shall be saved (verse 13). The wicked dead shall not live (verse 14). Following Torah obedience and His Awesome Name, Torah-keeping Yisrayah shall return to YHWH, pouring prayers and cries as great tribulation rages. The population will suddenly increase — presumably because the righteous dead shall be resurrected (at the second coming of Yahshua), which will occur (verses 14, 15 and 19). Pain and cries will be much because of sin (verses 16-18). But this happens only after the time of YHWH's indignation has passed, when the inhabitants of the earth are punished for their sins (verses 20–21).

Isaiah's same prophecy continues into chapter 27, where YHWH's judgment against the earth continues.

YHWH shall slay the dragon that is in the sea (verse 1; this is likely a prophetic allusion to Satan's Babylon the Great, the end-times world-ruling system that the books of Daniel and Revelation liken metaphorically to a dragon coming out of the sea, i.e., nations or humanity). Isaiah then goes into a discourse (verses 5–10) about Israel's restoration to her land, where she will experience spiritual revival and the land will yield an abundance of physical produce as well. What is the signal of the regathering of these exiled and scattered Yisray'lites?

Let's read verse 13

And it shall come to pass in that day that the great trumpet/shofar shall be blown, and they shall come who were ready to perish in the land of Assyria and the outcasts in the land of Egypt and shall worship YHWH in the holy mount at Yerusalem.

What is this gathering of the children of Yisrayah at the sound of the great trumpet, and when does it occur?

In the previous chapters, we see several dominant themes: judgment of YHWH against the nations — the enemies of Yisrayah in whose lands they have been held captive — Yisrayah being restored to her land, and now, in this verse, a regathering of Yisrayah at the sound of a great trumpet. Some believe that Yahshua's prophecy in Matthew 24:27–31 is a parallel prophecy to Isaiah's prophecy. Is Yahshua speaking about the regathering of Yisrayah after the great tribulation (Matt 24:29) and after his second coming (Matt 24:29–30), at which time he will send forth his angels to gather his people Yisrayah (literally, his elect, or picked-out chosen ones) from the four corners of the earth at a great sound of a trumpet (or shofar horn, verse 31)?

Furthermore, is this sound of a great shofar the very same great blast of the shofar that would sound in ancient Yisrayah every fiftieth year on the Day of Atonement (Yom Kippur), signaling the beginning of the Jubilee Year when all the captives were set free, debts were forgiven, and the land was returned to its original owners? The jubilee trumpet sounded, and the Jubilee Year was consecrated on Yom Kippur (Lev 25:9–10), while the year of release (as the Jubilee Year came to be known) actually started during the Feast of Tabernacles (Deut 31:10; cp 15:1ff; Exod 21:2; 23:10). This seventh-year release corresponds with the Jubilee Year, which begins at the end of the 49th year and at the beginning of the 50th year.

Furthermore, is this sound of a great shofar the very same great blast of the shofar that would sound in ancient Yisrayah every fiftieth year on the Day of Atonement (Yom Kippur), signaling the beginning of the Jubilee Year when all the captives were set free, debts were forgiven, and the land was returned to its original owners? The jubilee trumpet sounded, and the Jubilee Year was consecrated on Yom Kippur (Lev 25:9–10), while the year of release (as the Jubilee Year came to be known) actually started during the Feast of Tabernacles (Deut 31:10; cp 15:1ff; Exod 21:2; 23:10). This seventh-year release corresponds with the Jubilee Year, which begins at the end of the 49th year and at the beginning of the 50th year.

Isaiah 61:1–2, in an apparent reference to a future prophetic Jubilee release of the spiritual Yisray'lites' captives, speaks of proclaiming liberty to the captives. This event occurs in conjunction with the day of YHWH's vengeance or wrath, which occurs at the end of the age before the return of Yahshua. The day of YHWH's wrath corresponds to the seven trumpets and seven bowl judgements that He will pour out upon the earth as prophesied in Revelation (Chapters 8 through 12, 15 and 16). This is YHWH's judgment against Babylon the Great and culminates when Yahshua, at his second coming, destroys this evil one-world system once and for all (Rev 19:11–21). Therefore, it would seem that Yahshua's return will occur on an actual Jubilee Year. At that time, Babylon's enslaved captives (Rev 18:13) will be liberated. Among these spiritual captives, there will doubtless be Yisray'lites who will be set free, who will repent and return to YHWH, and whom He will regather and return to the Land of Yisrayah after a wilderness experience.

Trusting that understanding of these Scriptures is correct, then here is yet more evidence that the regathering of Ephraim [Yisrayah] to its land inheritance occurs after the wrath of YHWH and the fall of Babylon the Great, which occurs at the second coming of Yahshua.

Jeremiah 30

We have examined Jeremiah 30 in our discussion above on Jacob's trouble and the regathering of Yisrayah and Judah, as well as their return to the Land of Yisrayah; however, verse 11 contains additional details that we need to highlight.

Verse 11 reads,

For I am with you," says YHWH, *"to save you: though I make a full end of all nations whither I have scattered you, yet will I not make a full end of you: but I will correct you in measure and will not leave you altogether unpunished.*

YHWH says in verse 10 that He will save Yisrayah from the far land of their captivity and that Jacob shall return and rest — but after He will "make a full end of all nations."Through YHWH's judgment of the nations, he will correct and punish disobedient Yisrayah as well (verse 11, last part). This is an aspect of Jacob's trouble (see verse 7). Even as Jacob was wounded in his struggle with YHWH when he was returning from Laban, so the scattered Yisrayah will be wounded or punished because of the multitude of its iniquities and sins (or lawlessness; see verses 14–15). Like Jacob, the scattered Yisrayah will be brought low spiritually en route back to the Land of their inheritance (verse 14).

Jeremiah 31

Once again, this prophet of YHWH picks up the sorry saga of Yisrayah's (both houses of Yisrayah, verse 27) spiritual backsliding (verse 22) and its departure from the covenants of YHWH (verses 13–33). As punishment for its apostasy, Yisrayah was scattered among the nations of the world, from which YHWH promised to regather them (verses 8–10)—another prophecy that is yet to be fulfilled, since Ephraim has never in the past cried, "Arise, and let us go up to Zion unto YHWH our Father" (verse 6). In the twentieth century, some of Judah (the Jews) rallied and returned to Zion (the land of Yisrayah). To date, Ephraim (broadly speaking, the descendants of Yisrayah who have turned to Christianity) has not. Therefore, for Ephraim, this prophecy remains unfulfilled.

Then in verse 11, we read that,

YHWH has redeemed Yisrayah from the hand of him that was stronger than him, after which Yisrayah will return joyfully to Zion (verses 12–14). This verse was fulfilled in part when the Jewish exiles returned to Yisrayah from Babylon, but not all aspects of this prophecy have been fulfilled. For example, under Zerubbabel, Ezra, and Nehemiah, only a remnant of the Jews and some Levites returned from Babylon. Not all the tribes of Yisrayah returned from the north country, from the coasts of the earth, and from the islands afar off (verses 8 and 10).

Furthermore, the prophecy of verse 11 was fulfilled in part when the Jewish exiles were set free after YHWH judged Babylon, which fell to the Persians. The Persians then released the Jewish captives to return to the Land of Yisrayah. But since there are aspects of this prophecy that have yet to be fulfilled, it becomes evident that in the end times, YHWH will redeem enslaved Yisrayah and set her free to return to the Land after YHWH has judged the nations (as He did to Egypt before the First Exodus).

The timing of this redemption is fixed in verses 31 and 33, where YHWH speaks of entering a Marriage Covenant with both the house of Yisrayah (Ephraim) and the house of Judah (the Jews). Though Yahshua initiated this Covenant at His first coming on Passover, this marital covenant has yet to be finalised, as the writer of Hebrews indicates (Heb 8:8–13).

Zechariah 10

Zechariah further echoes his prophetic compatriots when he speaks of the houses of Judah and Joseph (i.e., Ephraim and Manasseh) being regathered from the nations and returning to the Land of Israel (Zech 10:6–10). Zechariah repeats Jeremiah's redemptive theme (verse 8) and links this with judgment against the nations that have held the people of YHWH captive (verse 11).

Although Zechariah prophesied while the exiled Jews were still returning from Babylon, many aspects of his prophecies remain future in nature. For example, the house of Joseph never returned with Judah, as he prophesied would happen (10:6). Furthermore, Chapter 10 opens up with the well-known Messianic two horse prophecy, the first part of which was fulfilled when Yahshua entered Yerusalem triumphantly riding a colt (Luke 19:30–38). Yet the second part of this prophecy is yet unfulfilled, but will be when Yahshua comes again — this time from heaven — riding a white war stallion to bring judgment upon the nations that have enslaved His people and oppose His rule (Rev 19:11–21). Zechariah's prophecy appears to envision a scenario where the captives of Judah and Ephraim will be freed or redeemed, enabling them to return to Zion in conjunction with YHWH's judgment of the nations, which, according to the Book of Revelation, occurs before and at the second coming of Yahshua HaMashiach.

Hosea 11:9-11

We find another piece of the puzzle as to the timing of Ephraim's return to the Land of Yisrayah in Hosea's prophecy to the northern kingdom of Yisrayah (i.e., Ephraim). In Chapter 11, the prophet picks up the lament of Ephraim's pitiable, spiritually backslidden condition and YHWH's sorrow over the plight of His beloved people. To bring His people back to Him, He will bring judgment against Ephraim (verses 8-10), but this will be in conjunction with His roaring like a lion, which a lion does when it is hungry (Amos 3:4), to send fear into the hearts of its enemies before attacking (Hos 11:10; Isa 5:29). When will YHWH "roar" like a lion? "On the day of His fierce wrath, when He will judge not only apostate Yisrayah, but the wicked heathen nations as well." When this happens, Ephraim will come trembling from the west (due west of Yisrayah is North America) and from the lands of spiritual Egypt and Assyria, where they have been held as spiritual captives (verse 12). Again, this prophecy has yet to be fulfilled. When the Jewish exiles returned from Babylon, they came from the east, not the west. Furthermore, those who returned to Yisrayah from Babylon (many did not return) were almost entirely from the kingdom of Judah, and not from the northern kingdom of Yisrayah, also known as Ephraim!

Amos 9:8-15

Once again, we see that YHWH's judgments will come upon the apostate house of Yisrayah, as YHWH allowed them to be sifted throughout all the nations (Amos 9:8–10). But restoration will occur! The tabernacle of David that has fallen will be raised up; that is to say, Judah and Ephraim will be regathered, return to the land of Yisrayah, and be reunited under a resurrected king David (see Ezek 37:15–28; cp., Jer 30:1–10, especially note verse 9). At that time, they will possess the lands of Edom and the heathens (verse 12). For Yisrayah to possess the lands of its enemies means that YHWH has first destroyed her enemies.

The timing of this prophecy is millennial, when the earth will yield its rich bounty, and YHWH will bring again the captivity of His people Yisrayah back to the Land of Yisrayah (verses 13–15).

Deuteronomy 30:1-9

Before his death, Moses prophesied what would occur to Yisrayah in the future. Some of these prophecies have been fulfilled completely, while others have been fulfilled only in part or not at all. For example, verse three says that YHWH will regather Yisrayah from all the nations to which He would scatter them because of apostasy. True, this prophecy was fulfilled in part when YHWH regathered some of the Jews [not all] from the one nation of Babylon. But this hardly fulfils the whole tenor of Moses' prophecy when he speaks about all the tribes of Yisrayah being regathered from all the nations to which they have been scattered.

Next, we note that this prophecy speaks not only about the regathering of Yisrayah and her return to her Land, but also about the spiritual revival of Yisrayah (her returning to Torah, verse 8) — another part of this prophecy that is yet to be fulfilled in a significant way. And Yisrayah's revival is tied to YHWH's judging the nations into which Yisrayah was scattered (verse 7), which, as we have seen above, occurs at the end of the age just before and at the second coming of Yahshua HaMashiach.

Further Evidence that Reveals Sins:

Having explored the BOC (Bible) evidence on yet-to-be-fulfilled prophecies, Yisrayah's Second Exodus, and the coming restoration into their Land, the ninth evidence below is significant to all Yisrayah preparing for the historical return to their Land of inheritance. The passage examines why many ancient Yisray'lites were unable to enter the Promised Land. As earlier mentioned, some prophecies are prototype or typological in nature as they recur to prove fulfilment events. In these latter days of the Second Exodus, some of the acts of the old would repeat themselves. To escape being destroyed (because not all Yisray'lites will enter the Land), a diligent disciple must learn those destructive sins that were displayed in the wilderness and begin to adjust themselves to the side of uprightness and righteousness.

Ninth Evidence:

The Reason Many Ancient Yisrayah Could Not Enter the Promised Land Would Repeat Again

What will determine any Yisrayah to return from the land of captivity into Yisrayah, the Land of inheritance, is to learn to keep away from sin. It's to master what happened during the First Exodus and juxtapose it with what is happening now, and possibly what will happen in the wilderness during the Second Exodus. During the First Exodus, many could not make it because they repeatedly committed the sin of unfaithfulness against YHWH and the leaders, He had appointed to lead His people back to the Land of Yisrayah. The BOC reveals that a similar situation would occur again. They would test or try YHWH, and YHWH would test them, at least, to find out if they have faith in Him to deliver them. Let's begin with the Table of the list of Ten Temptations that showcase how Yisrayah tested and sinned against YHWH during the First Exodus.

In Numbers 14:20-23

YHWH said, "I have pardoned according to your word; but in very deed — as I live, and as all the earth shall be filled with YHWH's glory — because all those men who have seen My glory and my signs, which I worked in Egypt and in the wilderness, yet have tempted Me these <u>ten times</u>, and have not listened to My voice; surely <u>they shall not see the land</u> which I swore to their fathers, neither shall any of those who despised Me see it.

Ten Times Yisrayah Tempted YHWH In The Wilderness

Temptations	Scripture	Situation/Location	Sin	Moses' Response	YHWH's Actions
1	Exodus 14:10-14	Pharaoh and Egypt army behind Yisrayah	Moses promises YAH will fight for them, and they should be quiet	Blocked Egyptians with cloud, divided Red Sea and destroyed the Egyptians as they chased	Blocked Egyptians with cloud, divided Red Sea and destroyed the Egyptians as they chased
2	Exodus 15:23-27	At Marah (Bitterness) they lacked drinking water	Moses cried to YHWH	YHWH showed Moses a tree which made the waters sweetTold if they would listen to YAH none of the diseases of the Egyptians would affect them	YHWH showed Moses a tree which made the waters sweet – Told if they would listen to YAH none of the diseases of the Egyptians would affect them

SECOND EXODUS OF YISRAYAH CHAPTER 13

3	Exodus 16:1-14	Wilderness of sin, with no food	None YHWH addresses directly Moses just relays the message not against him, but YHWH	YHWH proves people through law of manna, gives flesh (quail) and daily manna	YHWH proves people through law of manna, gives flesh (quail) and daily manna
4	Exodus 16:19-21	Wilderness of sin, gathering manna	Moses was wroth (burst in rage)	It bred worms and stank, melted	It bred worms and stank, melted
5	Exodus 16:22-30	Wilderness of sin, gathering manna	YHWH rebukes him, then as commanded he gathers a portion for memorial in Ark	YHWH asks Moses, how long will you refuse to keep my commandments and my laws	YHWH asks Moses, how long will you refuse to keep my commandments and my laws
6	Exodus 17:1-7	Rephidim: no water	Cried to YHWH – People were almost ready to stone him.	Commands Moses to spite the rock before the elders. YAH stands on rock – ater flows out when smitten.	Commands Moses to spite the rock before the elders. YAH stands on rock – ater flows out when smitten.
7	Exodus 32:13 4:35	At Sinai: Moses on Mt for 40 days to receive the Torah and Ten Commandments	Reminded YHWH of Covenant with Abraham, broke Tables of Law, made drink idol, put done	Would have destroyed the people or left them to an angel to lead them into the land. Turned wrath based on intercession and showed	Would have destroyed the people or left them to an angel to lead them into the land. Turned wrath based on intercession and showed

SECOND EXODUS OF YISRAYAH CHAPTER 13

				rebellion, renegotiated Covenant	glory – renewed a modified covenant.	glory – renewed a modified covenant.
8	Numbers 11:1-3		3 days from Mt Sinai; Taberah (Burning)	Nothing – YHWH addressed directly – when people cry to Moses though he prayed and stopped fire	YHWH sent fire which burnt amongst them – consumed those on outside of camp.	YHWH sent fire which burnt amongst them – consumed those on outside of camp.
9	Numbers 11:4 35		Kibrothhattaavah (Graves of Lust)	Moses upset – Cries to YHWH that the burden is too great. Doubts what YHWH will do.	YHWH puts spirit upon the 70; sends 3 feet deep of quail and while they eat (months' worth); as they ate sent great plague killing many	YHWH puts spirit upon the 70; sends 3 feet deep of quail and while they eat (months' worth); as they ate sent great plague killing many
10	Numbers 13:2514:39		Wilderness of Paran, at border of Canaan	Fell on face in prayer. Pleads for glory of name of YHWH despite people's great sin.	YHWH at first will destroy, but He pardons according to Moses' intercession. Promises to destroy all 20+ in wilderness. To wander for 40 years – one year for each day of spies in Canaan. All spies except	YHWH at first will destroy, but He pardons according to Moses' intercession. Promises to destroy all 20+ in wilderness. To wander for 40 years – one year for each day of spies in Canaan. All spies except

				Joshua and Caleb died immediately	Joshua and Caleb died immediately

SIN WILL STOP MANY

Further Sins:

Numbers 16:3

"You take too much upon yourselves, for all the congregation are holy, every one of them, and YHWH is among them. Why then do you exalt yourselves above the assembly of YHWH?"

Verse 1-3 Rebels Challenged Moses and Aaron's Leadership: Koran, Dathan, and Abiram led a coup to unseat Moses (leader) and Aaron (high priest) – accused them of high-handedness. These three men incited the 250 leaders from the 12 tribes of Yisrayah to rebel against the leadership of Moses and Aaron. The uprising against Moses and Aaron was no mere personality conflict; it struck at the heart of YHWH's authority and order among the Yisray'lites (verses 4-5). Moses brought their allegation to YHWH for judgment (verses 6-7). Moses reminded them that they were fighting against YHWH and requested that they appear before YHWH for judgment (verses 8-11). The trio of rebels refused to honour the invitation to appear before

YHWH (verses 12-14). Moses was furious and prayed to YHWH, "Do not respect their offering," reminding YHWH that they had accused him falsely, as he never coveted anything of theirs or behaved arrogantly. Eventually, they gathered at the door of the tabernacles of meeting, and YHWH appeared to all the congregation (verses 15-19). YHWH's anger instantly burned against the rebels. YHWH was set to consume them immediately, but Moses pleaded for the lives of the rebels, but to no avail (verses 20-24). When Moses discovered that YAH wouldn't spare the rebels, he told the people to depart from the rebels so that they would not be consumed with them (verse 25).

Moses now let out his anger against the rebels (verses 26-30):

"Depart now from the tents of these wicked men! Touch nothing of theirs, lest you be consumed in all their sins." "By this you shall know that YHWH has sent me [as the Leader] to do all these works, for I have not done them of my own will. [Moses represented YHWH before Yisrayah]. If these men die naturally like all men, or if they are visited by the common fate of all men, then YHWH has not sent me. But if YHWH creates a new thing, and the earth opens its mouth and swallows them up with all that belongs to them, and they go down alive into the pit, then you will understand that these men have rejected YHWH."

Ground Split & Swallowed Rebels (verses 31-36; see Ezek. 20:33-45; Hos. 2:16 17)

"Now it came to pass, as he finished speaking all these words, that the ground split apart under them, and the earth opened its mouth and swallowed them up, with their households and all the men with Korah, with all their goods. So, they and all those with them went down alive into the pit; the earth closed over them, and they perished from among the assembly. Then all Israel who were around them fled at their cry, for they said, "Lest the earth swallow us up also!"

"And a fire came out from YHWH and consumed the two hundred and fifty [250] men who were offering incense.

Complaints against Moses and Aaron [verses 41-49]

"On the next day, all the congregation of the children of Israel complained against Moses and Aaron, saying, "**You have killed the people of YHWH.**" Now it happened, when the congregation had gathered against Moses and Aaron that they turned toward the tabernacle of meeting; and suddenly the cloud covered it, and the glory of YHWH appeared. Then Moses and Aaron came before the tabernacle of meeting. And YHWH spoke to Moses, saying, "Get away from among this congregation, that I may consume them in a moment."

And they fell on their faces to intercede for the people (verses 46–50).

"So Moses said to Aaron (both men aborted their intercession), "Take a censer and put fire in it from the altar, put incense on it, and take it quickly to the congregation and make atonement for them (the people); for wrath has gone out from YHWH. The plague has begun." Then Aaron took it as Moses commanded and ran into the midst of the assembly, and already the plague had begun among the people. So he put in the incense and made atonement for the people. And he stood between the dead and the living, so the plague was stopped. Now those who died in the plague were fourteen thousand seven hundred, besides those who died in the Korah incident. So Aaron returned to Moses at the door of the tabernacle of meeting, for the plague had stopped."

Lessons Learnt:

YHWH appoints those who lead His Assembly. Anyone challenging such a leadership appointment challenges YHWH. There are two parts of provocation in the Number Chapter 16. Firstly, Korah, Dathan and Abiram – the rebels – incited the 250 leaders of Yisrayah to unseat Moses and Aaron because they thought they were overbearing. Unfortunately, the actions of the rebels were a direct challenge to YAH, who had appointed them. YHWH killed them despite Moses' initial intervention to plead for their lives. Secondly, the actions of the rebellious leaders influenced the people to also murmur against Moses and Aaron, claiming it was because of them. YAH killed those rebels, including the 250 leaders from the 12 tribes. The people's rebellion also backfired against them as YHWH destroyed them, killing 14,700 people. They didn't learn any lesson from what happened to the rebel leaders. YHWH is no respecter of anyone who undermines His work. The leaders He appoints are answerable to Him. He judges them by Himself. To embark on chastising whom YAH elects to lead His people is a direct assault on Him, and the consequence is swift and death.

YHWH RESOLVES THE INCESSANT COMPLAINTS

OFFICE OF THE PRIESTHOOD FINALLY RESOLVED

Miraculous Budding of Aaron's Rod. Here is the BOC excerpt:

NUMBERS 17 "And YHWH spoke to Moses, saying: **2** "Speak to the children of Yisrayah, and get from them a rod from each father's house, all their leaders according to their fathers' houses — twelve rods. Write each man's name on his rod. **3** And you shall write Aaron's name on the rod of Levi. For there shall be one rod for the head of each father's house. **4** Then you shall place them in the tabernacle of meeting before the Testimony, where I meet with you. **5** And it shall be that the rod of the man whom I choose will blossom; thus I will rid Myself of the complaints of the children of Yisrayah, which they make against you." **6** So Moses spoke to the children of Yisrayah, and each of their leaders gave him a rod apiece, for each leader according to their fathers' houses, twelve rods; and the rod of Aaron was among their rods. **7 And Moses placed the rods before YHWH in the tabernacle of witness.** **8** Now it came to pass on the next day that Moses went into the **tabernacle of witness, and behold, the rod of Aaron, of the house of Levi, had sprouted and put forth buds, had produced blossoms and yielded ripe almonds. 9 Then Moses brought out all the rods from before YHWH to all the children of Yisrayah, and they looked, and each man took his rod.** 10 And YHWH said to Moses, **"Bring Aaron's rod back before the Testimony, to be kept as a sign against the rebels, that you may put their complaints away from Me, lest they die." 11** Thus did Moses; just as YHWH had commanded him, so he did. **12** So the children of Yisrayah spoke to Moses, saying, "

"Surely we die, we perish, we all perish! 13 Whoever even comes near the tabernacle of YHWH must die. Shall we all utterly die?"

Unfaithfulness & Complaints Destroy

YHWH hates complaints [grumbling, protesting] from His people. If you have need, seek YHWH's face as Moses always did. Don't complain as if YHWH is no longer with you. He provides all the needs. Those who complain lack faith; they indirectly tell YAH, 'You are not able to solve the problem.' The only way to solve whatever problem is to go to Him in prayer and make your request known to Him. The rebels did not seek Moses and Aaron's attention. This is wrong! The rebel leaders thought they could unseat Aaron and take over his office as High Priest of Yisrayah. They then became confrontational and tried to force Aaron to give up his position, as they felt they also were set apart (holy). Thus, the leaders' conflict against Moses and Aaron led to their sudden death. After YHWH removed the wicked people in their midst, He intervened, and in Numbers Chapter 17, He resolved the matter with the sign and miracle of the "budding rod", which stopped the complaints (Numbers 17:1-13). These people continued to provoke YAH to anger without recourse to His love, goodness, kindness, faithfulness and His mighty power that brought them out of the hands of Pharaoh and Egypt.

Truly, YHWH is "slow to anger and abounding in steadfast love, forgiving iniquity and transgression," just as Moses said (Numbers 14:18; Ex. 34:5-7). Were it not for YHWH's patience and mercy, judgment would have occurred earlier. YHWH's mercies toward Yisrayah are a powerful illustration of 2 Peter 3:9, "YHWH is . . . patient toward you, not wishing that any should perish, but that all should reach repentance." YHWH endured for so long the complaints and unfaithfulness of His people. One must learn to love, trust, and obey His Word.

The complaints and acts of unfaithfulness exhibited above are some of the ways people test YHWH. If anyone must survive the Second Exodus of Yisrayah and make it to the Land of Inheritance, the person must beware of what happened to the fathers of old. YHWH does not spare those who rebel against Him.

Tenth Evidence:
Mammon Spirit Leads Pastors Away from the Truth

Mammon Spirit inhibits leaders from preparing Assemblies for the Second Exodus. This is a call to return to Torah-Law and to lead righteously.

This part of the evidence reveals different types of Pastors and Teachers who pretend to teach the Torah-Covenant Way but do not. Below, various ministers are revealed who corrupt assemblies of YAH, just as was shown during the First Exodus of Yisrayah. YHWH calls some, but many call themselves. No one who substitutes YHWH for 'mammon' is qualified to lead YHWH's congregation as Yisrayah is being prepared for the Second Exodus. If the Pastor goes astray, members will also go astray. The spirit that leads the Pastor is also the same spirit that leads the congregation. It's because of this that Yahshua HaMashiach warned against the pursuit of 'mammon', because behind it is the devil's spirit that ensnares its victims. Those held captive by the mammon spirit cannot enter the Land of Yisrayah during the Second Exodus. Yahshua warns against using the Name of YHWH to worship mammon. It's increasingly noticed that many Pastors and Teachers in assemblies being called out to follow YAHWEH's covenant instructions begin to deviate as soon as they join YAHSHUA's covenant family. What's wrong? A careful observation has revealed that the appetite for money and the desire to get rich quickly are, in part, the main causes of people drifting away. It's important that Torah education and training are adequately taught and received before an elected Pastor or teacher can teach others. Teachings are received during Shabbat meetings, Feast meetings, and within organised training schedules, so that the would-be Pastor learns the doctrine of YHWH as taught by Yahshua HaMashiach. Does it mean leaders do not understand Yahshua and the Apostles' warning regarding mammon? In Matthew Chapter 6:24, Yahshua HaMashiach warns concerning mammon:

"No one can serve two masters, for either he will hate the one and love the other, or else he will be

devoted to one and despise the other. You cannot serve both YHWH and Mammon."

In 1 Timothy 6:1-14, Apostle Shaul (Paul) continues with the Message of the HaMashiach concerning the mammon (money, wealth, riches) doctrine:

"If anyone teaches a different doctrine and doesn't consent to sound words, the words of our King Yahshua HaMashiach, and to the doctrine which is according to righteousness, he is conceited, knowing nothing, but obsessed with arguments, disputes, and word battles, from which come envy, strife, insulting, evil suspicions, and constant friction of people of corrupt minds and destitute of the truth, who suppose that righteousness is a means of gain. Withdraw yourself from such. But righteousness with contentment is great gain. For we brought nothing into the world, and we certainly can't carry anything out. But having food and clothing, we will be content with that. But those who are determined to be rich fall into a temptation, a snare, and many foolish and harmful lusts, which drown men in ruin and destruction. For the love of money is a root of all kinds of evil. Some have been led astray from the faith in their greed and have pierced themselves through with many sorrows. But you, man of YAH, flee these things, and follow righteousness, uprightness, faith, love, perseverance, and gentleness. Fight the good fight of faith. Take hold of the eternal life to which you were called, and you confessed the good confession in the sight of many witnesses. I command you before YHWH, who gives life to all things, and before Yahshua HaMashiach, who before Pontius Pilate testified the good confession, that you keep the commandment without spot, blameless, until the appearing of our King Yahshua HaMashiach."

Lawless Ministers: Mammon is a killer of doctrine and ministry. A Pastor must separate from the mammon doctrine, or he would share the mammon spirit with the work of YHWH. It's either that a minister takes time to understand the covenant commandments' instructions preached to him or he would be careless and entangle himself with the gospel of mammon, which is 'another gospel' being preached in some Christian churches today. Apostle Shaul instructs the ministers: **"keep the commandment without spot, blameless until the appearing of our King Yahshua HaMashiach"** (1 Tim. 6:14). Pastors are called to rely on YAHSHUA's Covenant commandments upon which His Ministry was built and the doctrine of the Father preached (John 7:15-18). YAHSHUA's work depended on following the Torah, the Law from which He taught the Disciples (Luke 24:27, 44-45). Without adequate knowledge and understanding, many ministers do not precisely know the goals and objectives that Yahshua HaMashiach set for His assemblies. Some leaders have thought that the work of YHWH is a quick way to make money.

Fame-Seeking Ministers: Many ministers feel underpaid, and as a result, they must seek out opportunities to earn money for position, fame, and recognition. Others think that if they don't take advantage of their congregation, they may labour in vain. Yet others believe that their leaders force them to work for them, and as a result, they must find ways to cut corners to be like them. When their desperation is not yielding fruit for them, they leave the assembly and form their 'own mission'. This is precisely what was discussed above regarding Dathan and Abiram, who fought against Moses and Aaron in the wilderness due to their leadership positions. When the eye is on money and not on YHWH, the individual deviates, and the ministry suffers. YHWH's anger is provoked by such rude behaviour. The Spirit does not operate in such a leader.

Treacherous Rebellious Ministers: Sometimes, one wonders if the work is for YAHWEH or for those treacherous rebels who work with insult and disrespect, as if they are working for their leaders. This is unfortunate! This kind of minister sneaks in through the back door; the back door because they're not trained or they are not patient enough to receive the true teaching of YHWH's Torah. Why are many in a hurry to lead? Most leaders believe that opening an assembly is a means to achieve quick gains, riches, wealth, and fame. Others feel it's all 'business'. Yet some believe that if they must work at all, they should be given sufficient funds to build an auditorium, a cathedral, or acquire a large house of worship so that everyone would notice they have arrived. In the Gentile nations, are the Pastors commanded to embark on building temples or to win souls? This is not to say worship must be done under the sun or rain in the open space. No! Not at all. Wisdom is the principal thing here. Do you know what your King and HaMashiach asked you to be doing for Him until He returns? When He says, "occupy till I return", do you understand Him? This is the reason you need Torah Covenant education.

Backbiting & Backstabbing Ministers: Furthermore, there are other types of Pastors – the 'money-begging pastors' – whose stock-in-trade is to backbite and backstab their assembly leaders. These sets of Pastors believe that whether they are going out for evangelism, a tour, outreach, or a crusade, or receiving a visitor, it's their right to ask, beg, and make it look as if it's their right to obtain every dime from their leadership before they do anything. All this money confusion is because someone did not receive the simple ministerial education necessary to run YHWH's house. YAH, that calls the Pastor opens the door of the Ministry. Joshua was told how he would receive YAH's blessings by depending on YHWH and the Torah. Those who choose money as their idol instead of YHWH as their Father still hold to their religious orientation, particularly such an orientation from Christianity, which ties everything they do to money and materialism. The mammon way is not YAHWEH's Covenant Way. The Mammon way of the Gentile leads people to believe that running an assembly is a money-driven venture. But does an Assembly need money? Yes, it does! YHWH provided the answer to it; Yahshua also offered an answer to it; the Apostles taught how to run the Assembly of YHWH. Is money the driving force behind the ministry? No! The Ruach Hakodesh [Holy Spirit] is the driver and mover of the Ministry. Men who develop an appetite for money do not know that they must learn how to fund the Assembly without compromising with the mammon of this world. Yahshua never compromised His ministry with the mammon of this world. Pastors should not, because of money, destroy the assignment YAHWEH commits into their hands. However, this is where the question comes in: 'Are these sets of people called by YHWH?'

Internet Fraudster Ministers: The BOC reveals that those who operate with the mammon spirit are not called by YHWH, who alone calls anyone (John 6:37, 44). They are simply running YAHWEH's Ministry as a personal business, seeking to grab funds here and there for their own selfish ends. These sets of ministers are behind computers, emailing assemblies or churches, soliciting for money, yet they are not servants of Yahshua. They are self-centred, money-conscious, and are not working for YAHWEH's Kingdom goal. They are not occupying as commanded by YAHSHUA. Money-making ventures are their objective, as they see those in the Gentile religions parade themselves with people's hard-earned money. Such people are not in the Ministry of YAHSHUA! They are computer fraudsters who use the name of the Assemblies and Yahshua to make money. The truth is that YAHWEH's Assembly is not driven by money. The Assembly needs money to do its work, but money is not the driver for achieving the work of the Heavenly Father. Consider here how YAHWEH worked with the fathers of old, including YAHSHUA, when they were called to occupy for Him and work as faithful servants so that the earth would be a glorious place for human habitation. Internet fraudster ministers do not think about their own salvation, nor the salvation of their victims.

Flee from Mammon worship: Those who corrupt themselves with mammon will corrupt their congregation. They would produce men and women who would not know the call of the Father, nor understand the Torah-Law they must eat day and night to get themselves prepared for salvation and the Second Exodus, which YAH is preparing the hearts of His people to understand. Mammon spirit will lead many away from obtaining the cloak of righteousness necessary for salvation. Mammon worship will take away the spirit of the Pastor, and he will end up teaching and preaching 'another gospel' and 'another messiah'.

In the end, such a Pastor will work in vain, and the gate of the kingdom will be closed against him (see Matthew 7:21-23). Flee from every appearance of mammon spirit!

Further Evidence: Timing of Second Exodus

Ephraim's Return to Yisrayah Coincides With the Beginning of the Millennial Era

We have already presented evidence above in several places where the regathering of the northern kingdom and southern kingdom of Yisrayah commences from the wilderness after YHWH's judgment of wrath against the nations of the world and the fall of Babylon, which occurs before and at the second coming of Yahshua. After this, Yahshua will establish His millennial kingdom on earth, which will last for 1,000 years, and a resurrected David will be king over a regathered and reunited Israel at the same time. Micah the prophet discusses this period with special emphasis on the millennial era as a time of regathering the lost and scattered Yisrayah. Let's see what he prophesies in this regard.

Micah chapter four tells us the time setting of Micah's prophecy: in the last days, when the house of YHWH will be established in Jerusalem on the Temple Mount (verse 1). From this same spot, Torah will rule all nations, and all nations will go up to Yerusalem to learn the ways of YHWH (verses 1–3). At the same time, peace will prevail on the earth, and wars will cease (verse 3, see Isaiah 2:2–4). This clearly is a future, millennial prophecy. The timing is in the last days after the second coming of Yahshua. In that same time, YHWH promises to regather the remnant of His people, Yisrayah, who were cast far off (or scattered, verses 6–8). Where will His people be delivered or redeemed from? They will come from a defeated Babylon, the enemy of Yisrayah (verse 10)!

Once again, we see a reiterated scenario of YHWH redeeming and regathering His lost and scattered people after defeating their enemies who have enslaved them. The time frame of this prophecy is millennial — presumably after the second coming of Yahshua and not before.

Rest From Her Enemies

Another clue as to the timing of Ephraim's return to the land of Yisrayah can be found in an interesting phrase that occurs three times in the Tanakh (or Old Testament) and once in the Epistle to the Hebrews.

In Deuteronomy 12, YHWH instructs the children of Yisrayah that as they go in to conquer the Promised Land, they must little by little defeat the heathens that are living there. As they are destroying the heathen idols, they are at the same time not to be walking in sin (i.e., Torahlessness, or "every man doing what is right in his own eyes," verse 8). They are to keep His Torah commands (verses 1, 5–7). In the process of Yisrayah's following YHWH's instructions, He promises to give them rest from their enemies (verse 10; see also 25:19 and Josh. 21:44; 23:1).

This idea of Yisrayah receiving rest from its enemies is echoed elsewhere in the Scriptures, not only when Yisrayah entered the Promised Land the first time under Joshua (Heb. Yehoshua), but also in the end times when redeemed Yisrayah will enter the same land under Yahshua HaMashiach. In fact, the writer of Hebrews draws a parallel between the first Joshua and the second Joshua (or Yahshua) and ties the idea of entering the Promised Land to that of a seventh-day Shabbat rest (see Heb. 4:1–9).

What we see from this is that, as the Torah-obedient children of Yisrayah were given rest from their enemies after defeating them, likewise, a similar scenario will occur in the end days when Ephraim returns to its promised inheritance in the land of Yisrayah. The writer of Hebrews likens this to the seventh-day Shabbat and seems to be suggesting that, as man rests on the seventh day, so **YHWH's people will enter the promised land under King Yahshua in the seventh millennia of man's existence on this earth**. This rest will last for one thousand years and is commonly referred to as the Millennium.

Ezekiel 33:21 to 39:29 — Chronology of Judgment and Restoration

The prophecies contained in these chapters appear to be a chronological summary of all that will happen to end-time Israel just prior to her being regathered and restored to the land of Yisrayah. It is a synopsis of the main points covered thus far in this book.

This prophecy begins in Ezekiel 33:21 ("in the twelfth year, in the tenth month, on the fifth day of the month") and continues through the end of chapter 39, at which time Ezekiel receives another vision for another time. This prophecy admonishes the watchmen (the prophets and spiritual leaders) of Yisrayah to be faithful to their duties to warn the city or the house of Yisrayah (33:7, 10, 11, 20) of impending danger should it come, and the judgments that will fall upon the house of Yisrayah if they fail to heed the watchmen's warnings to turn from wickedness (Torahlessness, Lawlessness). The Ezekiel 33 prophecy reveals a progression of events that provides another indication of the timing of Ephraim's return to the land of Yisrayah.

Let's now have an overview of this prophecy:

The prophetic watchmen warn the house of Yisrayah to repent of the sin of Torahlessness (chapter 33).

➢ YHWH rebukes the shepherds or pastors of the house of Yisrayah (in our days, this would refer to lukewarm Messianic Pastors, Christian pastors and spiritual leaders) who are self-serving hirelings and who are not ministering to, feeding or healing YHWH's lost and scattered sheep (see Evidence Tenth above) (chapter 34).

➢ YHWH promises to raise true shepherds after his own heart and will eventually set (a resurrected) David as king over his sheep who have been regathered from among the heathen nations (chapter 34).

➢ YHWH will judge and make Edom, the perennial enemy of Yisrayah, desolate (chapter 35).

➢ All the house of Yisrayah (all 12 tribes) will be regathered from the nations where they were dispersed and will be restored to their promised inheritance in the land of Israel after the judgment of Edom (chapter 36).

➢ Spiritual revival will occur among the 12 tribes of Yisrayah as YHWH continues to regather his people from the nations of the world as they are spiritually regenerated and repent of their Torahless ways (chapter 36).

➤ The land of Yisrayah will become a garden of Eden as YHWH's people serve and worship him, keeping the biblical feasts (Chapter 36).

➤ Ezekiel sees a vision of a valley of dry bones coming to life, which is the whole house of Yisrayah (both Judah [the southern kingdom] and Ephraim [the northern kingdom]) being physically resurrected and spiritually regenerated (Chapter 37).

➤ Then Ezekiel gives his famous two-stick prophecy, likening the two kingdoms of Yisrayah (the house of Judah and the house of Joseph, or Ephraim) to two sticks or tree trunks that will be brought together to become one tree in the hand of YHWH. David will rule over this reunited kingdom, and all will walk in the Torah ways of YHWH, who will make an everlasting covenant with his people and will make his tabernacle or dwelling place among them (i.e., a picture of the Millennium, chapter 37).

➤ Finally, we have the famous Gog and Magog prophecy of Ezekiel 38 and 39. It is prophesied that in the latter days, many nations (currently Muslim nations and Russia) will come against Yisrayah when it is dwelling safely in the land (verses 8, 11, 14), resulting in YHWH being sanctified in the midst of his people (verses 16, 23). YHWH will answer the invasion of Gog with the fire of his wrath (verses 19–

22). Fire and judgment will fall upon Gog (39:1–20). This could very well be a picture of the end times battle of Armageddon that will occur at Yahshua's second coming (Rev 14:14 20 and 19:18). As a result, YHWH will be glorified in the eyes of the heathen because of his judgments against Gog, and the house of Israel will recognise that YHWH is their Elohim (verses 21–24). YHWH will then bring back the captivity of the whole house of Yisrayah (i.e., all 12 tribes, verses 25–29). If this is a prophetic picture of the famous battle of Armageddon, then this is also a likely picture of the fall of Babylon the Great (Rev 18 and 19). [More revelation is required about God and Magog – and will serve as an update to this book].

We see from this chronological scenario that YHWH's judgment falls on heathen nations or enemies of Yisrayah (39:21). This occurs at the same time that lost and scattered Yisrayah begins to wake up spiritually as to their true identity as Yisray'lites (39:22). At the same time, the heathen shall know who the House of Yisrayah is (verse 23). YHWH will have mercy on Yisrayah and regather scattered Yisrayah to their promised land (verses 25–29)

CHAPTER 14: CONCLUSION

In the above study, massive scriptures were presented to trace the lost and scattered Yisrayah, whom YHWH promised redemption and restoration back to their land. These same prophecies also give us clues as to when the two Houses of Yisrayah [Judah and Ephraim, i.e., 'Israel'] will unite and return to the land. Tangentially, two facts stood out as particularly noteworthy when this study was compiled.

First, for about a thousand years, the prophets of Yisrayah discussed the subject of Yisrayah's dispersal among the nations, their regathering, and subsequent return to the Land of Yisrayah. This was not a subject they neglected nor passed over lightly. Some of the books of the Latter (Minor) Prophets are devoted entirely to discussing the destiny of the two houses of Yisrayah. Additionally, each of the Major Prophets allocated dozens of chapters to this subject matter (i.e., Second Exodus). How so many modern Biblical scholars and teachers can be so dismissive, if not outright ignorant, of this subject is impossible to comprehend and explain, if not for the fact that only YHWH reveals His Covenant to the people He calls. Afterwards, He said that, **"The secret things belong to**

YAH Almighty Father, but the things that are revealed belong to His children" (Deut. 29:29).

Second, another wonder while compiling this study is the fact that YHWH the Father revealed to Yisrayah in the wilderness that they would not serve Him in the land of Canaan, which they were returning to possess. He told them to desist from the worship of the Gods of the Gentiles because if they disobey, the Gods of the Gentiles they serve would ensnare them and take their hearts and worship away from Him, and He would disown them and scatter them into the Gentile nations until they repent. The judges and the prophets revisited YHWH's predictions to them periodically. Why didn't they recall the warnings? Why did they go on sinning and sinning until they were entangled in idol worship and were driven away into nations till today? The answer is in what YHWH foretold: **'Idols ensnare their victims.'** This is also true: **'Worship of anything other than the Name of the Creator – YHWH – will entice and ensnare the victim. The result is ruins!'**

Third, the fact that becomes apparent once one has studied the subject of Yisrayah's return is this: the biblical prophets form a unified choir of voices that were saying the same thing for a thousand years. Furthermore, they corroborate each other over and over again about the events and timing of Yisrayah's regathering and return to their Promised Land – this is called the Second Exodus of Yisrayah.

The Themes The BOC Repeated And Highlighted In This Study Include:

- Yisrayah (all 12 tribes, i.e., the northern kingdom/Ephraim and the southern kingdom/Judah, or the Jews) will be regathered and return to the Land of Yisrayah. This is the future and is about to happen [although some are in the land already – but according to the prophets, they and the foreigners occupying the land now will undergo judgment leading to the cleansing and refinement of the land before the remnant [Judah] that will be left and other Yisray'lites returning could live peaceably in the land forever – see Zechariah 13].

- The Scriptures reveal a repetitive, cyclical paradigm of Yisrayah's apostasy and redemption. The apostasy will be purged; the Name of YHWH will be restored to their lips; Torah [Law] will be renewed as the only lamp and light for the people's knowledge of truth.

- A second exodus from the nations is coming that will be like, but greater than, the first exodus from Egypt.

- Yisrayah will go through a time of wilderness testing or judgment to humble her, which will bring her to repentance for the sin of Torahlessness or Lawlessness (transgression or breaking of the Law). Yisrayah's return to the Torah is a precondition for her return to the land of Yisrayah. Without knowledge of the Torah, there will be no Second Exodus. The people must have YHWH's knowledge, or they would perish.

- A confederacy of nations led by Edom will attempt to prevent Yisrayah from returning and entering the Promised Land. This is known in the BOC, i.e., Bible, as Jacob's trouble. YHWH will allow this to happen to discipline and refine His people; their judgment will draw them to know Him better and bring glory to His awesome Name in the midst of His repentant and returning people as He helps them to destroy their enemies, preventing them from entering the land.

- Only after YHWH gives Yisrayah rest from her enemies and destroys those who have been holding them captive will Yisrayah be free to return to her land inheritance. When this happens, Yisrayah will have peace and dwell safely in the Land of Yisrayah with a resurrected David ruling over them and the Messiah ruling over the entire world. This is the millennial reign of the HaMashiach.

- All of these prophecies shall occur in the last days and coincide with the great and terrible day of YHWH's wrath and the coming of Yahshua HaMashiach to establish the Kingdom of YHWH on this earth.

- Those who plotted the theory of 'rapture' and those deceived by it will be disappointed. At that time, they will realise how much the devil deceived them into believing a lie! The kingdom Yahshua preached, and He told His people that it's 'near thee', is the Kingdom of the Father, which He will set up and govern as the Father appointed Him.

Based on these facts, the conclusion seems inescapable that a series of events will transpire in the last days, coinciding with YHWH's end-times judgment against the nations of the world (known as the wrath of YHWH), just before the second coming of Yahshua, that will help to bring about the beginning of the return of Ephraim to YHWH and His Torah. Ephraim may return in two or more different groups, as Judah returned from Babylon in various groups.

1. From various prophecies and biblical narratives, it seems that Ephraim's repentance and return to the Land of Yisrayah will first involve at least two sub-groups of Ephraim. The first group is a small and faithful Torah obedient remnant from Ephraim that has kept faith in Yahshua (they will escape the great tribulation into the wilderness because they kept the Word of YAH and His Commandments – Rev. 3:8, 10; Rev. 12:6, 14; Rev. 14:12); and they would come through a wilderness experience, a time of testing (for the disobedient who would still be holding to the Gentile religious way) just before Yahshua's return. It is this group that Yahshua will lead into the Promised Land at His second

coming. The 144,000 Yisray'lites from all 12 tribes that are mentioned in Revelation Chapters 7 and 14, as well as those who have come out of the great tribulation (Rev. 7:9–17), will take part. These same redeemed Yisray'lites from all 12 tribes will return with Yahshua at His second coming as the warrior bride to destroy the enemies of Yahshua and His people (Rev. 19:1–15; Jude 14). 2.

2. The next and larger group of Ephraimites to return to the land of Yisrayah will do so after the second coming and at the beginning of and during the millennial reign of Yahshua. This group will be comprised of scattered Yisray'lites. Once Babylon the Great is defeated, Yahshua's earthly Kingdom will be set up in Yerusalem, and the Torah-Word of YHWH will go forth from that city (Isa. 2:3; Mic. 4:2). Ephraim will begin to learn who they are spiritually. A way will then be made for them to return to their spiritual and physical heritage in the land of Yisrayah via a highway in the wilderness (e.g., Isa. 11:16). This is likely the spiritual harvest of souls, which the fall biblical Feast of Tabernacles (or Sukkot) prophetically pictures.

Similarly, in modern times, not all of Judah (the Jews) returned to the land of Yisrayah at once. It has been a gradual process that began in the nineteenth century and has continued to this day. Presently, only half of the Jews are living in Yisrayah.

The question for the reader then is this: if our conclusion is correct, which group will you be a part of — the smaller group of redeemed Yisray'lites (referred to as Yahshua's warrior bride) that returns to the Land of Yisrayah with Yahshua at His second coming, or the larger group, or the lost-souls group, that must go through all of YHWH's end-times judgements, including the great tribulation and wrath of YHWH?

A Call to Action:
What Can You Be Doing NOW?

The subject of preparedness is currently a topic of discussion within the Hebrew Covenant Roots Movement. Many teachers are holding seminars and offering advice on how to navigate the upcoming economic and political challenges they believe will befall believers. Some are even selling supplies on their websites, while others are advocating the purchase and stockpiling of guns, gold and grub [all for defence in the coming days of 'Jacob's trouble']. While being a modern-day Joseph and preparing physically for the lean times ahead is always a wise move, more importantly, it would be good to give you a list of suggestions on how to prepare spiritually for the wilderness times that YHWH's end-time generation people will go through. You can ensure that you will be ready to be a part of the first group of redeemed Israelites who will return to the land of Israel with Yeshua at his second coming.

- Repent of sin (i.e., breaking YHWH's Torah commandments, 1 John 3:4). Bring your life into conformity to the Torah (YHWH's instructions in righteousness as revealed in the books of the law and as elucidated throughout the rest of the Scriptures) to the most significant degree possible in your daily walk. This is YHWH's desire for the end-times saints (Rev 12:17; 14:12). Those who don't will suffer YHWH's judgment along with the wicked (Rev 18:4). In returning to Torah-obedience, you will be helping to fulfil biblical prophecy, since Ephraim's return to Torah is a precursor to his returning to the land of Israel.

- Love YHWH-Yeshua the Messiah with all of your heart, soul, mind and strength by keeping his Torah commandments (John 14:15; 1 John 2:3–6). In so doing, you will be on YHWH's "right side" and not on his "wrong side" and will be more likely to be the recipient of his divine protection and provision during the hard times to come.

- Recognise that if you are a faithful and blood-bought believer in Yeshua the Messiah, you are a part of redeemed Israel (Eph 2:11–19; Gal 3:29), and you are grafted into the spiritual olive tree of Israel (Rom 11:13–24). Embrace your spiritual identity as a one-new-man Israelite and a son of Abraham!

- Understand how the restoration of the two houses of Israel is a necessary precursor to Yeshua's second coming (see Acts 1:6–8 and 3:21).

- Ask yourself what you can do to help fulfil Yeshua's command to help gather in the lost sheep of the house of Israel (Matt 10:6; Acts 1:6–8).

- Educate yourself from the Scriptures on what it means to be a redeemed Israelite. Start by reading the definitive book on this subject, Redeemed Israel, by Batya Wootten (available at www.keyofdavidmarketplace.com). Then share the truth of the restoration of the two houses of Israel with as many people as possible.

- Support the ministry work of those who are teaching about and reaching out to lost and scattered Israel. Support these ministries with your prayers, finances, and help, and utilise your spiritual gifts to advance the kingdom of YHWH.

YISRAYAH'S SECODND EXODUS IS FAST APPROACHING

Yisrayah is going home. The brilliant sunshine is already cast upon the land, awaiting the people to return to their Land of inheritance.

REFERENCES

Arikibe, G.C. (2018), Yahshua's Greatest Commandments: Laws of Love and Liberty Revealed – *The Ten Commandments*, Published by Assembly of the Living Yahweh, U.K.

Arikibe, G.C. (2025), In the Book of Covenant Yahweh Is Not God, Yahweh Is Yahweh, He Changes Not. Published by Assembly of the Living Yahweh, U.K.

Arikibe, G.C. (2018, Babylon Is Fallen, Published by Assembly of the Living Yahweh, U.K. Book of Covenant (2024), *Sacred Name Bible*, Assembly of the Living Yahweh, U.K.

Douglas R. Frayne and Johanna H. Stuckey (2021), A Handbook of Gods and Goddesses of the Ancient Near East. Three Thousand Deities of Anatolia, Syria, Israel, Sumer, Babylonia, Assyria, and Elam. *Published by Eisenbrauns University Park, Pennsylvania*

John Day (2002), Yahweh and the Gods and Goddesses of Canaan, Journal for the Study of the Old Testament Supplement Series, 265. *Published by Sheffield Academic Press Ltd, London.*

Ya'acov Natan Lawrence (2018). What Is the Second Exodus and When Will It Occur? *Source*: *Waters in the Wilderness, A Teaching Ministry of Hoshana Rabbah Biblical Discipleship,* **An Article cited:** *4/08/18*

About The Author

Dr. Goodwins Arikibe is a Covenant Bible teacher, preacher, writer, educator, leadership mentor, and business consultant. He discusses critical issues affecting the scattered Israelites in the diaspora. He reviewed why they were dispersed and examined what they need to do for their Second Exodus and restoration to the Land of Yisrayah in these last days. The central theme of his ministry outreach is to propagate YHWH's covenant instructions.

Dr. Goodwins Arikibe is the Lead Pastor of Assembly of the Living Yahweh (ALY), a multidimensional congregation headquartered in Stoke-on-Trent, United Kingdom. He is the Coordinator of Israel in Diaspora Global Network. He holds an Advanced Diploma in Theology, a Bachelor's Degree in Business Education, a Master's Degree in Business Administration, and a PhD in Leadership and Organisational Performance.

In 2014, Ruach Hakodesh (Holy Spirit) revealed YAHSHUA, the true Anointed One [Messiah], and the Father YHWH to him. For three and a half years, under the guidance of the Spirit, he relearned the Book of the Covenant. Currently, he teaches the Word of Truth as it was originally given to Yisrayah from the Torah [the first five Books of the Bible or Book of the Law]. Goodwins is a prolific author and counsellor of the Word. He has written over fifteen books (some yet to be published) on spiritual and secular topics, including Leadership and Organisational Performance, Becoming a Servant Leader, Book of the Covenant, Yahweh Is Not God, and Second Exodus of Yisrayah, among others. He travels extensively with his wife as a team, conducting teaching conferences and seminars at various Assemblies, Churches, Ministries, and Educational Training institutions worldwide. Dr. Goodwins is happily married with five children and grandchildren.

NOTES

MORE BOOKS BY AUTHOR

1. IN THE BOOK OF COVENANT YAHWEH IS NOT GOD

In the Book of Covenant Yahweh Is Not God

Dr. Goodwins Arikibe

The hidden truth is revealed. YAHWEH, the Creator of Heavens and Earth, is not God. But "God" [a generic title] is whom the world worships. But why? YHWH does not bear the title 'God' or 'Lord'. He is the Creator of Gods. This Book reveals what Pastors and Teachers have been hiding for ages. YHWH says the consequence for not serving and worshipping Him based on His Set-apart Name is eternal death. Does that surprise you? Discover the truth from the pages of this Book. Please read it with your Book of the Covenant [Bible] shown below. Be blessed for your obedience!

Click Here

https://books.by/covenant-venture-books/in-the-book-of-covenant-yahw

OR

https://www.amazon.co.uk/BOOK-COVENANT-YAHWEH-NOT-GOD-ebook/dp/B0FKZH2VDQ

OR

https://covenantventuresglobal.com

2. WHAT ISRAELITES MUST KNOW AS THEY PREPARE FOR THE SECOND EXODUS

Book of the Covenant [Sacred Name Bible]
Dr Goodwins Arikibe

The Difference Between the Book of the Covenant (BOC) and the Bible

The Heavenly Father warns that there should not be addition or subtraction in His Word. Unfortunately, in the Bible, this instruction has been violated. For instance, His Sacred Name "YHWH" was removed; the Saviour's Name, "YAHSHUA" was removed. These were replaced with "the Lord God" and "Jesus Christ", respectively. This is grave disobedience that violates Exodus 20:7. Also, the Bible replaced the 7th day

Sabbath with 1st-day Sunday worship. The Annual Feasts of Passover, Pentecost, and Tabernacles were replaced by Pagan Feasts, e.g., Easter, Christmas, and New Year. The Bible teaches that 'by **faith and grace**' <u>alone</u> one shall be **saved,** without recourse to obedience to YHWH's Torah and Commandments, which are the whole duties of man (Deuteronomy 10:12-13,20, Ecclesiastes 12:13, Ezekiel 20:21, etc). The Bible is a religious book that teaches the traditions and commandments of men (Matthew 15:1-9). On the contrary, the BOC restores the 'Covenant' and teaches the Sacred Names of YHWH and YAHSHUA, the holy Sabbath Day, the Annual Feasts, etc. Idol names and titles associated with the Sacred Names are removed in the BOC as YHWH commanded. The BOC revives the "Covenant with YHWH", which **people <u>must obey</u> and have <u>faith in YAHSHUA</u> for their righteousness and salvation** (Deuteronomy 6:25). The BOC warns that those who forget YHWH to serve and worship Gods shall perish with those Gods. YHWH declares:

Deuteronomy 8:19-20 *"It shall be, if you shall forget YHWH your FATHER, and walk after Gods, and serve them and worship them, I testify against you today that you shall surely perish. As the nations that YHWH makes to perish before you, so you shall perish, because you wouldn't listen to YHWH your FATHER's voice."*

Jeremiah 10:11 *"You shall say this to them: 'The Gods that have not made the heavens and the earth will perish from the earth, and from under the heavens.'"*

Jeremiah 10:25 *"Pour out Your wrath on the nations that don't know You, and on the families that don't call on Your Name [YHWH]; for they have devoured Jacob. Yes, they have devoured him [Israel], consumed him, and have laid waste his habitation.*

My Dear Reader, your Bible teachers do not know the Father YHWH, nor do they know YAHSHUA the Saviour. They forsake His everlasting Covenant. These and more are the reasons BOC is the only Sacred Book that teaches true repentance and guides people to YAHSHUA, who is the Way, the Truth and the Life to YHWH the FATHER and the eternal Kingdom. This book can be accessed on

https://covenantventuresglobal.com

Or

https://books.by/covenant-venture-books/in-the-book-of-covenant-yahw.

3. IS CHRISTIANITY A REPLACEMENT OF COVENANT-KEEPING ISRAEL?

Christianity & Israel, the Covenant-keepers

Dr. Goodwins Arikibe

This book answers the question, 'Is Christianity a replacement of Covenant-keeping Israel?' It examines who a Christian is. It explains what Christianity is in relation to Israel and its Covenant Way. Christianity as a religion is far different from the Covenant given to Israel. Israel was promised the Seed and the Land. Are these promises fulfilled? Without a grasp of the concept of Israel, the Covenant, and Christianity, one may remain ignorant and miss the Kingdom. This book thoroughly investigated these subject matters, including:

- What righteousness and alvation mean to a covenant-keeping Israelite.
- Faith, Grace and the Law, which work together for salvation.
- Israel as a nation and 'rapture' into heaven. What the BOC teaches.
- Who is the Messiah of Israel and Christianity? Are there two Messiahs?
- The expiry time of the Gentiles, and the Second Exodus of Yisrayah to their Land.

The whole book can be accessed free of charge on www.livingyahweh.com.

4. ISRAEL, LAND, BLESSINGS & SALVATION

Israel, Land, Blessings & Salvation

Dr. Goodwins Arikibe

Who is Israel? This is a question that many who are Gentile-Israelites may not even be able to answer, except if they read a book such as this. But whoever uses the BOC can easily respond to this vital question, including proffering answers about the Land, the blessings and salvation they were promised. Are you an Israelite or a Christian? There is much to glean from this book, particularly regarding who Israel truly is and the other promises bestowed upon it in these last days. You can access this book for free at www.livingyahweh.com.

5. WHO IS YOUR SAVIOUR: YAHSHUA OR JESUS?

Who Is Your Saviour: Yahshua or Jesus?

Goodwins Arikibe

Assurance of salvation depends on who one worships. The wrong choice of the Saviour will spell doom. The BOC commands that YHWH alone must be worshipped. Baptism, which is a compulsory part of the Covenant, requires immersion in the water by the Salvation Name so that the Set-apart Spirit will be given to lead into all truth (Acts 2:38, John 16:13). This book reveals exactly the Salvation Name given to humanity for their eternal life [John 17:2-3]. The religious confusion that hoodwinks unsuspecting believers into failing to discover their faithful Saviour is exposed in this book. It teaches the fruits and characteristics of the faithful Saviour and exposes the false-messiah that deceives the whole world. Learn about the ancient Baal, whom people still serve today. Does the "name" people serve and worship matter? Yes! That's the main reason the FATHER issued severe warnings about the "name" one worships. This is where this book is very profound. The Baal Gad, the Lord God, and Jesus Christ, who dominate the Bible people read, insist they are the actual names. Is it true? Who are they? Furthermore, the Bible teaches that GRACE is the only means for salvation. How true is it? Is there anything deliberately omitted that you do not know? You ought to find these out in this book for your salvation. What then is the gift of the Spirit, and why was it given? In all these, what did your pastor teach you? The author carefully researched through the pages of the BOC to provide astonishing answers that have eluded many for so long.

You can access this book free of charge at www.livingyahweh.com [Go to: Publications/Books].

6. SATAN'S DECEPTION REVEALED

Satan's Deception Revealed

Dr. Goodwins Arikibe

The Book of the Covenant reveals who your enemy is. Your adversary has powerful tools that cause humanity to fall, no matter how they resist. The weapons of the enemy that ensnare and prey on souls have been dug out. Besides, Satan is a 'hijacker' of what belongs to the people of YHWH, and he took away so much from them, including their salvation. This book takes you through to discover: what deception and falling away mean; who the real false messiah is, and his false church; false prophets and false pastors who ruin people's salvation; the seal of revelation, etc. This investigative book has done the work for you. Providing knowledge to the reader corrects erroneous beliefs that lead them to make wrong choices. This book guides a curious kingdom-seeker to the way and the truth of YAHSHUA and the Kingdom, which those who diligently seek Him find. The book can be accessed at www.livingyhawh.com

7. YAHSHUA'S GREATEST COMMANDMENTS

Yahshua's Greatest Commandments
Dr. Goodwins Arikibe

Many read the Bible yet have not come to the full knowledge of these quotes:

"If you love Me, keep My commandments." John 14:15

"If you keep My commandments, you shall abide in My love;

Even as I have kept My Father's commandments, and abide

In His love." John 15:10

This book provides the Father's **keys** of LOVE and KNOWLEDGE that YAHSHUA promised, which only the obedient receive for salvation. Understanding of the quotations above, which run through the entire Gospel of truth, and their application in real-life situations, draws an individual closer to the Father and the Saviour. This book probes what Satan hates most — the Covenant Commandments of YHWH. Although some knowledge has been provided in the book – '**Becoming a Servant Leader**', you're invited to discover YAHSHUA's Greatest Commandments. The fear and love of the FATHER are dependent on obeying His commandments and living by them. Whoever acknowledges Him both in obedience and reverence shall be saved. *"Therefore, fear YHWH, and give glory to Him; for the hour of His judgement is come: and worship Him that made heaven, and earth, and the sea, and the fountains of waters"* [Revelation 14:7]. The commandments of YHWH are a behaviour and character-moulding tool given to those who would obey Him and worship Him. It is the mirror that enables the obedient to see themselves and make necessary adjustments. It is the sailor's compass. It is a soldier's weapon to overcome at all times. Besides these, do you want to know the hidden revelation that this book really teaches? For further understanding, read the whole book at www.livingyahweh.com.

Remain blessed in YHWH's Name!
HalleluYah!!
Amein!!!

GENTLE APPEAL

DONATE

If this message has been a blessing to you, please consider showing your appreciation by purchasing some copies of the book(s) for your beloved brothers/sisters, friends, or well-wishers. By doing so, you'll be contributing to the dissemination of the Good News to those who are being saved. Better still, please donate to enable us to print and publish these materials and distribute them to millions of perishing Israelites scattered across nations, awaiting to hear the Good News of YAHSHUA HaMashiach. By choosing to either buy or donate, you are not only lending a hand to augment the huge production expenses, but you are also being part of evangelism – reaching out to perishing souls, which this project is all about. Covenant Venture @.http://covenantventuresglobal.com May Abba YAH who called you, bless you!

About The Book

Hidden for generations, the truth is now being uncovered — prophecy is coming true before our eyes. In the Second Exodus of Yisrayah, Dr. Goodwins Arikibe reveals one of Scripture's most profound revelations: the restoration and return of YHWH's scattered people to their promised land. With clarity and spiritual authority, he exposes the deception of the "rapture". He clarifies the true divine plan — the Second Exodus of Yisrayah, a movement of faith, repentance, and restoration for all who belong to YHWH's Covenant.

Through ancient prophecies, historical truths, and divine revelation, Dr. Arikibe guides readers to rediscover their identity as YHWH's covenant people. He explains why they were scattered among the nations, how they lost their spiritual heritage, and what must now be done to prepare for the great return. This book serves as both a revelation and a roadmap — a call to repentance, obedience, and renewal through the Torah Covenant, guiding the faithful back to the Father's promise.

More than just a book, Second Exodus of Yisrayah is a divine summons — a prophetic message for all who seek truth, restoration, and the fulfilment of YHWH's eternal plan. It challenges every believer to awaken from spiritual slumber, return to the Covenant, and take their rightful place in the unfolding redemption of Yisrayah. The signs are clear, the call has gone out, and prophecy is being fulfilled before our very eyes. The time is near. The question remains — are you ready for the Second Exodus?

www.ingramcontent.com/pod-product-compliance
Lightning Source LLC
Chambersburg PA
CBHW071146070526
44584CB00019B/2676